THE QUILTING PATCHWORK & APPLIQUE PROJECT BOOK

THE QUILTING PATCHWORK & APPLIQUE PROJECT BOOK

DOROTHEA HALL

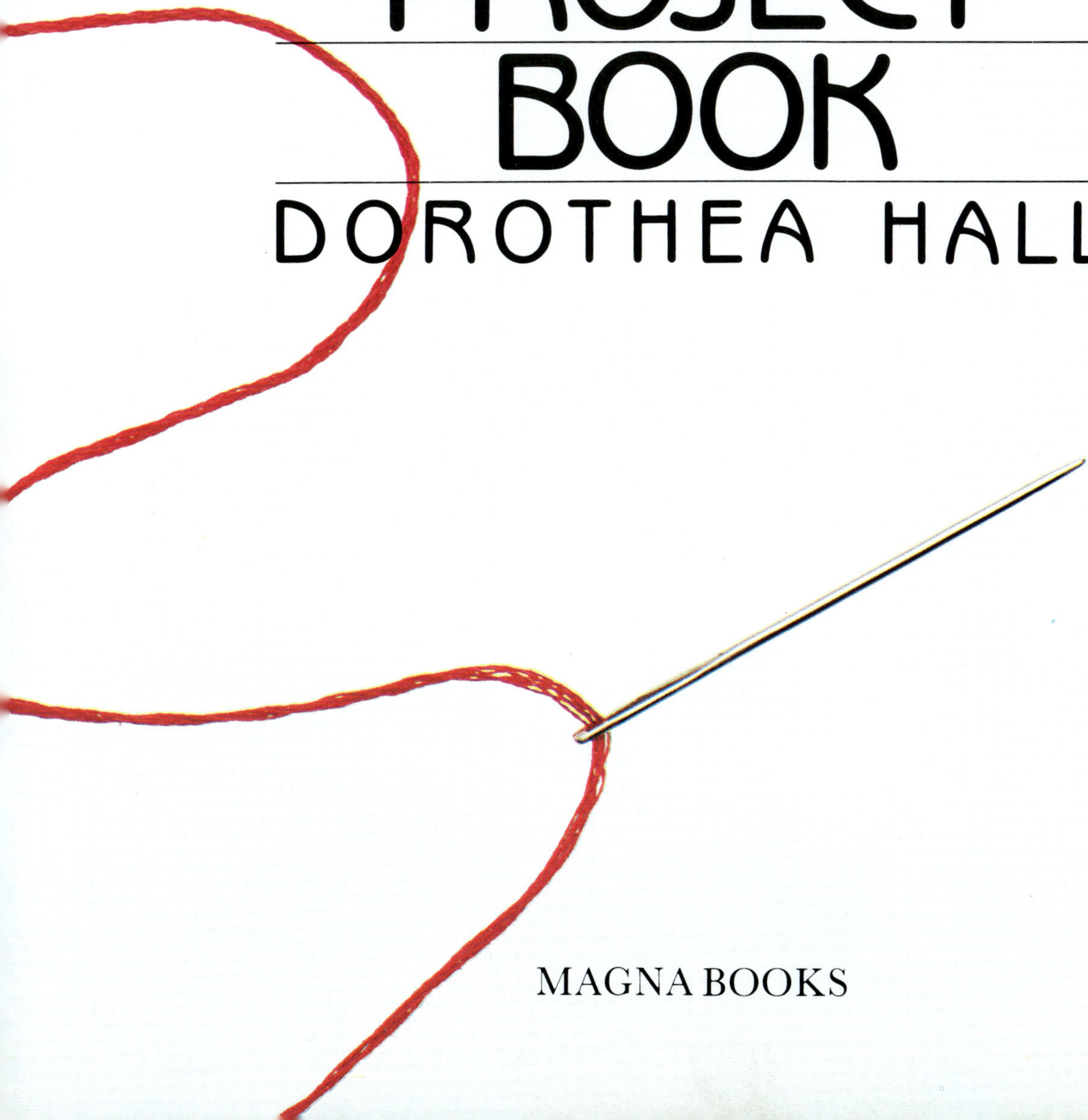

MAGNA BOOKS

A QUARTO BOOK

This edition published 1989 by
MAGNA BOOKS
Magna Road, Wigston
Leicester, LE8 2XH

ISBN 1 85422 058 6

This book was designed and produced by
Quintet Publishing Limited
6 Blundell Street, London N7

Art Director: Peter Bridgewater
Editors: Nicholas Law, Josephine Bacon
Artwork and Illustrations:
Joan Hutchinson, Donald Bason

Typeset in Great Britain by
Central Southern Typesetters, Eastbourne
Manufactured in Hong Kong by
Regent Publishing Services Limited
Printed in Hong Kong by
Leefung-Asco Printers Limited

• CONTENTS •

INTRODUCTION	6
BASIC EQUIPMENT	9
QUILTING TECHNIQUES	17
QUILTING PROJECTS	28
PATCHWORK TECHNIQUES	47
PATCHWORK PROJECTS	63
APPLIQUĒ TECHNIQUES	89
APPLIQUĒ PROJECTS	99
WHERE TO FIND EXAMPLES OF QUILTING, PATCHWORK AND APPLIQUĒ	122
BIBLIOGRAPHY AND ACKNOWLEDGEMENTS	123
GLOSSARY	124
INDEX	127

• INTRODUCTION •

IN RECENT YEARS there has been an astonishing growth of interest in all fabric crafts, but none so enthusiastically sustained as in quilting, patchwork and appliqué. For many people, the terms 'quilting' and 'patchwork' are synonymous with patchwork quilt, and although they are traditionally combined in certain types of quilt-making, each technique is a needlecraft in its own right – since there are many bedcovers made in patchwork that are not quilted and there are those that are quilted, but not patched or appliquéd.

However, on a domestic level, the 'evolution' of all three needlecrafts is very closely linked with the development of the 'quilt'.

Although bedcovers, made by quilting, patchwork and appliqué, have been made by rich and poor alike all over the world from China to Peru, and have been a vital form of creative expression for countless women over the past 300 years, their individual beginnings go back to ancient history. Unfortunately, owing to the perishable nature of textiles, few original examples have survived, but various references are made in both early writings and on ancient architectural frescoes and carvings. Possibly the oldest recorded example of quilting is a Siberian carpet estimated to have been made during the 1st century BC. This was discovered on the floor of a tomb during the Koslov expedition in 1924–5, and is now in the Leningrad Department of Archeology of the Academy of Sciences. The earliest known example of patchwork is a votive hanging which was found in the Cave of the Thousand Buddhas in India, and dates from the 6th century AD – although records show that both patchwork and appliqué were used in ancient Greece and in Egypt as early as 1000 BC. It is also known that traders from ancient China sold mosaic patchwork made from silk and brocade, and that in India, tents were highly decorated with hangings and friezes of appliqué and quilted designs. Turkish foot-soldiers wore quilted garments under their armour for warmth and to prevent chafing, as did the Chinese.

Like other traditional needlecrafts, their exact origins are not known, but all three techniques are thought to have begun in the East (where weaving and trading in woven fabrics began) and then travelled via the Oriental trade routes to Asia, Europe and the West. It must have taken about 2,000 years for these needlecrafts to reach Britain, during which time various adaptations were made – changes related to domestic economy and local prevailing climatic conditions – and so there developed the individual styles that we know today. To survive the severely cold winters of northern countries, for example, warm quilted garments, carpets and bedcovers were made with thick interlinings of sheep's wool or rags, which later came to be known as wadded quilting. To eke out sufficient fabric for the top layers – which would be homespun and relatively scarce – odds and ends and even the good parts of old garments would be salvaged and pieced together, thus making a simple type of patchwork. In more temperate climates thinner interlinings and lighter forms of quilting evolved, notably corded and padded (Italian and Trapunto). Here very fine silk and linen ground fabrics were used, and often combined surface embroidery and pulled thread work, so that the finished effect became more and more decorative. Two of the earliest surviving pieces of Trapunto quilting are a pair of Sicilian quilts, dated 1395, which are beautifully worked on natural linen with brown thread. In each case, the entire surface is divided into rectangular shapes, filled with complex pictorial scenes depicting figures, animals and lettering from the legendary story of Tristram.

These skills are believed to have been introduced into Britain by the Crusaders on their return from Europe during the 12th and 13th centuries. Eventually, quilting frames were devised and the art of quilt-making in Britain flourished. All-over designs were found to be more durable than earlier random stitching, and all kinds of scroll-like patterns and pictorial designs became popular. Quilting, patchwork and appliqué were combined in many forms, and needlework in general became more complicated. Appliqué was used to display colourful heraldic devices on standards and colours, heralds' tabards, surcoats and flags, and on ecclesiastical banners and vestments. Symbolical motifs cut from rich velvets, silks and damasks were applied to equally sumptuous ground fabrics and lavishly embroidered with silk, and pure gold and silver threads.

From the time of the Middle Ages, appliqué in Europe was a highly sophisticated craft worked by professional embroiderers specializing in ecclesiastical, heraldic and all other official and civic regalia – as it still is today.

By the late 16th century quilting in England was a firmly established trade. It continued through the 1700s when fashionable garments, such as waistcoats, petticoats and hats, were decoratively quilted for the wealthy, as were complete sets of bed furnishings.

As the taste for more exotic designs in fashion and home furnishings grew, great quantities of printed fabrics began to be imported from India. Their superior quality and immense popularity soon threatened European production, so taxes were levied on all imported fabric. In an effort, therefore, to use every scrap of chintz, women began to cut up the exotic 'palampore' designs, which had previously been used whole for bed hangings and coverlets, and to apply separate motifs rearranged on plain cotton grounds – thus making the first appliqué furnishings. These were elaborately quilted and often lavishly embroidered using the technique called *broderie perse,* or Appliqué Perse. Gradually, as more printed fabrics became available, dressmaking and furnishing remnants were utilized to make patchwork – which, in a way, was thought to resemble the colourful and expensive printed chintzes – and its popularity increased. So much so, that by the end of the 18th century it had been taken up as a pastime by the more leisured middle classes and elevated to a decorative needle art. Patchwork was adopted and used it with great panache on all furnishings, from chair seats, mantlepiece and window pelmets, to cosies, antimacassars, and coverlets. Silks were mixed with satins in crazy patchwork, and further decorated with embroidery, fringes, braids and bobbles.

Despite changes in fashion and the introduction of commercially quilted fabrics, quilting in 19th-century Britain still flourished in many country districts, mainly in Yorkshire, Durham, Northumberland and several areas in south Wales where each community maintained its own traditional style of design, and individual quilters took great pride in their craft. To meet the demand for finely stitched quilts, a thriving cottage industry developed, even though by the late 1800s, the weekly earnings of a woman outworker would be about half that of a farm labourer. In certain areas of Wales and England, itinerant quilters travelled from home to home where they would stay with families for several weeks to replenish their stock of quilts.

Meanwhile, during the 1700s, settlers moving out to the New World had taken these skills to America. With limited supplies of fabric, patchwork was used as a quick and thrifty means of providing whole fabric for much-needed bedcovers – and thus began the great American patchwork tradition. In order to speed up piecing, the block and set were devised whereby plain strips of fabric were set between pieced blocks. This provided a new design element and a grid on which hundreds of patchwork patterns have since been based.

As patchwork developed and spread across to the West coast, a dazzling selection of new patterns and variations was created, each one with its own fascinating name such as Rocky Road to Kansas, Lincoln's Platform and Slave's Chains – many of them of immediate topical interest reflecting the political and social changes that took place. In both England and America, quilting parties or 'bees' became important social events, particularly for women, when neighbours would meet to share in quilting the patchwork tops. Each family took great pride in having a fair number of quilts – some for every day and others for special visitors and celebrations. The very best quilts were show pieces only, and may have survived simply because they were treasured heirlooms handed down through the family – and now, like other fine needlecrafts, are seriously sought after by collectors. For many anonymous women in history, their sewing is the only long-lasting thing to have survived.

In more recent times, machine-made blankets, central heating and the duvet have all contributed to the decline in homemade quilt-making – but the innate desire to create remains. Apart from the current spontaneous revival in quilt making, much energy has been rechannelled into contemporary quilting, patchwork and appliqué, evolving over the years into new and exciting art forms. Where the general approach is more experimental and self-expressive, individual designers have excelled, for example Pauline Burbidge with her Floating Triangles, and Eng Tow's Grey Shadows. Their work has given fabric crafts a value and an entirely new status – and in some instances should be judged as pieces of fine art.

The book shows a wide range of projects, illustrating both traditional and contemporary techniques, and it offers the modern needlecrafter the opportunity to recreate some of the most beautiful patterns of our time.

CHAPTER ONE

BASIC EQUIPMENT

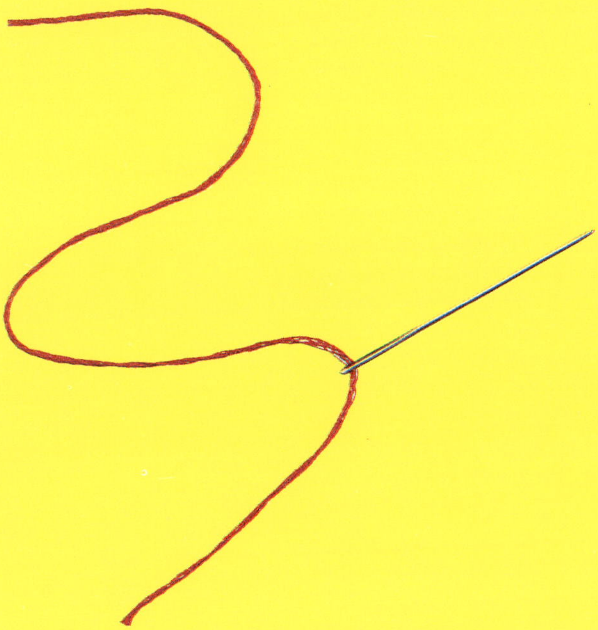

THE BASIC EQUIPMENT needed for quilting, patchwork and appliqué is not elaborate and can be bought at most department stores or needlework and art suppliers. When you begin to collect your tools and equipment together, you will probably find that you already have several items in your workbox or around the home.

• GENERAL DRAWING EQUIPMENT •

FOR DESIGNING, marking fabrics and making templates you will need rulers (both plastic and metal), and a set square (right-angle triangle), a protractor, a pair of compasses and a range of coloured crayons, lead pencils and chalk pencils—a set of felt pens is also useful for making your own designs. There are various proprietary 'magic' markers available for transferring designs to fabric. These are particularly useful for quilting, where it is crucial to have a lightly marked design that does not permanently stain the fabric. You will also need a sharp craft knife.

PAPER

Use cartridge (sketching) paper, shelf paper or artist's detail paper for planning designs, where several sheets can be taped together for working out very large patterns.

Graph paper is recommended for planning scaled patchwork designs and borders and for shaping templates. Isometric graph paper is extremely helpful for constructing certain patchwork templates such as the hexagon and equilateral triangle.

You will need tracing paper or tissue paper for transferring designs. Dressmaker's carbon paper is also used for transferring designs to fabric and gives a fairly long-lasting mark. It is available in several colours including red, yellow, blue, black and white. Choose the colour nearest to your background fabric or thread, and also white, or other light colours, to show up on dark fabrics.

Notepaper is the ideal weight for backing papers used with hand-sewn cotton or silk patchwork. Thicker fabrics, however, may need slightly heavier papers. The paper should be sufficiently firm for its edges to be felt through the folds of the fabric.

CARD, ABRASIVE PAPER AND ACETATE

Templates for all three techniques of quilting, patchwork and appliqué can be made from these materials to suit your own designs. Thin ticket card (thin cardboard) is generally recommended for templates used in quilting and patchwork projects of average sizes. Abrasive paper (a fine sandpaper, for example) is especially good for gripping the fabric but, with repeated use, it has the disadvantage of wearing out at the edges. Both card (cardboard) and abrasive paper templates can be strengthened with tape, and duplicates can always be made. For very large projects, where the templates have to withstand repeated use, it is a good idea to use a more durable material such as acetate. This is available

__Right:__ The basic equipment __1__ Setsquare __2__ Notebook __3__ Compasses __4__ Drawing pins __5__ Plastic eraser __6__ Pencil sharpener __7__ Fixative __8__ Spray diffuser __9__ Shears __10__ Craft knife __11__ Steel rule __12__ Felt-tip markers __13__ Technical pens __14__ Non-clogging ink __15__ Cartridge paper __16__ Squared paper __17__ Tracing paper __18__ Sketch book __19__ Brushes __20__ Watercolours __21__ Gouaches __22__ Conté crayons __23__ Charcoal __24__ Chalks __25__ Pencils

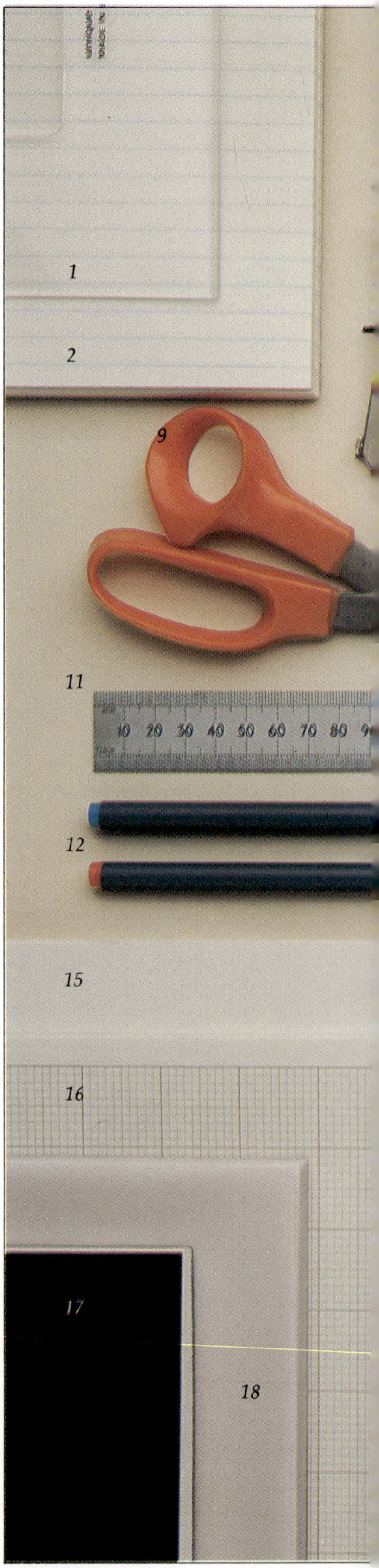

5
STAEDTLER
MARS-PLASTIC
4
6
7
FIXATIVE
57 ml
8
10
19
20
21
DESIGNERS GOUACHE
22
23
24
25
13
14
FW

Plus
NYLON MENDING
SYLKO
435
20 Needles

***Left:** Most needleworkers prefer a container that is both light and easily portable. The lined basket shown is an excellent example – it is pretty and capacious at the same time, and holds a wonderful selection of sewing materials and equipment.*

from art supply shops and can quite easily be cut to shape with scissors or a craft knife and ruler.

TEMPLATES

Quilting stencils are used in a similar way to templates for transferring designs to fabric. Although it is not difficult to make your own stencils from parchment, there are several traditional and modern designs available at craft suppliers. Templates for hand-sewn patchwork, such as the shell, hexagon and diamond, can also be bought from craft shops in a range of sizes. They are made from thin metal or plastic and are produced either as two solid shapes, one 6mm (¼in) larger than the other all round, or as a window template where the outer edge is 6mm (¼in) from the inner edge. In each case, the larger shape is used to cut out the fabric and the smaller shape, or the inner edge, is used for cutting out the backing papers. This gives a 6mm (¼in) seam allowance all round the fabric patch. These templates can also be used for marking quilting designs (*see* Quilting techniques, page 20).

• GENERAL SEWING EQUIPMENT •

A GOOD SELECTION of pins is needed including fine lace pins for delicate fabrics, dressmaker's stainless pins for general use, and glass-headed pins for pinning together several thicknesses. Being longer than average, the glass-headed pins are much easier on the fingers for pushing through bulky layers of fabric. You will also need a measuring tape and a dressmaker's tracing wheel for transferring designs, using the carbon paper method. Many craftworkers who do not use a thimble for ordinary hand sewing will find that one, if not two, are essential for quilting. A second thimble is often used on the first finger of the hand under the frame to guide the needle back through the fabric. A 2cm (¾in) wide cotton tape is needed for stretching the layers of fabric into a quilting frame.

NEEDLES

It is as important to practise obtaining the correct size needle and thread to suit your fabric and the way you work, as it is to use the correct needle for the job in hand.

For hand quilting, you will need quilting needles about 2.5cm (1in) long or size 8 or 9 betweens, which are slightly longer. For ordinary hand sewing and appliqué, a selection of sharps is required and for surface embroidery, crewel needles. For padded and corded quilting, use a large-eyed bodkin and for marking quilting designs, a round-ended tapestry or rug needle.

THREADS

It is important to choose the thread that will give the best results for your particular needs. Either match the thread to the fabric being used, silk thread for silk fabric, for example, or, in the case of quilting, use quilting thread. Quilting thread is smoother and stronger than ordinary cotton threads and comes in a fairly good selection of colours. Otherwise, No. 50 or No. 60 heavy duty mercerized cotton is an excellent alternative. Cotton/polyester threads and synthetic threads tend to knot and fray and are not generally recommended for hand sewing. However, as with other hand-sewing threads, they can be drawn through a block of beeswax which should strengthen them and prevent twisting.

For hand- or machine-sewn patchwork, No. 60 cotton thread is best while for appliqué use general sewing threads. For surface embroidery select coton à broder (the single-strand medium-weight cotton thread), stranded embroidery or pearl (sometimes called perlé) threads.

SCISSORS

For accurate cutting, use sharp dressmaker's shears, and keep them for cutting only fabrics so as not to blunt the blades. For snipping into corners and curves, when doing padded quilting, and for cutting threads, small embroidery scissors are good. General purpose scissors are needed for cutting paper and card.

FRAMES

Rectangular slate embroidery frames and large quilting hoops are ideal for hand sewing small items of quilting or appliqué, whereas for very large items a quilting frame is recommended.

A quilting hoop consists of two rings, usually made from wood, which fit closely one within the other so that the fabric is kept evenly stretched. The outer ring has a screw attachment for adjusting the tension.

Slate embroidery and quilting frames come in different sizes and weights. They are usually made from wood and constructed in much the same way. They have two rollers with tapes attached and two stretchers with slots at the ends to take the rollers and a series of holes into which pegs or screws can be fitted. These are adjusted to give the right amount of tension to the fabric. The size of a frame is measured across the width of the tape. Both frames can be fitted with table or floor stands to leave both hands free for stitching.

SEWING MACHINES

A sewing machine is an excellent labour-saving piece of equipment useful for quick quilting, piecing patchwork blocks and stitching on appliqué patches, as well as for stitching very long seams needed in making up items and for many finishing processes.

For best results, choose a machine that will give a good straight stitch, and, if possible, with a reverse stitch for starting and finishing, and a zigzag stitch for applying fabric patches and quick seaming.

IRONS

An iron is an essential piece of equipment and a sound investment for any fabric craft.

A thermostatically controlled steam iron generally gives the best results and is especially good for pressing seams really flat. It is quite important to have your iron and board close to your sewing area so that you can get used to the professional way of pressing seams as you sew.

FABRICS

Making a personal collection of fabrics is one of the most exciting aspects of working with fabric crafts, and plays an important part in the creative process of designing. Accidental arrangements of colours and patterns may trigger off new design ideas, often when least expected. All kinds of fibres in plain and mixed coloured patterns can be used. However, for quilting, patchwork and appliqué, certain fabrics work better than others.

Generally, smooth, closely woven fabrics such as dressweight cottons, brushed cottons, fine linen, lightweight wool, lawn, poplin, satin, silk or sateen work best. It is better to avoid synthetic, crease-resistant, or very stretchy fabrics as they are more difficult to handle. Heavier damasks, velvets, corduroys, suitings and tweeds combine well together and can be used for bigger machine-sewn projects.

For shadow quilting, a semi-transparent top fabric such as voile, muslin, organza or other sheer silk is used.

Cotton fabrics should be pre-washed and ironed while still damp, to test for colour fastness and shrinkage. Avoid using any fabrics where the dyes may run.

With the exception of corded quilting, where an open-weave fabric is used, the backing fabric should be made from the same fibre and of the same quality as the top fabric.

Other more unusual fabrics suitable for certain types of patchwork or appliqué are felt, plastic-coated fabrics and leather, including suede, chamois and different hides. As turned-under hems are not required, items such as fashion garments, accessories, cushions, hangings and toys can be quickly machine-stitched. However, as leather and felt cannot be washed, the cleaning requirements should be considered before going ahead with a project.

WADDING

Synthetic wadding (batting) is both lightweight and washable and comes in various standard widths and thicknesses. The layers can easily be separated, which means that thinner or thicker waddings (batts) can be made to suit individual needs. The 56g (2oz) and 112g (4oz) weights are popular for quilting while the thicker 224g (8oz) variety is used for tied quilting. Alternative waddings include cotton and wool domettes (woven, fluffy, light-blanket weight), and cotton wadding. Cotton wadding tends to move and separate during washing, which means that it should be closely quilted. It is also more difficult to sew. All three alternatives give a flatter finish and are heavier than synthetics which is an advantage for hangings.

Loose polyester or cotton fibre is used for padded quilting, and three-dimensional quilting.

QUILTING CORD

This is used for corded quilting and may be unspun soft fleece or white cotton cord. It is available in different thicknesses and can be bought by the metre (yard) from most needlecraft suppliers.

Alternatively, thick loosely spun knitting yarns like Lopi wool, or soft embroidery threads make excellent substitutes. In fact, coloured yarns can be combined with a semi-transparent top fabric to give unusual shadowy effects.

A selection of stranded embroidery threads.

Opposite left: *A variety of needlework frames that can be used for quilting, appliqué and embroidery. The advantage of using a frame with a stand is that both hands are left free to work. The palette is used to keep lengths of thread tidy.*

CHAPTER TWO

QUILTING TECHNIQUES

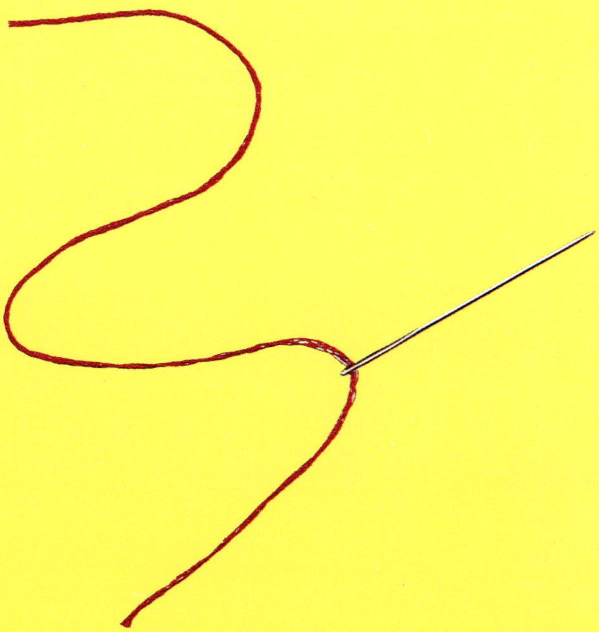

QUILTING has moved on a long way from when it was used as protective padding under the armour of twelfth-century knights and crusaders, and later for warm bedcovers and clothes—from which time the rich and long-lasting tradition of quilting design developed.

Although quilting is still used for stitching very beautiful and practical items following traditional quilting methods, many craftworkers prefer to experiment using the various techniques as a means of creative expression for making relief and free-standing forms. Before one can really begin to innovate and enjoy creating individual art-forms, it is a good idea first to understand the basic techniques in order to reach a personal style of working.

Essentially, quilting involves decoratively stitching together two or three layers of fabric using any of the following techniques.

Wadded quilting (English) is the traditional method and has a soft layer of wadding inserted between two outer layers which are held in place by working small stitches over the entire surface, either by hand or machine.

Padding (stuffed) quilting (Trapunto) has two layers of fabric and the design is outlined by hand or machine stitching in a similar way to wadded quilting. The stitched areas are then stuffed from behind with loose wadding to give a rich, sculptural effect.

Corded quilting (Italian) has two layers of fabric and the design is made by working pairs of narrow parallel lines of stitching in free-style or geometric patterns, either by hand or machine. Cord is then threaded into the resulting channels from behind to give a raised decorative effect.

Shadow quilting involves stitching together a solid and a semi-transparent top fabric. The design is outlined in a similar way to padded quilting and filled from behind with either coloured fabrics, mixed threads, sequins or beads to give the design an unusual effect of diffused colours.

FABRICS

Both plain and patterned fabrics can be used but light-toned fabrics create deeper shadows and will emphasize the quilting stitches—as will those with soft, lustrous surfaces—whereas patterns tend to hide the stitches. Soft, smooth fabrics such as cotton, poplin, calico, silk, satin, crêpe-de-chine and cotton/wool mixes are ideal for general quilting projects. Certain felt fabrics and supple chamois and gloving leathers are eminently suitable for fashion accessories.

QUILTING DESIGNS

Some of the simplest quilting designs are stitched directly through the fabric layers without pre-planning the arrangement. In patchwork quilt-making, for example, each geometric shape is outlined either in the seam or just outside, or, alternatively, patches can be

Top: *Early twentieth-century English quilt, worked in the north, probably in county Durham or Northumberland. The design shows a large central cross within a circle, and decorative shell motifs in the corners. The whole of this beautifully stitched quilt is surrounded with a chintz border.*

Above: *A selection of traditional borders showing plain and feathered twists, plaited chains and running feather designs, plus swagged crescents, to be used as a continuous band around a design or combined with corner motifs.*

Opposite above and below: *Traditional motifs of circles, flowers, leaves, fans and hearts, used singly or repeated to make composite shapes for central designs, or corner motifs.*

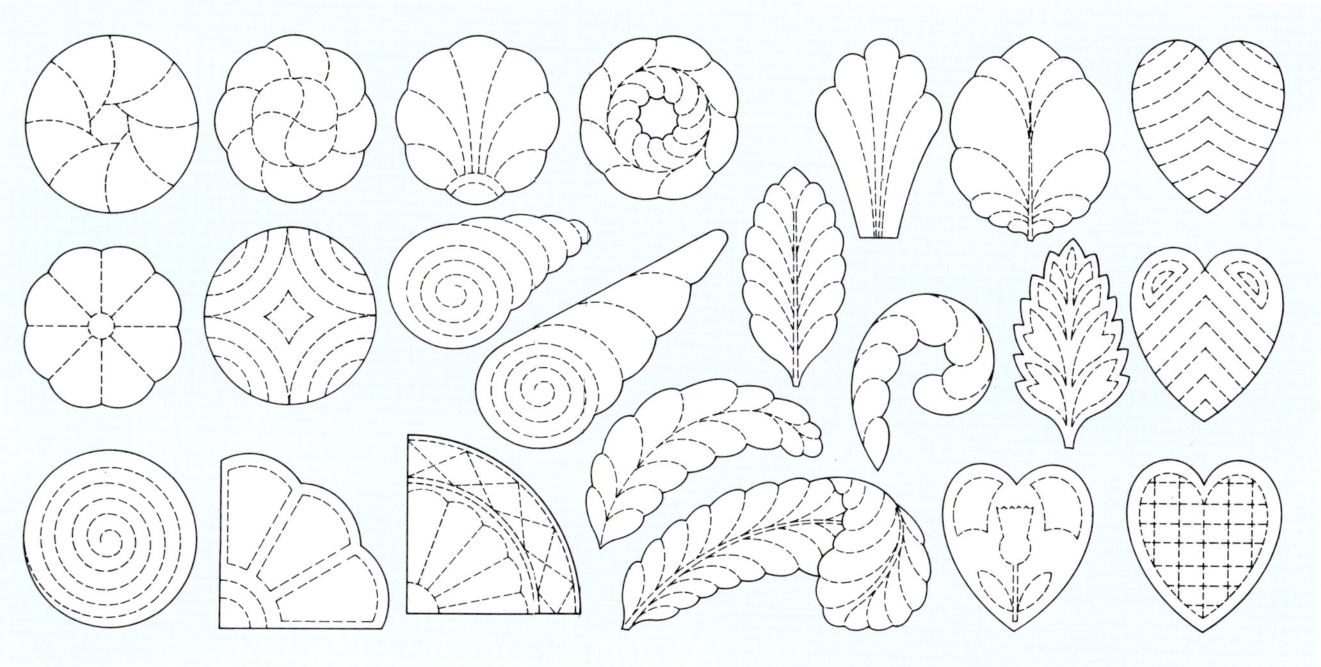

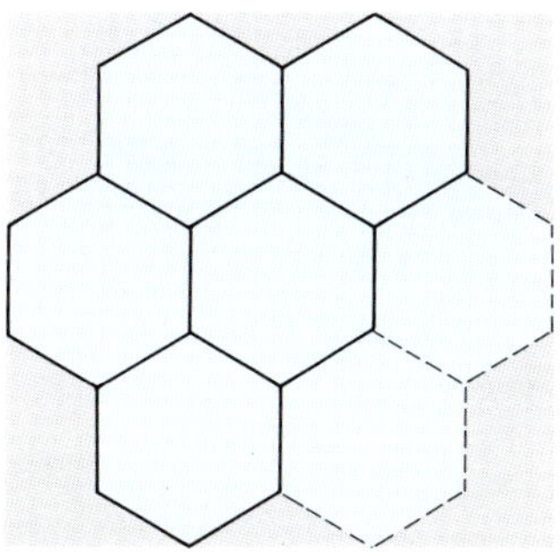

filled with contrasting geometric patterns. Appliqué shapes can also be emphasized with several contour lines, as in Hawaiian appliqué work, or freely stitched lines can be repeated at random over an entire surface.

Before choosing a design, decide whether a traditional or contemporary approach is best for the item you plan to make. Traditional designs are generally more formal and symmetrical and are better for quilts, coverlets and cushions. Contemporary designs tend to depict informal subjects in an asymmetrical way and are more suitable for hangings, pictorial scenes, clothes and accessories.

TRADITIONAL DESIGNS

A traditional design is carefully built up to give a well-balanced overall effect. Single images are placed around a prominent central motif, linked with background 'filler' patterns and usually bordered with corner motifs.

Spirals, flowers, leaves, lovers' knots and hearts, fans, feathers, shells and chains are all typical traditional motifs. As well as templates, sheets of traditional designs are available which can either be traced directly on to fabric, or cut up and rearranged to suit your own needs. On most quilting patterns the inner shapes indicated by broken lines are filled in freehand after transferring the outline. The inner lines on stencils are already punched out so that they can easily be filled in.

Background patterns (left) consisting of straight lines can be marked directly on to the fabric using a ruler and coloured pencil. Masking tape is also an effective way of marking simple straight lines. Other backgrounds involving units such as the hexagon and shell are best transferred by template or carbon paper.

Borders around a design must be marked accurately and at right angles to each other. It is a good idea to needle-score two parallel lines to the width of the border as a guide for keeping the patterns straight. Make sure the template size fits evenly into the length of each border, adjusting the corners to it.

CONTEMPORARY DESIGNS

Contemporary designs reflecting everyday images often follow a more relaxed style and range from simple contour quilting, through nursery shapes and alphabets, to pictorial landscapes and large figurative or abstract compositions—colour and mass being used as an artist would treat a painting.

WADDED QUILTING

Wadded quilting uses a layer of wadding (batting) between two outer fabrics, and as its name implies, is traditionally made for warmth. It is perfect for all kinds of quilts and throws, jackets, trousers, waistcoats and mitts, as well as a decorative finish for bags and accessories and many household items such as cushion sets and rugs egg, tea- and coffee-pot cosies.

PLANNING A DESIGN

Many traditional designs for wadded quilting (where templates are used to build up the pattern) can easily be adapted for padded quilting and shadow quilting.

Your design will, to some extent, be governed by the size of the finished object you plan to make. In order to hold all three layers securely, plan your design to cover the entire area. For quilts and coverlets, for example, it is best to emphasize the centre and borders, and, on garments, to fit the shape or movement of the body.

Symmetrical arrangements can be worked out first as a quarter repeat before completing the final design. Whatever your design, it should have contrasting shapes and textures and be worked out on paper before marking the fabric.

TEMPLATES

A template can either be a complete motif, such as the outline of a flower or leaf, or a small unit repeated within a larger motif, such as the petals of a flower.

To make a template simply trace the design on to ticket card (thin cardboard) and cut out, or cut out the motif from the tracing, stick that on to ticket card, then cut out.

Where a pattern is to be built up from a repeated unit, notch the edges of the template to show where the shapes meet up.

CUTTING THE LAYERS

Following the grainlines, cut the three layers of fabric (top, wadding (batting) and backing) slightly larger than the finished size, as quilting tends to shrink the work. If, on large items, the top and backing fabrics need to be joined from several widths, place a full width in the middle with half widths at each side—in this way a centre seam is avoided. Join wadding in the same way, butting the edges together and securing with herringbone stitch.

MARKING THE FABRIC

It is much easier if the top fabric is marked before the layers are assembled together. First lightly press the fabric into quarters to find the centre, and make any other divisions helpful for placing or constructing your design. Transfer the design to the right side of the fabric using one of the following methods. Mark the main outlines first, then add background patterns and borders.

MARKING THE BACKGROUND

For marking straight lines, use a coloured pencil or round-ended needle and a long, flat ruler. Lines can be overlapped or crossed to make lozenge, diamond or basket patterns (*see* page 19).

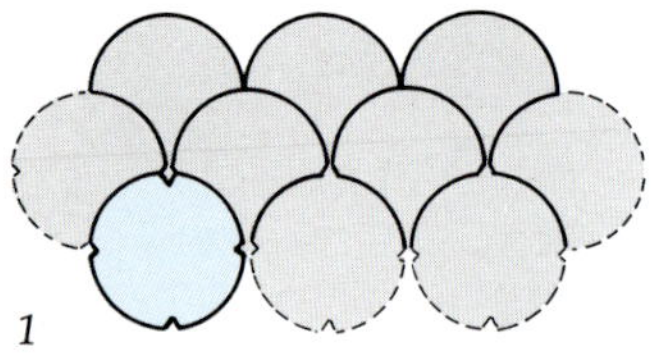

1

2

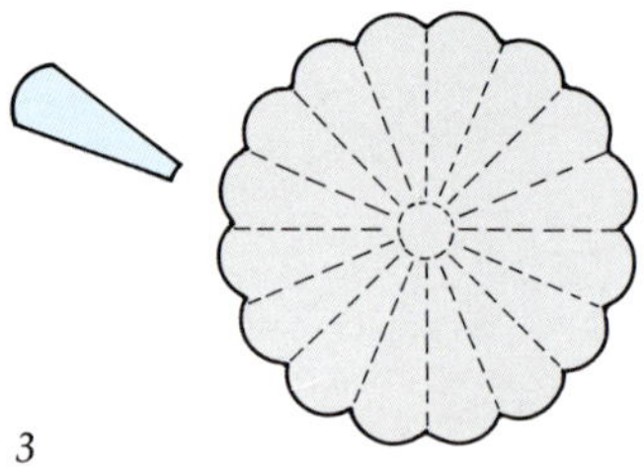

3

__1__ Making an all-over shell pattern using a single template.
__2__ Twisted border showing the template and corner construction.
__3__ Rose motif showing the single template and the central ring, which is always marked.

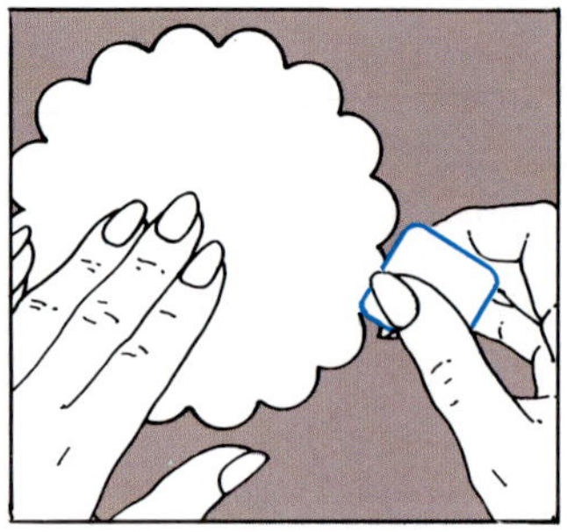

Using a template 1 *Place the template on the right side of the top fabric and lightly draw around the edge with sharpened tailor's chalk or a coloured pencil, repeating the marks as needed.*

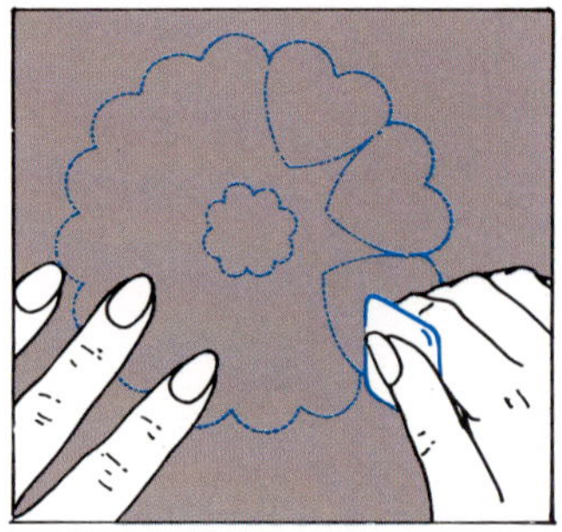

__2__ Remove the template and fill in the details by hand, or use a smaller template of the correct segment. Always mark the centre ring to avoid confusing lines crossing in the middle.

Above: *On large items that need joining, place a full fabric width in the middle so that the seams do not interrupt the central quilted design.*

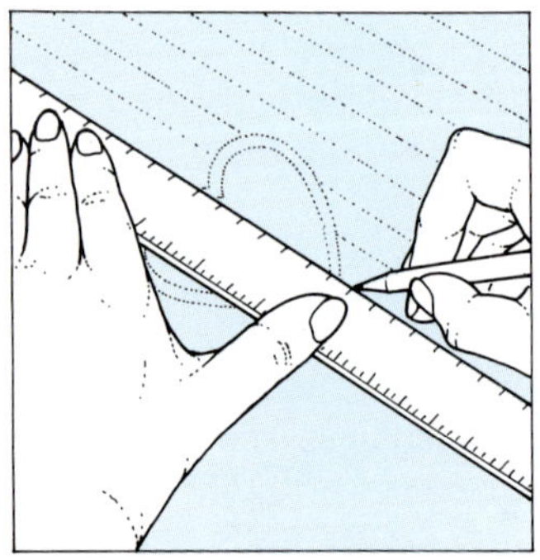

Above: *Use a long ruler to mark all background patterns.*

Opposite: *Detail of an eighteenth-century English quilt expertly embroidered in shaded colours using silk thread on a satin ground. The background pattern uses a trefoil-shaped template, and is quilted in whipped running stitch.*

NEEDLE MARKING

A clearer line is indented if the top fabric is placed on a padded surface. An ironing board is ideal for small items, or larger projects can be marked on a table covered with a soft blanket. Prepare the top fabric with the centres marked, and, holding the template in place, mark the outline with a round-ended tapestry or rug needle. Hold the needle almost parallel to the fabric and press the tip downwards while guiding it around the edge of the template.

USING DRESSMAKER'S CARBON PAPER

This method is relatively quick and reliable and suitable for opaque fabrics. Choose a light coloured carbon paper for dark fabrics but, for other colours, a close tone is better. This prevents any excess carbon from staining

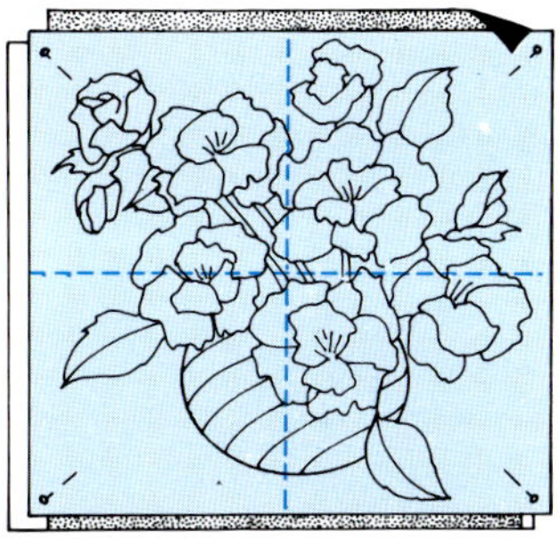

***Using dressmaker's carbon paper* 1** *Pin the design on the right side of the fabric matching the centre lines, and slip the carbon paper between, carbon side down. Avoid pinning through the carbon paper.*

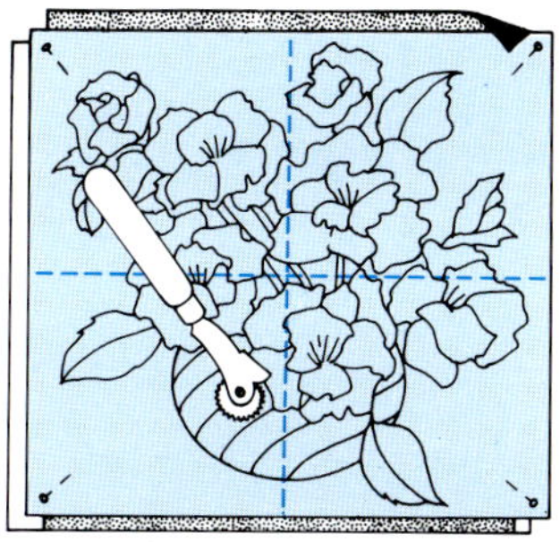

2 *Carefully go over the lines with a tracing wheel or an empty ballpoint pen. Try not to press on the surrounding area to prevent transferring unwanted marks.*

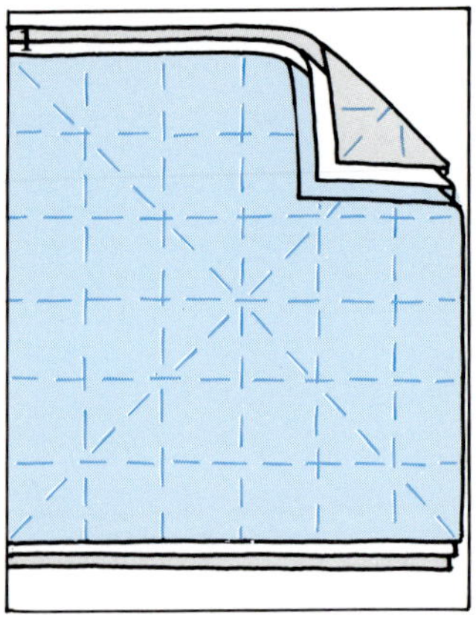

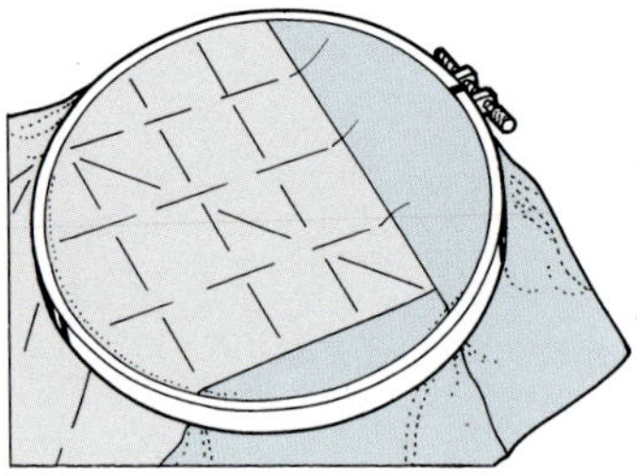

Above: *Extra pieces of fabric stitched to the edges will allow you to quilt into corners, using a hoop.* ***Left:*** *Layers of fabric arranged in the correct order.*

the fabric and rubbing off on to the quilting threads. Although it will wash off, carbon staining can be an unnecessary irritation. Draw your design on tracing paper.

PREPARING TO QUILT

Although wadded quilting can be worked in the hand, a quilting hoop or frame is recommended. This keeps the layers together and evenly stretched. A quilting hoop can be used for large items by moving it along after completing a section. Work should not be left in a hoop indefinitely as this may badly crease the fabric.

USING A HOOP

Assemble the layers on a flat surface, first placing the backing wrong side up, the wadding next, and then the marked top fabric right side up. Pin and tack the layers together, covering the area with several rows of tacking stitches worked across in both directions, first diagonally through the centre and then in rows about 6cm (2½in) apart. Avoid knots (which can be difficult to remove from the finished quilting) by working outwards from the centre, leaving half the length of thread in the centre when tacking one half row, and returning to rethread and complete the row in the opposite direction. Smooth out any wrinkles as you stitch.

Put the hoop in the centre of the work and gradually work towards the edges as each area is completed. In order to quilt the edges, pieces of similar fabric should be tacked around the work. This extends the area and makes it possible to keep the edges evenly stretched while quilting.

USING A FRAME

For working large projects such as a full-size quilt, a quilting frame is recommended. On the whole, the advantages of using one outweigh the disadvantages: the work will crease less; little or no preparatory tacking is needed; more than one person can work at the frame; and you can stitch right up to the edges using both hands. However, the main disadvantage is its size, which means that it cannot be moved around as easily as a smaller frame.

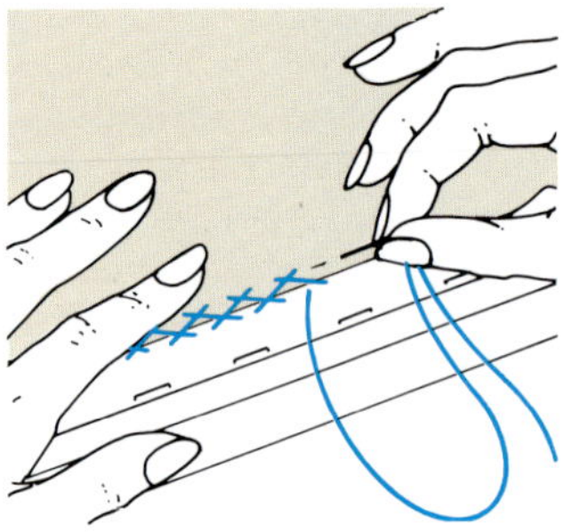

Using a frame 1 *Using herringbone stitch and working outwards from the middle, attach the backing fabric to the webbing on each roller. Wind the surplus fabric around the back roller, leaving an area of about 30–50cm (12–20in).*

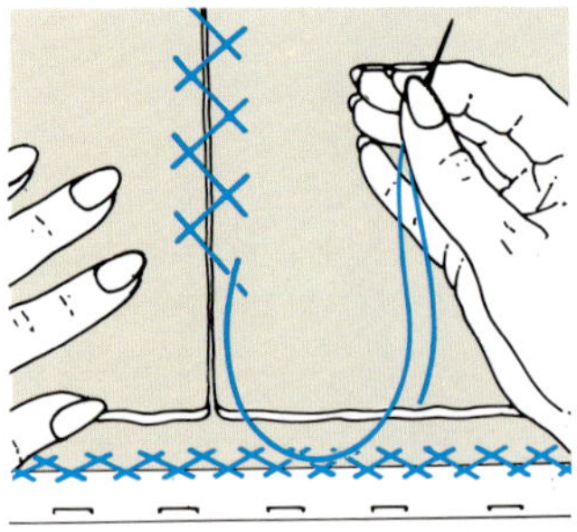

2 *Spread the wadding evenly over the backing and, if necessary, butt the edges together and herringbone stitch to secure, avoiding a centre join where possible.*

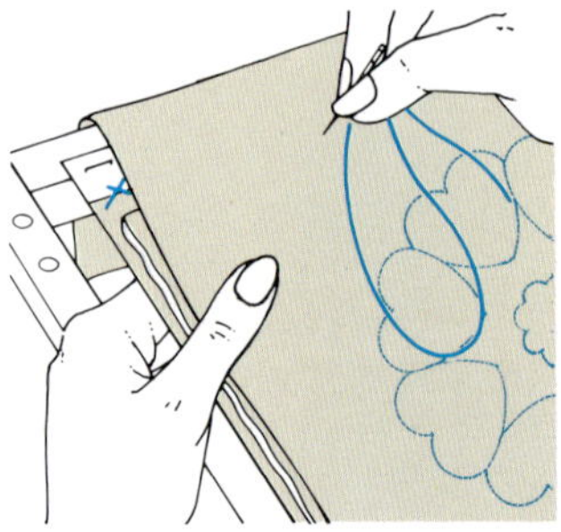

3 *Place the marked top fabric over the wadding. Smooth flat and tack the layers together along the front edge, allowing the surplus fabric to hang over the back roller. Pin all layers close to the back roller about 2cm (¾in) apart.*

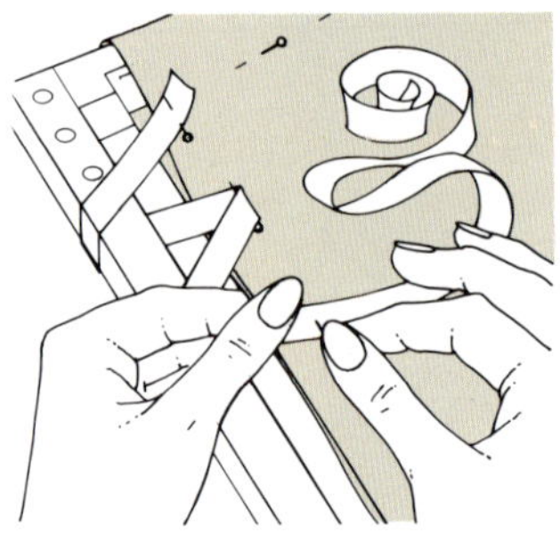

4 *Position and secure the stretchers so that the work is springy rather than tightly stretched. Hold both sides of the work in place with cotton tape. Loop the tape around the stretcher and attach with pins, stretching the work evenly on both sides.*

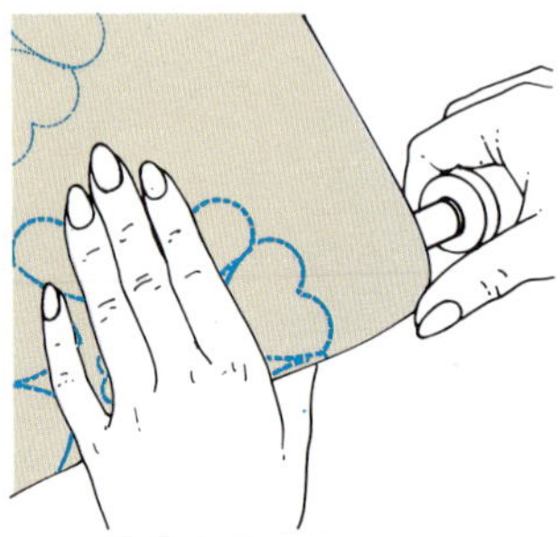

5 *Quilt the exposed area working from the front to the back roller. Loosen the tapes and stretchers and wind the finished quilting round the front roller. Restretch the fabric and repeat the process as needed.*

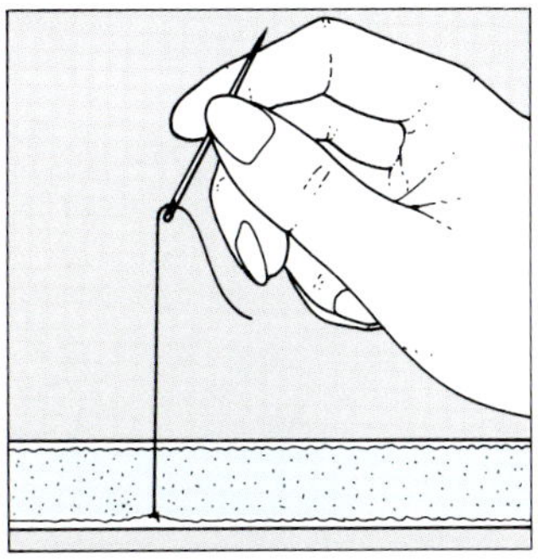

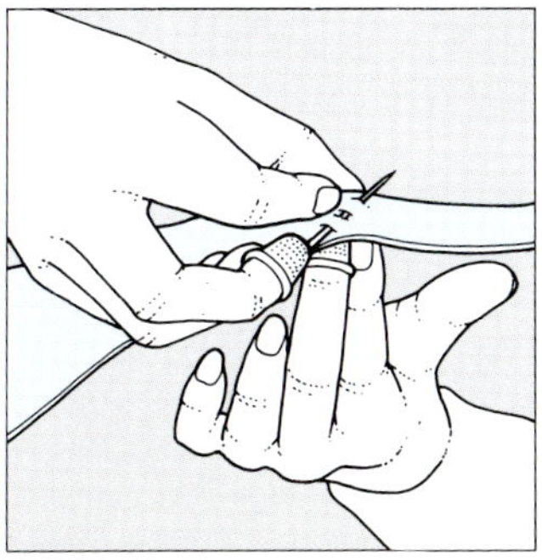

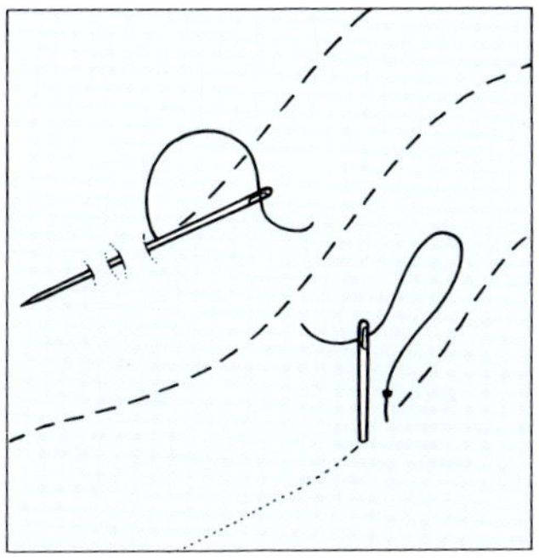

Below: *Orange Saddle. This enchanting child's horse saddle is thought to have belonged to an Indian prince. It is made completely from tussore silk, and quilted with simple linear patterns.*

***Hand quilting* 1** *Use a fairly short thread, about 50cm (20in) long. Wax the thread and knot the cut end to prevent twisting. Bring the needle out and pull the knot through the backing, leaving it caught under wadding.*

2 *With a thimble on the second finger of the sewing hand, make several stitches. Keep the thumb pressed down on the fabric just ahead of the needle while the other hand below, feels the needle and guides it back through.*

3 *To finish, make a knot close to last stitch and take thread through to back. Pull knot through catching it under wadding, and cut thread. Working with several needles in a design is easier than stopping and starting new threads.*

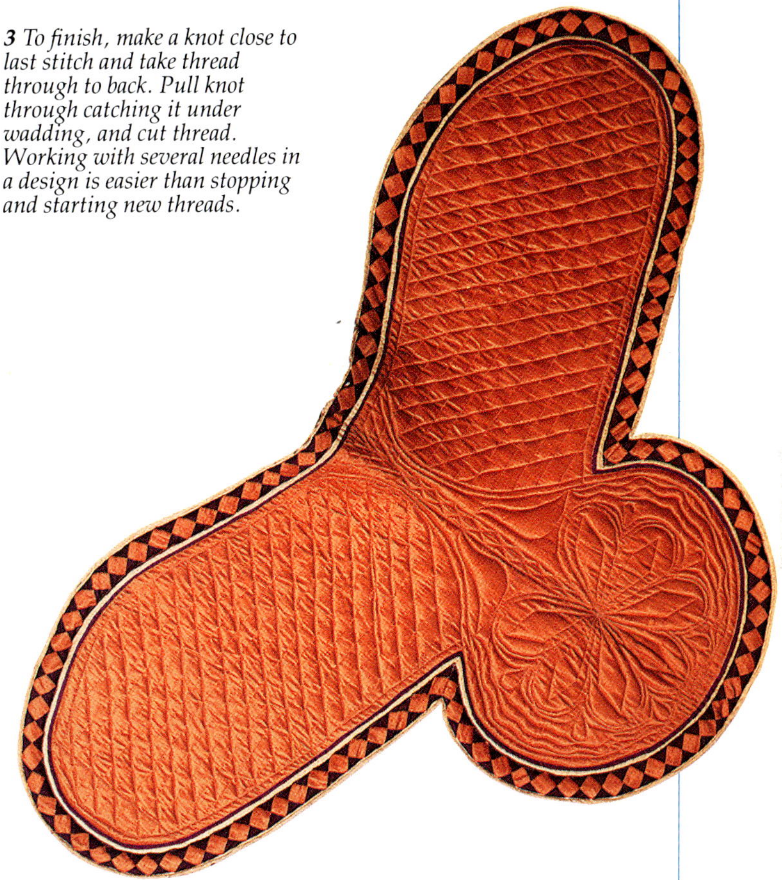

HAND QUILTING

Hand quilting is usually worked throughout with small, even running stitches taken through all three layers of fabric, and it should appear to be the same on each side—making a completely reversible fabric. However, the stitch length should be adjusted to the size of the thread and the thickness of the wadding used, bearing in mind that regularity is more important than the size of the stitch. Back stitch and chain stitch also work well but, for best results, keep to the same stitch in a single piece of work.

MACHINE QUILTING

Machine quilting is fast and direct and appeals to many contemporary quilters mainly because they can express their ideas quickly, and, perhaps, more spontaneously. Machine quilting, however, produces a harder line and lacks the beautiful softness of hand quilting.

Pin and tack the layers together as for hand quilting, and stitch the design, working outwards from the middle. Use a medium length stitch and loosen the tension if the wadding is very thick. You may also need a larger needle.

It may require several attempts and specific practice in order to machine a line exactly straight or to follow flowing curves and make perfect circles. Use both hands to feed the fabric under the needle and do not machine faster than you can comfortably control the fabric.

Finish the quilting and neaten the threads by first pulling them through to the back of the work. Thread them into a needle and make a small back stitch. Pass the needle through the wadding, bring it out a short distance away and cut close to the surface.

A quilting bar can be fitted to the sewing machine and provides an excellent guide for stitching parallel lines. After marking and stitching the first line, adjust the bar so that it rests on the previously stitched line.

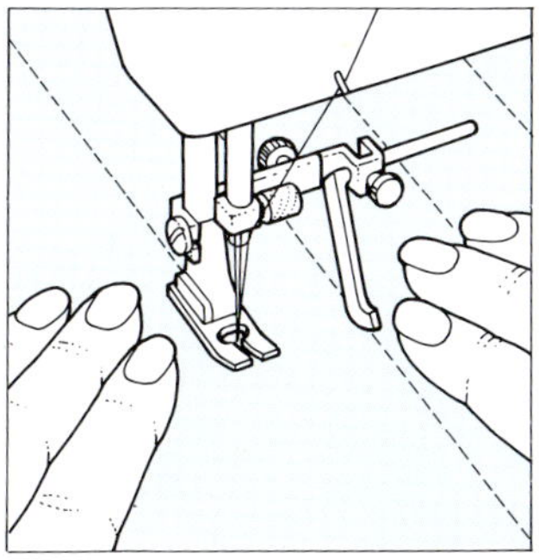

Left: *Using the quilting bar, complete the first line and repeat as needed. Stitch very long lines in alternate directions to avoid puckering underneath.*

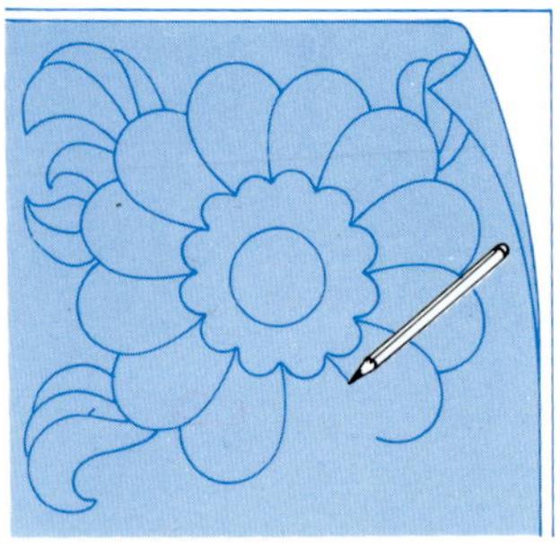

Padded quilting (Trapunto)
1 Cut out the main fabric and backing to the same size and transfer the design, in reverse, to the backing fabric, using dressmaker's carbon paper.

2 Place both fabrics wrong sides together and, working outwards from the centre, tack diagonally and vertically in both directions.

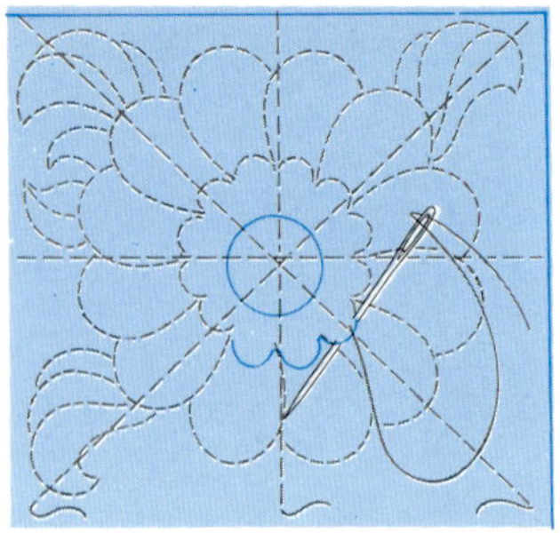

3 Outline the design with small running stitches by hand or machine, taking care to pick up both layers. Work from the centre out.

4 Remove the tacking threads and then, working from the wrong side, snip the backing in the middle of each area to be padded using small embroidery scissors.

5 Using a round-ended bodkin or a small crochet hook, stuff the shapes with teased-out wadding.

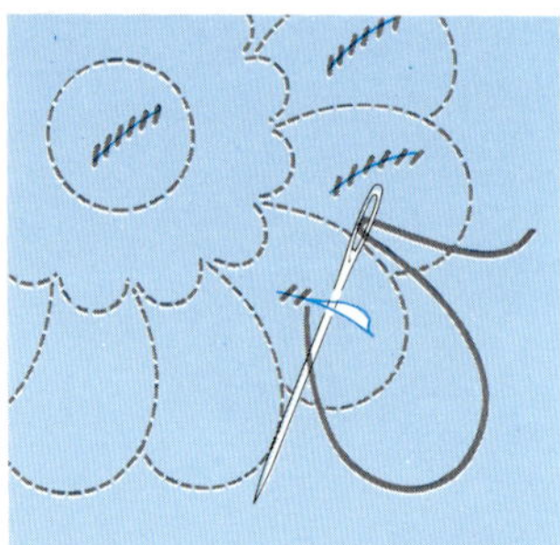

6 Carefully mould each shape, periodically checking the effect on the right side. Finally, slip stitch the openings together, and neaten the finished work with a lining.

PADDED QUILTING (TRAPUNTO)

Padded (stuffed) quilting is a purely decorative technique using two layers of fabric where certain areas of a design are padded from behind, which gives the surface a pleasing, undulating texture.

The depth of the moulding can be varied to create shallow relief or highly raised effects for both traditional and contemporary designs. The technique offers great scope for utilizing more unusual top fabrics such as stretchy nylons and knits, velvets, velours and taffetas, as well as the more usual varieties. For the backing, choose a soft, open-weave fabric such as muslin, scrim or voile. When planning your design, each area to be padded must be completely enclosed to make a good shape. Use padded quilting for pillows, bags, and pictures, picture frames and hangings.

***Below:** This modern three-dimensional cushion takes padding a stage further. The knitted hand holding a tent-stitched miniature cushion conceals a greetings card pocket. Knitted strips, felt leaves, and embroidered flowers decorate the surface.*

Above: *Border design of interlocking triangles, which, when filled with cord, gives a pleasing contrast to the plain centre.*

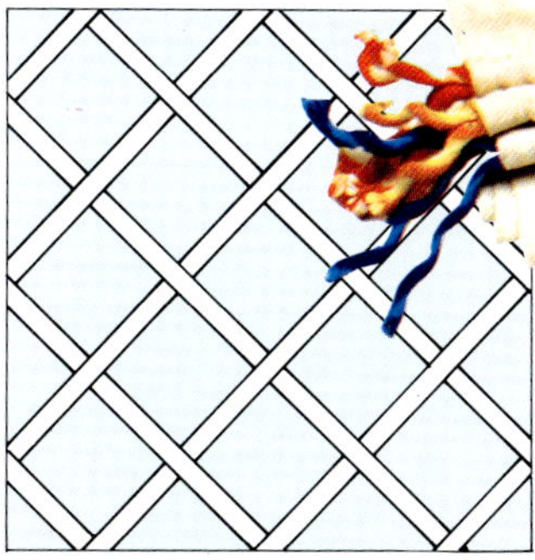

Above: *All-over trellis pattern constructed with interwoven parallel lines.*

Corded quilting (Italian)
1 *Transfer your design to the backing fabric and pin the two layers together, right sides outward. From the centre, tack diagonally and vertically in both directions, adding more lines of tacking on larger projects.*

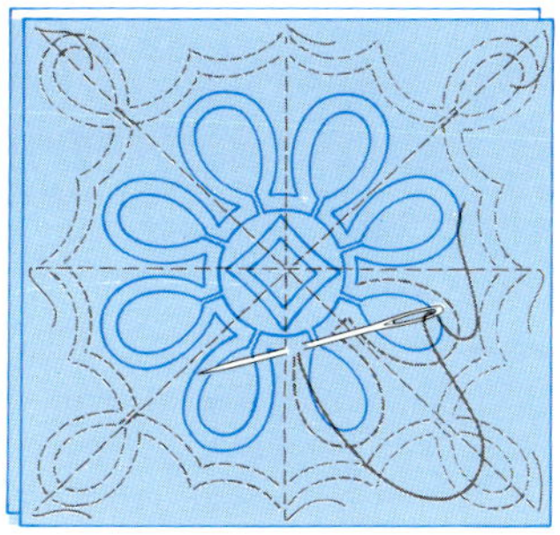

2 *Working on the wrong side, hand sew around the design using small running stitches, being careful to stop and start new channels as suggested by the design. Simple designs can be machine sewn.*

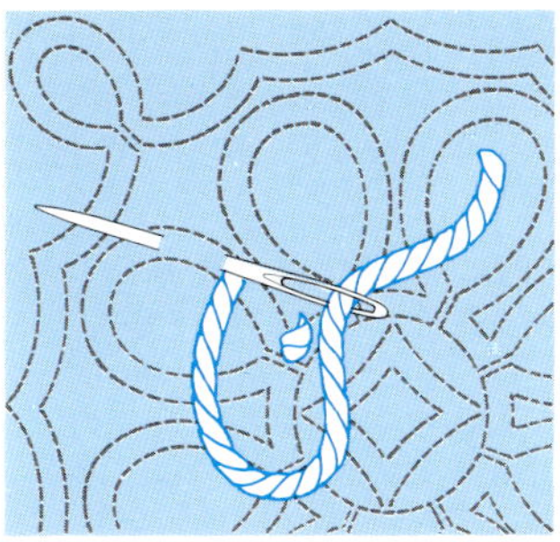

3 *With the wrong side facing, separate the backing threads, or snip into the channel, and insert a bodkin threaded with quilting cord. It is best to have a short length of cord in the needle and not to pull the cord too tightly. Pass it through the channel a little at a time, bringing it out at angles and curves.*

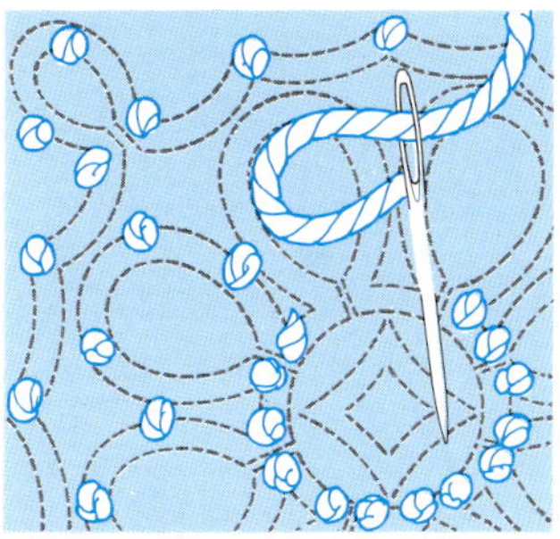

4 *Reinsert the needle into the same hole leaving a small loop of cord on the surface—these will eventually become eased into the channels.*

Above: *Experimental cording on narrow strips of calico. The strips are corded with hand-dyed piping cord before being woven, and secured by hand, to form an unusual textured fabric.*

CORDED QUILTING (ITALIAN)

Corded quilting uses two layers of fabric and has, as its name suggests, a ridged, linear appearance. The designs are carefully worked out in pairs of parallel lines, which are later filled with cord or quilting wool. The whole effect is of flowing continuous movement. Many traditional designs are based on geometric lines involving intricate tracery and beautiful interlaced patterns, as well as detailed flower arrangements and naturalistic figures in domestic scenes.

Corded quilting can be worked by hand or machine and is most suited to a closely woven top fabric and a loosely woven backing, as in padded quilting. Linen and linen scrim are the traditional fabrics used—these are hardwearing and launder well—with a cotton cord or soft yarn for the quilting. Although piping cord now makes a good alternative it gives a slightly harder effect. Incidentally, all cords should be washed first to prevent shrinkage later on.

An important design consideration, using the two-layer technique, is to carefully plan on paper the exit and entry points for threading the cord. Try to bring out the needle at corners and junctions to give clear definition to your design.

For a smart, sophisticated look work the quilting in fabrics such as moiré silk or taffeta for dress panels and accessories, and choose cotton, linen or cotton/wool mixes for coverlets, cushions and pillows.

Above: Shadow quilted trees, stuffed from behind with coloured felt and fabrics, make an unusual repeat design.

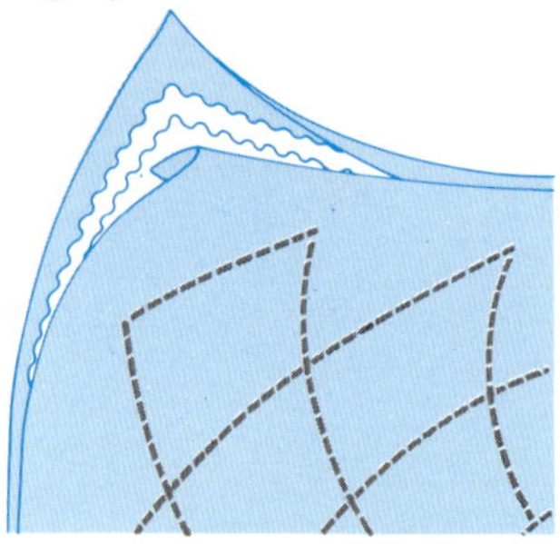

Reversible edge 1 *Trim the wadding back to the finished size, and, if needed, trim the top and backing to within 1.5cm (½in) of the wadding. Turn both fabric edges to the inside, lapping one edge over the wadding.*

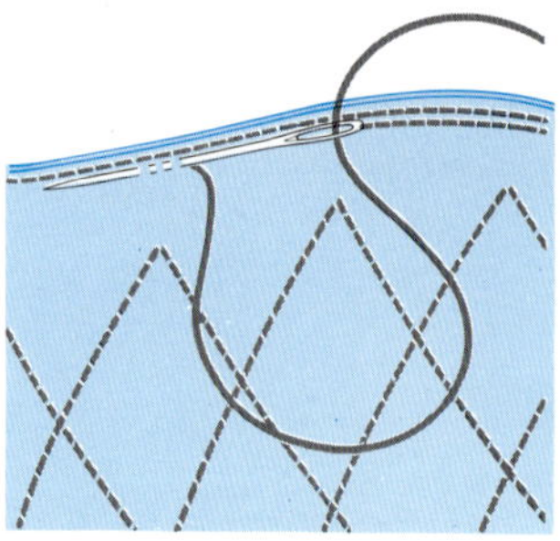

2 *Press and pin the edges together and then stitch round the quilt as close to the edge as possible, catching in the wadding. Stitch a second line 6–15mm (¼–½in) further in.*

SHADOW QUILTING

Shadow quilting is a variation of padded quilting using two layers of fabric with coloured insertions under the semi-transparent top layer to give the design fascinating effects in soft, muted colours. Organdie, voile, sheer silk and nylon knits are all suitable top fabrics. Muslin or scrim can be used for the backing, and a variety of bright, even vibrant coloured fabrics or threads for the filling. As colours become subdued (shadowy) under the top fabric, quite shocking contrasts can be used. Sequins, glitter fabrics and threads, even beads, felt and foil offer scope for originality.

Designing for shadow quilting has the same basic limitations as padded quilting. Individual shapes are enclosed with stitching, either by hand or machine, and padded from behind in exactly the same way.

Use shadow quilting as spot motifs on garments, for bags, cushion sets, pictures and pieced-quilt blocks—even for mock jewellery.

FINISHING

There are several ways of finishing the edges on quilted work depending on the function of the particular item. Quilts and coverlets, for example, can be self-neatened (making the edge reversible)—bound, bordered or piped—whereas garments and accessories usually need to be cut out from the quilted fabric and finished as instructed in the pattern.

Remove the work from the frame, take out all the tacking threads, and finish the edges using one of the following methods.

BINDING

Use either commercial binding, which is available in different fabrics and widths, or cut your own bias strips from the fabric used. For large items such as quilts, long strips are needed and should be made following the instructions given on the opposite page. You will need fabric at least 50cm (20in) wide.

BORDERED

For this type of border, where an extension of the backing is used to edge the quilting, shown opposite, you will need to allow extra backing and wadding in your initial calculations.

PIPING

Piping gives a professional finish to a quilt edge, where it is inserted between the top and backing fabrics. It is also an attractive trim for cushions and garments, for example, when it is stitched into the seams as they are made up.

You will need matching or contrasting coloured fabric and piping cord of a suitable thickness. No. 4 is a popular choice. See the opposite page for piping quilts and cushions.

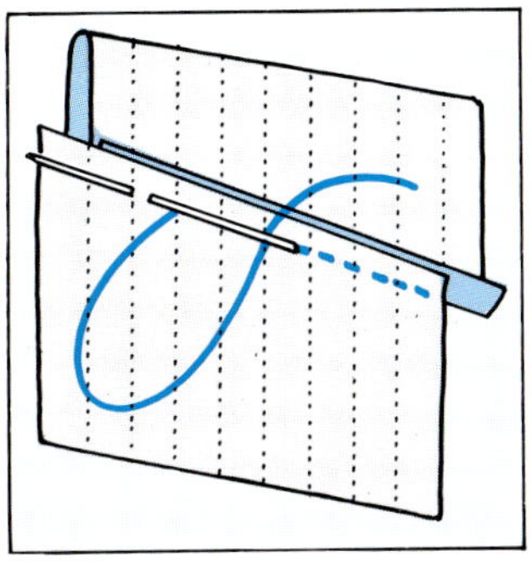

Binding 1 *On the wrong side, mark the fabric with diagonal lines 5–8cm (2–3in) apart and trim off the corners. With right sides together, fold the fabric in half on the straight grain and stitch with one strip extending beyond the seam at each side.*

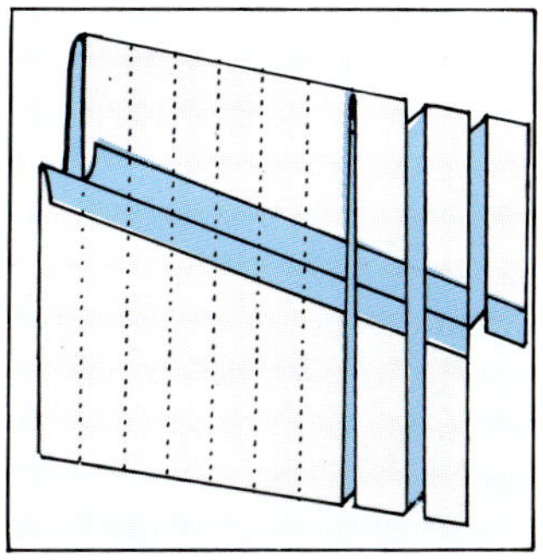

2 *Press the seam open. Begin at one end and cut around the tube of fabric on the marked line to give a long, continuous bias strip with already finished seams.*

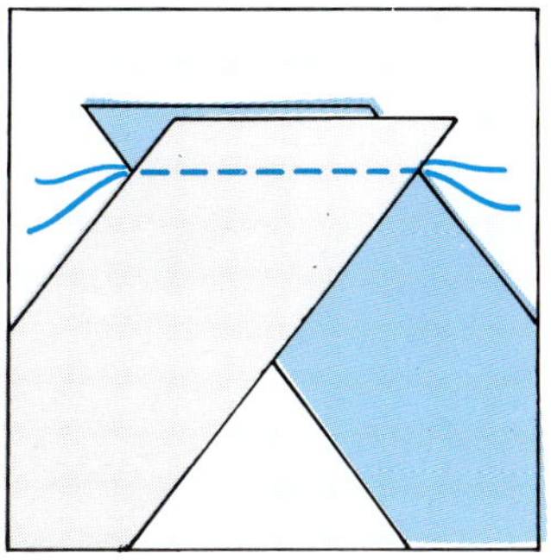

3 *Calculate the length of binding needed and cut to size allowing extra for all seams. Join the ends together, and any intermediary seams, as shown and press the seams open.*

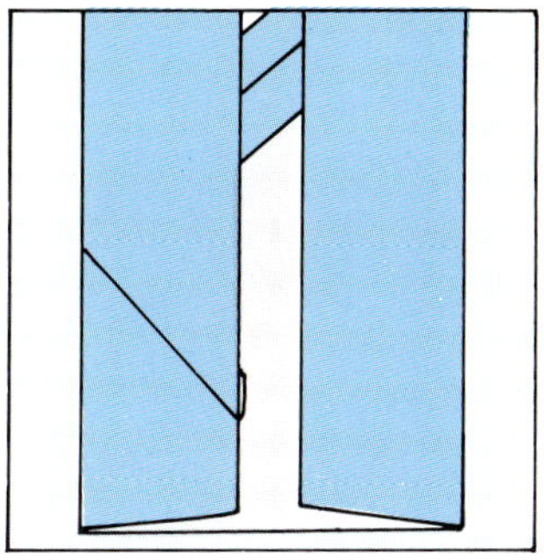

4 *Press the edges towards the middle with the right side outside.*

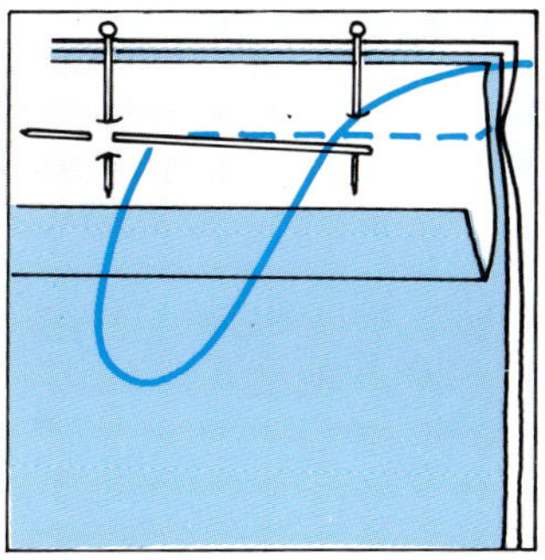

5 *With edges even and right sides together, pin the binding to the quilted item. Using matching coloured thread machine stitch or hand sew along the foldline through all layers.*

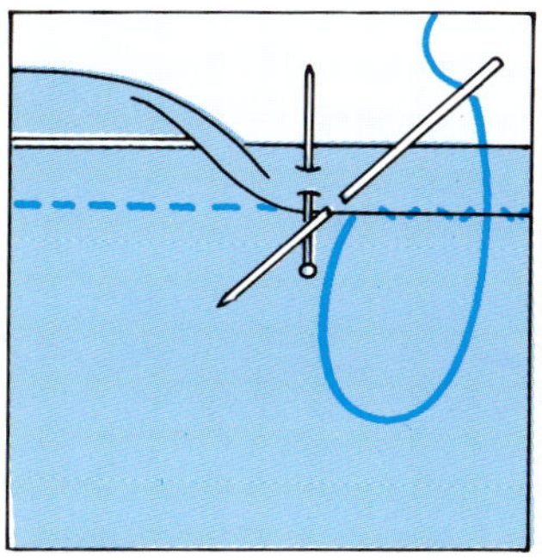

6 *Turn the binding to the wrong side and pin to hold. Using a matching coloured thread, slip stitch over the previous stitching.*

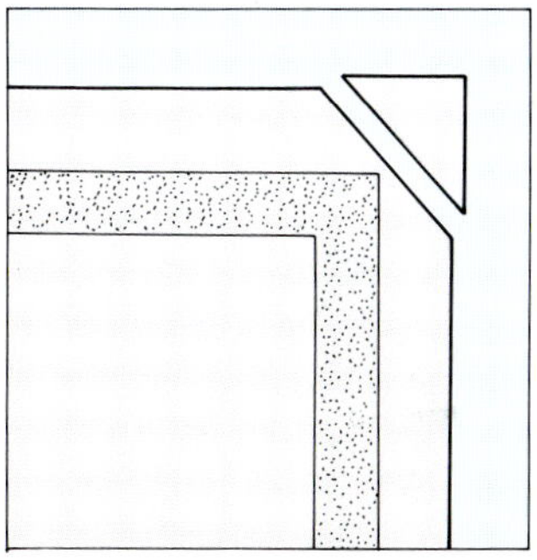

Bordered 1 *Trim the excess backing to twice the width of the border required plus 1.5cm (½in) for turning. Cut the wadding back to the finished width of the border, and cut off the corners, as shown.*

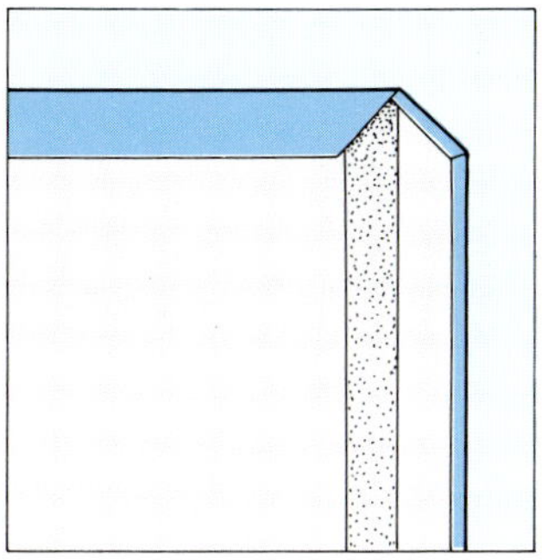

2 *Turn under the raw edge and press, and then fold the border over the wadding to the front and pin in place. Mitre the corners, as shown.*

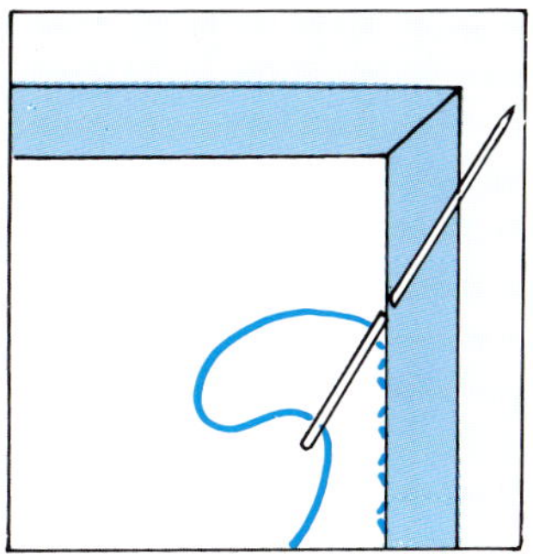

3 *Stitch either by machine or hand, taking care to hand sew neatly and securely across the mitred corners.*

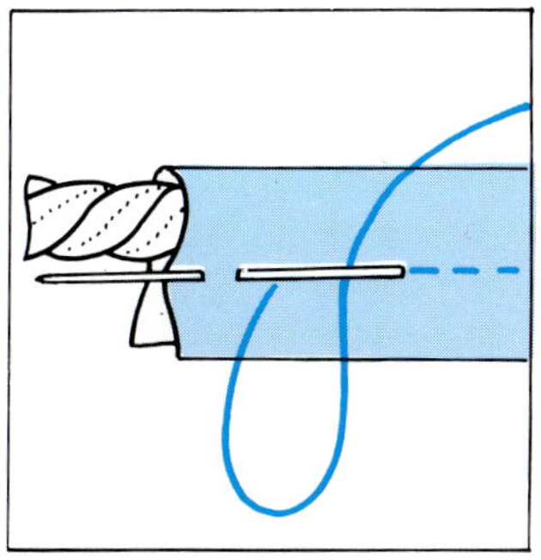

Piping 1 *Cut the required length of bias strip by the circumference of the cord plus 3cm (1¼in) for seam allowances. Place the cord inside the strip right side outside, and stitch across close to the cord either by hand or machine using a piping foot.*

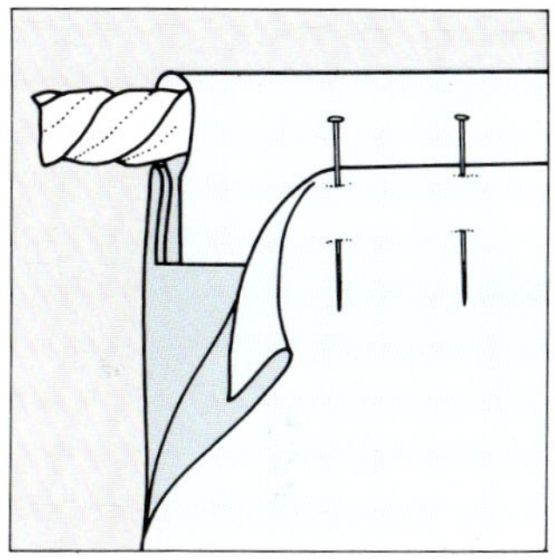

2 For quilts, *tack piping to quilt right sides together and raw edges even. Stitch close to previous stitching and press seams to the wrong side. Turn in edges of backing, pin over stitchline and slip stitch in place.*

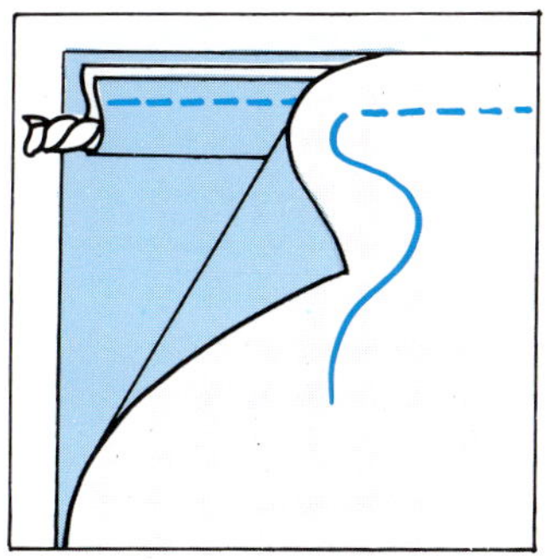

3 For cushions, *tack the piping in place with right sides and raw edges even. Ease piping around corners clipping into edge. Cover with second layer of fabric, tack and stitch through.*

CHAPTER THREE

QUILTING PROJECTS

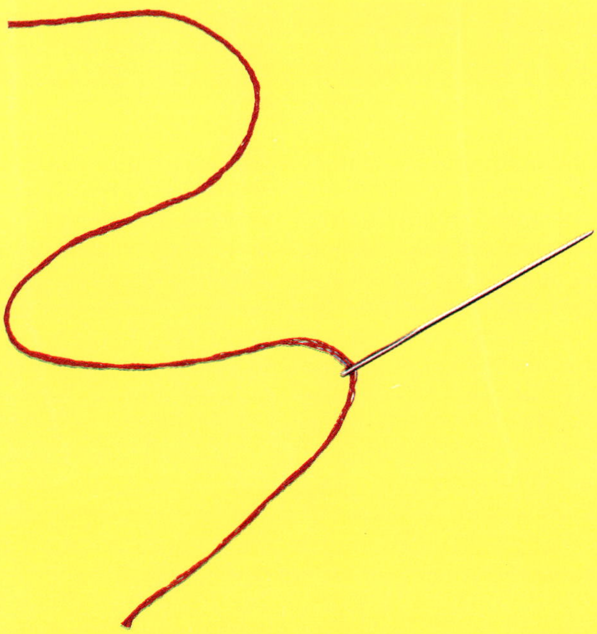

Left and far left: *Feather Circle. Diagram showing a quarter section of the design.*

Opposite: *This baby's crib cover entitled Purple Hearts is made from a cream cotton/wool mixture, and quilted in varying tones of purple coton à broder.*

• WADDED QUILTING-HAND SEWN •

FEATHER CIRCLE

NOT ALL TRADITIONAL QUILTING need be worked on plain fabric with matching coloured thread. Designs can be simplified and interpreted in contemporary fabrics, threads and colours to suit present-day settings. Glamorous silks with beautiful faint watermarking, wild silks with lightly textured surfaces, heavy sateens, slipper satin, several types of upholstery satins and silks, all with soft, lustrous surfaces, can be used together with heavier silk threads or coton à broder in contrasting or variegated colours for the quilting, and piping, backing fabric or lining picked out in a slightly stronger colour. This could be softly patterned (a fabric from an existing interior scheme) in diagonal stripes, pin-head spots, ikat fabric, plain cotton or satin to offset the shape. Cushions worked like this often have greater impact made in sets. Here the designs could be varied but linked by using the same accent colours or vice versa, choosing harmonizing well-balanced colours. Use traditional quilting designs for all sizes of cushions and bolsters, a bedside rug, sofa throw, quilt, and, in carefully worked out proportions, on garment cuffs and yokes.

For the cushion project, choose a soft lustrous fabric, such as sateen for the top and either the same or a contrast backing, as preferred. The diagram gives a quarter section of the design which should be enlarged to the size required (*see* page 91), 36–40cm (14–16in) being a popular size. Transfer it to the top fabric, using dressmaker's carbon paper in a closely matched colour so that it will not show too strongly. Reverse the tracing on the centre lines to complete the design. Borders are easier to transfer this way rather than by having to adjust a template to fit.

Prepare the layers as for wadded quilting and work the design in contrasting coloured coton à broder, working outwards from the middle.

Make up the cushion with a toning contrast piping around the edges (*see* page 27 for piping, and page 97 for making up a cushion cover).

PURPLE HEARTS

Old quilting techniques combine perfectly with new design ideas in this enchanting baby's crib cover. The design shows the traditional heart motif repeated over the entire quilt, using a simple square grid in a modern way.

Interestingly, the grid lines are treated as a feature of the design and contrast well with the quilted texture of the heart motifs. Here, each heart is outlined in purple and filled with a different combination of line patterns in shaded colours, picked up from the binding fabric. The quilt is made from a cream-coloured cotton/wool mixture and bound with a narrow floral print of the same mixed-fibre fabric. It uses a fine layer of synthetic wadding for the interlining and coton à broder for the quilting. The size fits a standard crib of about 64cm by 77cm (25in by 30in). The quilt is completely reversible.

Alternative fabrics such as shot taffeta, glazed cotton, satin or crêpe-de-chine may be used where single motifs would make especially attractive cushions, or repeated on larger quilts and coverlets and given a surrounding plain border.

For the project cut out the front and back sections to the correct size, following the instructions in quilting techniques. Fold the top in quarters, lightly press, and tack the creases to make guidelines for transferring the design. Make a template as shown below, using 6mm (¼in) graph paper glued to thin card (cardboard). Draw a 15cm (6in) square and mark the border lines 6mm (¼in) apart. Draw a heart freehand in the centre (or enlarge the design to scale). Then, draw a diamond as shown and mark its edges at 6mm (¼in) intervals. Join the dots to make a diagonal grid, as a guide for marking the filling patterns. Cut out the heart and trim the outer edges square.

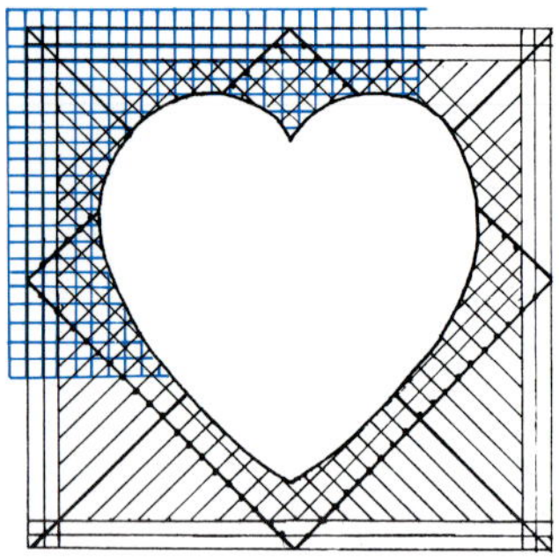

Above: *Heart-shaped template constructed on graph paper.*

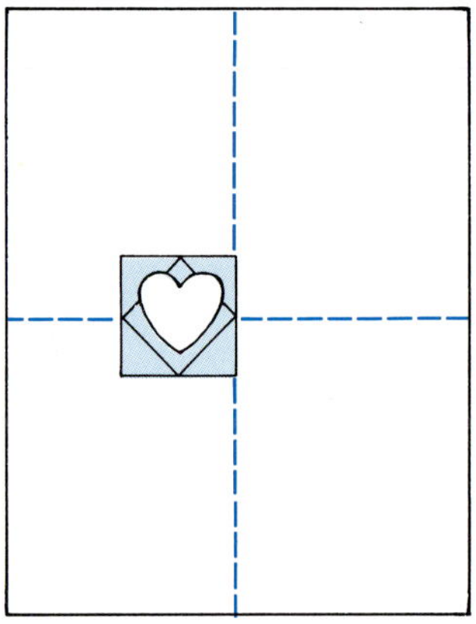

Right: *position for first template.*

Position the template as shown, secure with masking tape, and, using a coloured pencil, mark off dots for the grid lines and transfer the motif, repeating it over the entire area. Then, using the diagonal grid, and a ruler, fill each heart with a different line pattern. Join up the dots to mark the intersecting grid lines, adding the correct number of lines to the outer border.

Remove the guideline threads, and prepare the layers as for wadded quilting. Using a hoop, work the horizontal grid lines in shades of blue and the vertical lines in shades of turquoise. Outline the hearts in purple and quilt the patterns in various graded combinations of blues and greens. Complete the quilting and bind the edge with a fabric cut on the bias grain.

OCEAN WAVE WITH WINDOWPANE

Japanese quilting, known as *sashiko,* is used on this colourful 'wrap and tie' cushion. *Sashiko* originated in rural Japan where the women of fishing and farming communities used it to decorate most of their outer garments. Coats, jackets, aprons, gloves and socks were quilted mainly in white on a dark blue cotton fabric, essentially for warmth. Beautiful, often complex-looking all-over patterns are quilted with running stitch, using a simple grid system. The grid is stitched first and the squares are filled in with designs. One garment may have one or many designs often separated with asymmetric lines. Frequently in more sophisticated *sashiko,* used especially to decorate the traditional *obi,* naturalistic motifs and designs are superimposed on a background of geometric patterns in imitation of elaborate woven silks.

Use *sashiko* quilting either as an all-over pattern or as inset blocks or panels for a jacket, waistcoat, trousers, dressing gown, bag, baby carrier, crib cover or wall hanging.

For the cushion project use bright coloured cottons. The separate outer cover, is a simple rectangle, which is quilted and then bound around the edges with a contrast colour. It is tied over a 30cm (12in) square pad covered with plain fabric in a third contrast colour.

Make a full-scale tracing of the design from the diagram given—a 5cm (2in) square grid is used but this can be adjusted to suit any size cushion. Using carbon paper, transfer the design to the top fabric. Assemble the layers as for wadded quilting, using the same fabric for the top and backing. Quilt the design with a contrast coloured thread and working a slightly longer running stitch—about 3mm (⅛in). Work the grid first, then fill in the ocean wave and windowpane patterns, using a darker-toned thread. Bind the edges of two opposite sides—the shorter length first—and then bind the other sides with extended ties (for binding *see* page 27).

Cover the pad following the instructions given and place it diagonally on the cover and fasten with bows.

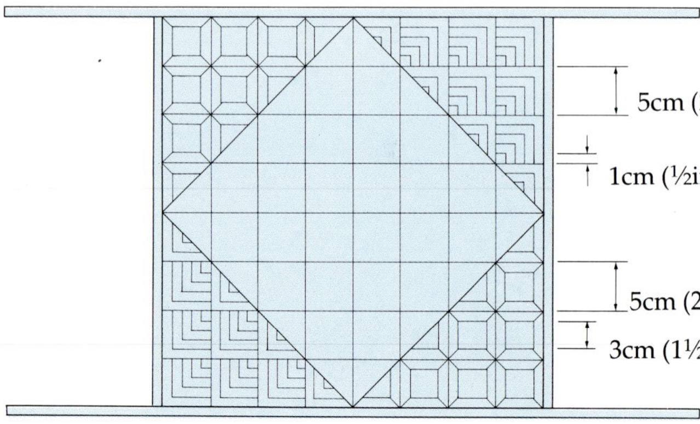

TORTOISE-SHELL AND PAMPAS GRASS

FORMAL *SASHIKO* (Japanese quilting) combines stylized motifs and patterns with clear, primary colours to create strikingly simple designs, as in this contemporary wall hanging.

Reflecting traditional Japanese restraint, the design uses just two asymmetrically placed motifs quilted in contrasting patterns on a bright red ground. Both patterns, known by the delightful names of Tortoise-shell and Pampas grass, are worked in black coton à broder in running stitch and back stitch.

Dressweight cottons are used throughout including the borders and backing, with a thin layer of synthetic wadding placed between them to give a little extra 'body' to the quilting.

Cotton is the traditional fabric used in *sashiko* and gives an authentic touch to the design which may be worked alternatively on the back of a kimono-style jacket, blouson top, dressing gown, or floor cushion.

For the project a 66cm (26in) square is ideal for either a wall hanging or floor cushion, and approximately 26cm (10in) square for a jacket motif. Enlarge the design on to tracing paper (*see* page 91) to the size required. Cut out the correct sections from two contrasting coloured fabrics using the tracing as a measurement guide—remembering to add seam allowances. Join together the central square and the surrounding border neatly mitring the corners (*see* page 61).

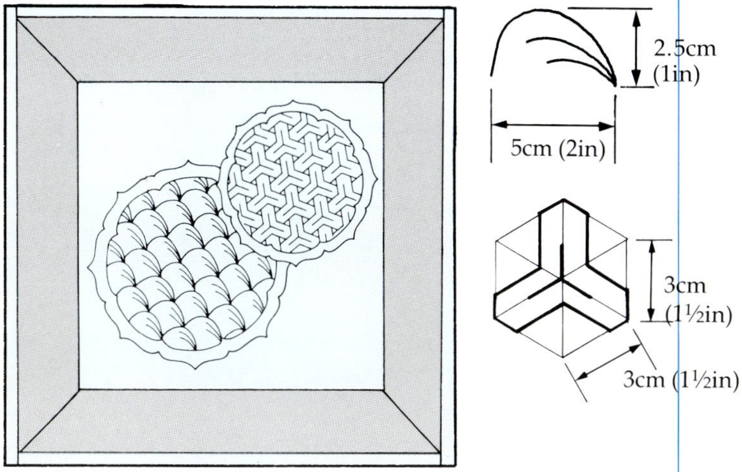

Using dressmaker's carbon paper, transfer the design as shown, and prepare the layers as for wadded quilting. Working outwards from the middle, quilt both patterns using running stitch before outlining the motifs in back stitch. Quilt the border seam to secure all layers, and cover the edges with straight-cut binding (*see* page 27).

Opposite: *Ocean Wave with Windowpane. This delightful 'wrap and tie' cushion cover, quilted in sashiko, uses just two simple geometric patterns.*

Right: *Tortoise-shell and Pampas Grass. The wall hanging, worked in formal sashiko, shows a stylized, asymmetric design filled with two typical Japanese patterns – tortoise-shell and pampas grass.*

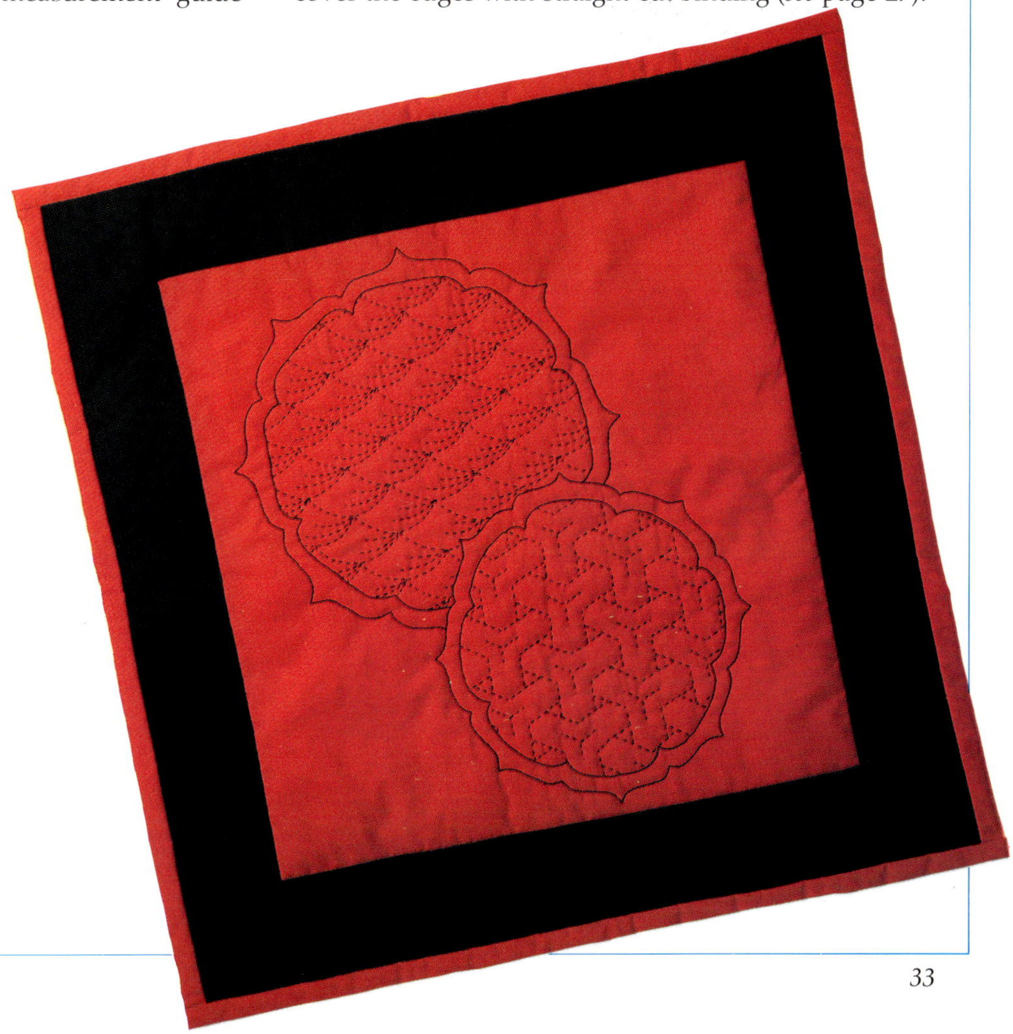

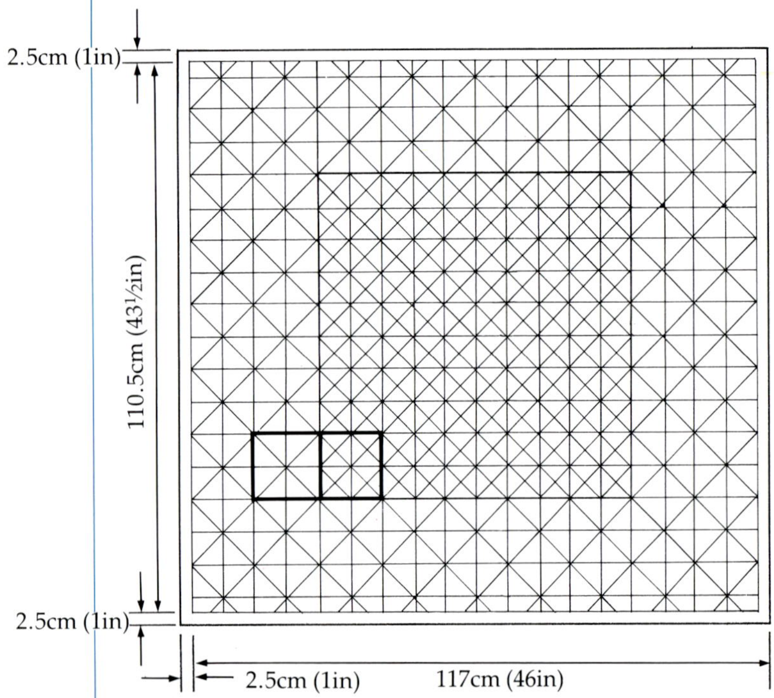

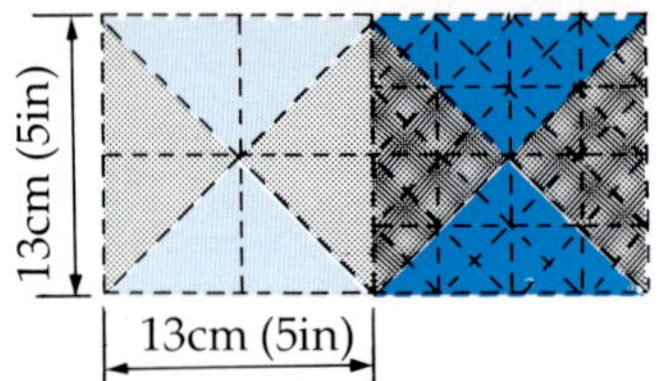

Above and right: *Squares and Diagonals. Repeat patterns showing sprayed design and quilting lines.*
Below: *This contemporary fabric chessboard made from raw silk patchwork, is lightly wadded and quilted along the seam lines.*

• WADDED QUILTING/MACHINE SEWN •
SQUARES AND DIAGONALS

THIS COLOURFUL contemporary wall hanging combines wadded quilting techniques with spray-dyeing and quilted geometric patterns to give contrasting densities of colour and texture. The same quilting pattern is worked over the entire surface in two different scales—a similar arrangement might also be used on other plain, striped or spotted fabrics, for example.

Fabrics with a smooth surface, such as cotton, sateen or synthetic satins, work well for spray-dyeing. Here, the appropriate areas of the design are masked out with film, and, using a spraygun with a splatter cup (or a toothbrush) with disperse dyes—these are commercial fabric dyes which should be bleedproof—the pattern is sprayed on gradually building up colour densities from small dots. The finished design is then 'fixed', usually with steam from a boiling saucepan. This technique is eminently suitable for quilts, floor cushions and rugs, sleeping bags, dressing gowns or baby carriers.

For the project interpret the sprayed effect by making a scaled drawing of your design based on a square grid with a central diamond, as shown in the diagram given below, and by indicating the colours.

Press the pre-washed fabric flat and lightly mark the design. Mask out the correct areas and spray the design, building up colour patterns from splattered dots. Seal the dye and prepare it for quilting following the manufacturer's instructions.

Assemble the layers as for wadded quilting, and, working from the middle out, quilt the central design, using the quilting bar (*see* page 23). Complete quilting the outer border and finish the edges (*see* page 26).

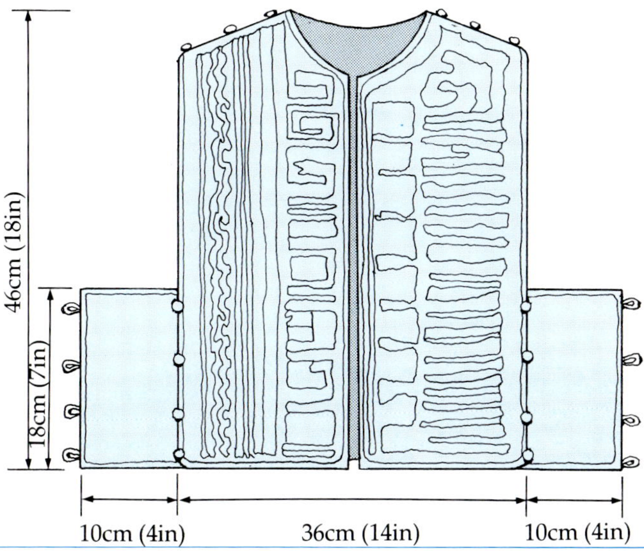

Above and left: *Paint Box. Silk waistcoat, with a free-style quilted design based on an open paint box.*

PAINT BOX

After a little experience of machining straight, geometric patterns, it can be quite stimulating to try a freer approach. Lines of quilting can be purposely made crooked and yet, worked within the confines of a basic idea, can still suggest freedom and spontaneity. Areas of lively textures are created by simply 'taking your machine needle for a walk' and one area contrasted against another to form an all-over pattern.

Use Jap silk (habutai or Chinese silk), sateen, soft cottons or very fine wool for a waistcoat or jacket (or other similar garments) so that the finished quilting is supple enough to wear comfortably. For a floor rug, floor cushion or bolster cover, firmer more hardwearing fabrics should be selected.

Right: *Rippling Stream. This spray-dyed and machine-quilted silk bag is cut out and quilted in one piece, finished around the edges with bias binding and decorated with padded appliqué flowers.*

Below: *Detail of padded appliqué flower showing which petals to attach to the purse (**left**) and detail of the pattern for cutting out the main fabrics which can also be used as a quilting quide (**right**).*

For this project the unusual design for this charming waistcoat was inspired by a child's paint box. After making several preliminary line drawings, the final design and quilting technique emerged.

The waistcoat is very simply shaped—the two sections for the front are quilted, as shown in the diagram. The back section and side pieces are left unquilted and are each attached to the corresponding edges of the front sections by tiny buttons. The back section could also be quilted in a similar freestyle fashion.

Enlarge the pattern on to tracing paper, first checking your own measurements across the shoulders and from the centre back to the waist. Adjust if needed, and add seam allowances all round. Cut out each section and draw in the relevant design. Choose Jap silk for the top layer, with light-weight wadding and pre-washed calico underneath. Transfer the design using dress-maker's carbon paper and secure the layers as for machine quilting. Using ordinary sewing thread, quilt the design by lowering the feed dog and using the darning foot without a frame.

Make up each section with a piped edge (*see* page 27). Attach buttons to the waistcoat fronts and the shoulders on the back section. Work thread loops to fasten.

RIPPLING STREAM

Free machining offers fresh scope for interpreting movement and mood in a design. These freely expressed lines running diagonally across the fabric suggest gently flowing water. A single blossom, half appliquéd to the flap, gives real style to this handsome purse. Soft fabrics, such as silk, crêpe-de-chine and egg-shell-finish satins, are ideal for making all kinds of bags, sachets, cushions, belts, or dressing gown collar and cuffs.

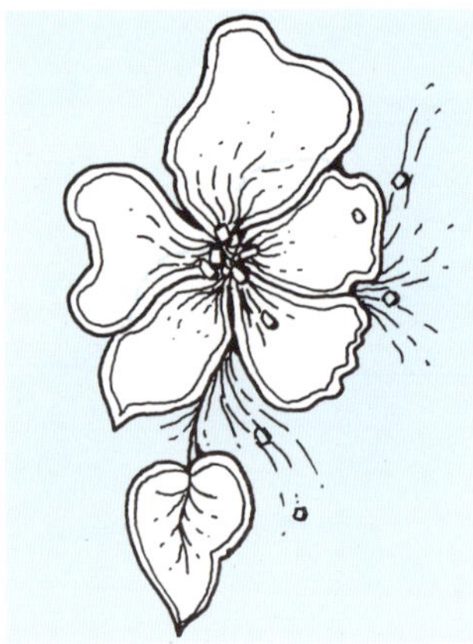

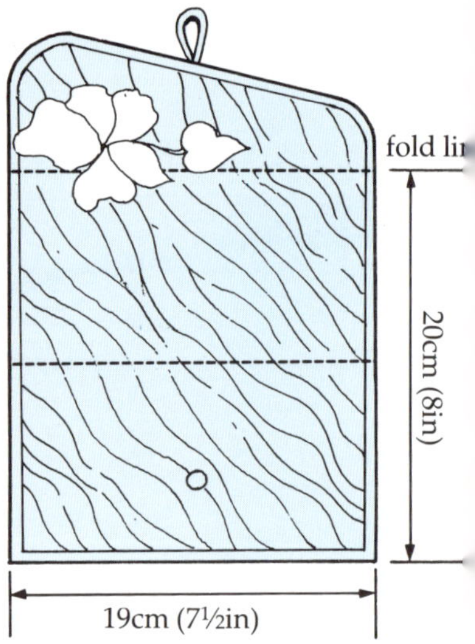

For the project lightly spray-dye the main fabric of the purse to give a shaded effect. Alternatively, commer-cially shaded fabrics can be used, or plain fabrics with the colour changes suggested by different sewing threads. Jap silk is used for the top and bottom layers, and a light synthetic wadding inside. Allow extra fabric for the appliqué flower and leaf motifs.

Enlarge the design on to tracing paper, and, using dressmaker's carbon paper, transfer the design to the top layer. Then cut out a back and a top section for the flower and leaves, each from the correct coloured fabric.

You will also need a button, fabric loop and sufficient bias-cut fabric in a contrast colour to go around the flap and to join the purse together down the sides. Assemble the layers as for machine quilting, and, with a darker-toned thread, machine the lines diagonally across, working from the middle outwards.

Bind around the edges, covering the straight short side first. Fold the purse and continue to bind the edges together, enclosing the raw edges to neaten. Make up the flower motif and leaves as shown below, zigzag stitching the edges with contrast colours. Appliqué the motifs to the flap, stitching down the leaves but three petals only of the flower. Hand embroider veins on the leaves and the flower centre, adding a few bugle beads to highlight the effect. Attach a small fabric-covered button and loop to fasten.

DANCING WAVES

A more formal, symbolic water design is suggested by machining evenly spaced wavy lines over the entire surface. In this delightful quilted wall hanging, pastel coloured fragments of fabric are appliquéd on top suggesting flotsam gently moving on the waves.

Fabrics with a smooth surface and a slight sheen, such as sateen, silk, and good quality cotton satins, are best for showing off the quilting in a wall hanging, but heavier fabrics would be more suitable for floor rugs.

For the project use the wave template given, spaced at 2.5cm (1in) intervals across the fabric. This works well on any size of hanging or rug design. Prepare your top and bottom fabrics and a lightweight wadding, allowing slightly more width than the finished size needed as for machine quilting. Cut out the template and repeating the curve, mark the first wavy line down the centre on the right side of the fabric. Stitch the first line, loosening the tension on the sewing machine if needed. Attach the quilting bar and set it to 2.5cm (1in). Quilt the next line with the bar resting on the previous line and working in the opposite direction. Complete the quilting on one side working alternately in opposite directions to prevent the fabric puckering. Repeat on the other side and finish the edges by close zigzagging in a contrast colour. Trim the fabric to the stitching.

Appliqué the coloured triangles at random. Outline with zigzag stitch and neaten the ends on the back. Working on the wrong side, hand sew the turnings on both short edges to make channels for hanging.

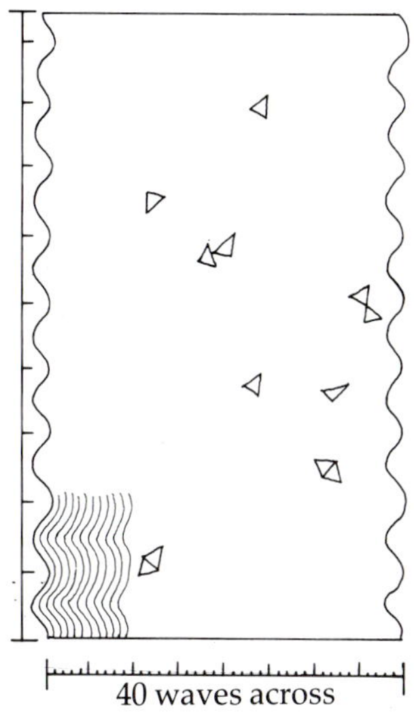

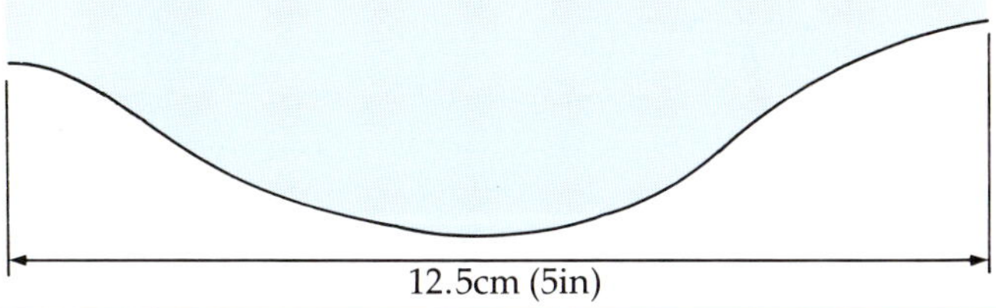

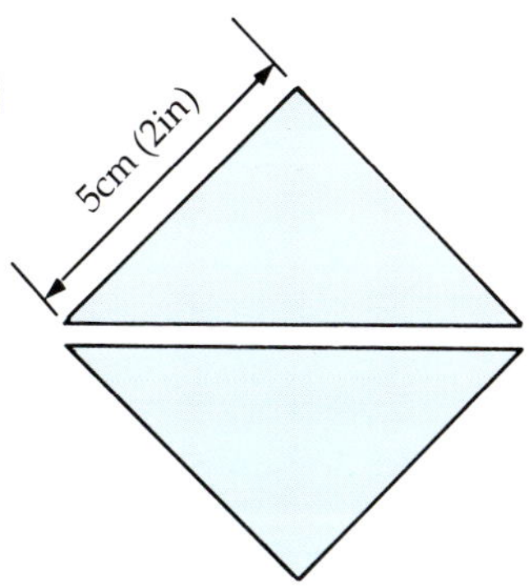

***Above:** Dancing Waves. Trace patterns for the waves (**left and top right**) and appliqué pieces of flotsam (**right**).*

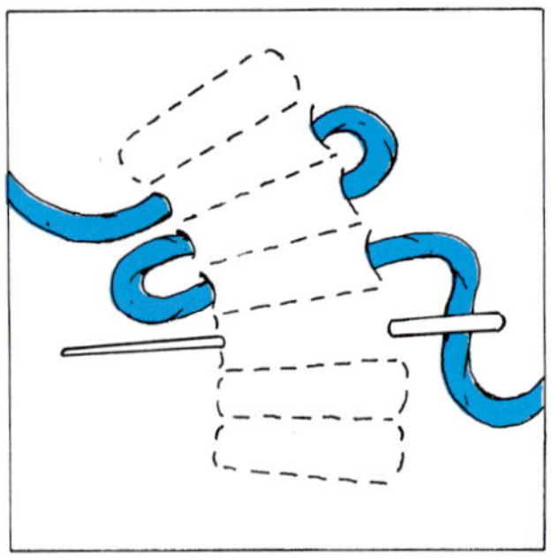

Above: *Fruit Basket. To cord quilt the handle, use a single strand of quilting yarn and insert the needle through the backing fabric, from right to left. Pull through and reinsert it in the next channel from left to right. Continue in this way, leaving a small loop at each end. Do not pull tightly, otherwise the twisted cane handle effect will be lost.*

Right: *Enlarge the design – adding more border lines for a larger size, or omitting them to fit a smaller cushion pad, if preferred.* **Below right:** *The design combines both padding and cording techniques. Fruit motifs are realistically padded to stand out in relief from the wicker basket, which is neatly described with cording.*

• PADDED QUILTING •

FRUIT BASKET

THIS CHARMING eighteenth-century style design lends itself perfectly to hand-sewn quilting and combines both padding (Trapunto) and cording techniques.

The design is best worked in either plain cotton, sateen, silk or satin for a soft, lustrous effect, and it can be used for cushion sets, crib covers and matching pillows, nightdress sachets, or tea- and coffee-pot cosies. You could also repeat the design over larger coverlets or frame a single design for a picture—as a start for an embroidery collection.

For the project enlarge the design on tracing paper. An ideal size is 40cm (16in), but adjustments can easily be made to fit a larger pad by adding more lines around the border, or, for a slightly smaller pad, by removing the existing border line.

Using dressmaker's carbon paper, transfer the design centrally to the backing fabric, remembering to reverse the design. Choose matching coloured threads for outlining the design so as not to compete with the raised effect of the padding. Tack the layers together as for padded quilting and complete the padding referring to the section on corded quilting for the basket and border. Follow the diagram given for the handle, complete the padding, and then, using short straight stitches, work small crosses on the tops of the fruit and suggest the strawberry seeds to finish.

When you pad the fruit, try to make the shapes in the foreground slightly fuller than those behind, to add to the realistic effect. Make up the cushion following the instructions on page 97.

Above: *Soft sculptured teapot and lid made from quilted cotton and synthetic wadding. The staining inside is applied with tannin-coloured acrylic paint.*
Left: *Marzipan sweetmeats individually made from hand-dyed chiffon, stuffed with wadding and finished with felt stalks. Each sweet (small fruit) is placed on a circle of stiffened net and arranged in a fabric covered box, 12cm by 10cm ($4\frac{1}{2}$in by 4in).*

VANESSA

In contrast to the blistered effect, traditional Trapunto quilting also provides the opportunity for creating on a broader scale all kinds of fabric sculpture. Here, in this contemporary picture, the design features a child's doll boldly and skilfully moulded using a mixture of quilting and fabric dyeing.

A cotton stockinette fabric is used for the figure—this type of stretchy fabric responds amazingly well to padding and shaping, and to fabric dye. The wittily placed right hand is made separately and applied after shaping the figure, as are the hair and embroidered

***Above left and above:** Vanessa. Emphasize the body contours first by quilting to varying depths, and then, using pale pink fabric paint, highlight the roundness by painting in the shadows.*

features. The applied background uses plain and printed cottons to suggest the corner detail, with shadows painted and stitched in darker tones to give a greater realism.

For the project instead of an embroidery frame, the quilting is worked on a picture stretcher—ready to be framed later on. Make a full-scale drawing—about 40cm by 58cm (16in by 23in)—and following the instructions in Quilting techniques, transfer it in reverse to a light calico backing. Make a separate template for the right hand. Staple the fabric over the stretcher with the outline on the underside. Then stretch a layer of stockinette on top—not too tightly. Working from the underside, backstitch around the figure stitching around the wrist only of the right hand.

Pad each section of the doll in turn, and then, working from the right side and back stitching through the padding, suggest the form as in the diagram. Pull the stitches tightly in areas like the eye sockets and dimples to suggest depth, and less tightly for rounder shaping. Make the right hand, and attach it by the wrist and palm, leaving the fingers loose. Outline the eye sockets with stem stitch, the irises and eyelashes with straight stitch, and the mouth with satin stitch. For the hair, use sewing thread to catch overlapping curls of crewel wool in place. Complete the shaping by applying pale pink fabric dye to suggest nicely rounded forms.

Cut out the background fabrics using templates cut from the original drawing (*see* Appliqué techniques). Apply each one, following the outline closely and stapling the outer edges over the stretcher. Using fabric dye paint shadows to suggest the floor, and stitch the remaining background shadows with darker toning embroidery threads.

• CORDED QUILTING •

CIRCLES AND QUATREFOILS

CORDED QUILTING, worked closely over an entire surface area, gives a very pleasing blistered effect. Designs can be worked with different thicknesses of cord to raise certain parts of a design higher than others, and to suggest an illusion of perspective, as shown in the pillow.

Fabrics with a matt surface, such as linen, firm cotton, fine wool and brushed cottons, are best for this type of design. Slightly narrower channels are used in the quatrefoil to give it the appearance of being behind the circle. Instead of quilting cord, use stranded embroidery cotton, pearl threads or coton à broder for more intricate shaping. Though it is rather exacting work and time-consuming, corded quilting gives very satisfying results. Use it on small, precious pieces such as a set of scatter cushions, pot-pourri or lavender sachets—with an open-weave backing to allow the perfume to escape —or as a centre motif on a pram or crib cover.

For this sweet-scented herb pillow project choose a smooth, plain coloured linen or cotton for the top and backing, and an open-weave linen for lining the top layer. Enlarge the design on tracing paper. Transfer it to the lining fabric using dressmaker's carbon paper.

Assemble the layers as for corded quilting, and, using either back stitch or running stitch, outline the design carefully, making the correct channels with the circles on top. Use matching quilting thread, or one or two tones darker, to emphasize the design. Thread the circles with eight strands of embroidery thread and the quatrefoils with six strands to differentiate the two heights. With bias-cut matching fabric cover sufficient No. 4 piping cord to go around the edge (*see* page 27). Make up the pillow as for a cushion (*see* page 97), positioning the piping between the seams. Add a handful of sweet-scented herbs or pot-pourri inside the pad before inserting it in the cover.

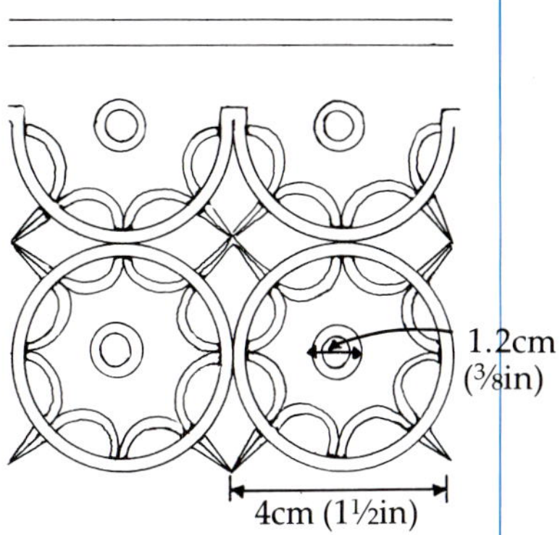

Top and above: *Circles and Quatrefoils. The outer edge and the construction of the two motifs.* ***Left:*** *The overall plan of the whole design.*

Left: *Double Celtic Knot.*
Above: *A quarter section of the design. When completing the double knot, make sure the two bands are correctly interlaced in each section.*

• CORDED QUILTING •

DOUBLE CELTIC KNOT

INTERLACING DESIGNS are traditional favourites for corded quilting techniques, ranging from simple trellis patterns to more complex knot formations, as in this contemporary cushion cover.

Here, the design gives a pleasant shadowy effect and shows an interlaced double knot worked in two tones on a white cambric ground. The entire design is outlined in lighter and darker tones of blue and green embroidery threads, and the resulting channels filled with deeper tones of purple and blue knitting yarns. Acrylic yarn is preferred for its softness so that the finished cushion cover remains soft and pliable.

Toning mauve cambric is used for the backing and for binding the edges, and the closure secured by oversewing. Other semi-transparent fabrics such as voile, batiste or lawn would make suitable alternative main fabrics, and the design could also be used for a crib cover, sofa throw or nightdress sachet.

Certain interlacing designs can be puzzling to work. To avoid unnecessary complications, it is important when stitching the channels to make sure they follow an 'under and over' sequence throughout.

For the project the diagram gives a quarter section of the design which should be enlarged to the size required and then transferred in reverse on the centre lines to complete the design. An overall measurement of 46cm (18in) square is a popular size for a cushion. Go over the outline with a black felt pen and then tape the drawing to a firm work surface. Tape the cambric on top and lightly trace the design through.

Back the cambric with mull (a heavier muslin) and assemble the layers as for corded quilting. Working from the right side, outline the channels with running stitch using two tones of No. 8 pearl thread (eg work the outer channel throughout in pale turquoise and slate blue and the inner channel in pale blue and deep green). Following the instructions given fill the inner channel with purple yarn and the outer channel with a matching deep blue yarn.

Make up the cushion cover and then bind the raw edges with straight-cut cambric. Insert the cushion pad and finally either oversew the closure or insert a matching coloured zip.

• SHADOW QUILTING •

TRIO

THIS FORM OF shadow quilting uses contemporary fabrics and images in a delightfully fresh way. Collections of shiny, bright coloured sequins, beads and threads are sewn under sheer fabric into 'pockets' of varying shapes.

Transparent fabrics of all kinds can be used for decorative items. Traditional voile, muslin and organdie will give a crisp finish while modern synthetic sheers, being much softer and more pliable, are perhaps better for this kind of shadow quilting. Some of the knitted sheers available may be too stretchy, which is a point to bear in mind when buying.

This is the perfect technique in which a beginner can experiment by making small and beautiful pieces such as the pincushion shown or scatter cushions, a purse for a special gift or a bridesmaid's confetti bag, for example, or balance several triangles into a fantastic mobile.

For the project you will need a light-coloured cotton or silk backing to show off the design, a synthetic sheer top layer, and two bright, contrasting fabrics for the border and the pincushion back, plus a selection of mixed-coloured sewing threads and bright red star-shaped sequins.

Make a full-size drawing, and transfer it to the backing using dressmaker's carbon paper. Arrange cut threads and two or three sequins alternately in the triangles. Place the sheer fabric on top, pin and tack each section closely. Zigzag stitch the centre triangles first, then apply the inner border in separate strips (*see* page 57), to form the outer edges of the triangles and to enclose the sequins. Apply the outer border in the same way. Make up as a small cushion, stuff with teased-out wadding, and hand sew to close. Decorate the centre with a thread tassel, tightly bound before stitching through a bead.

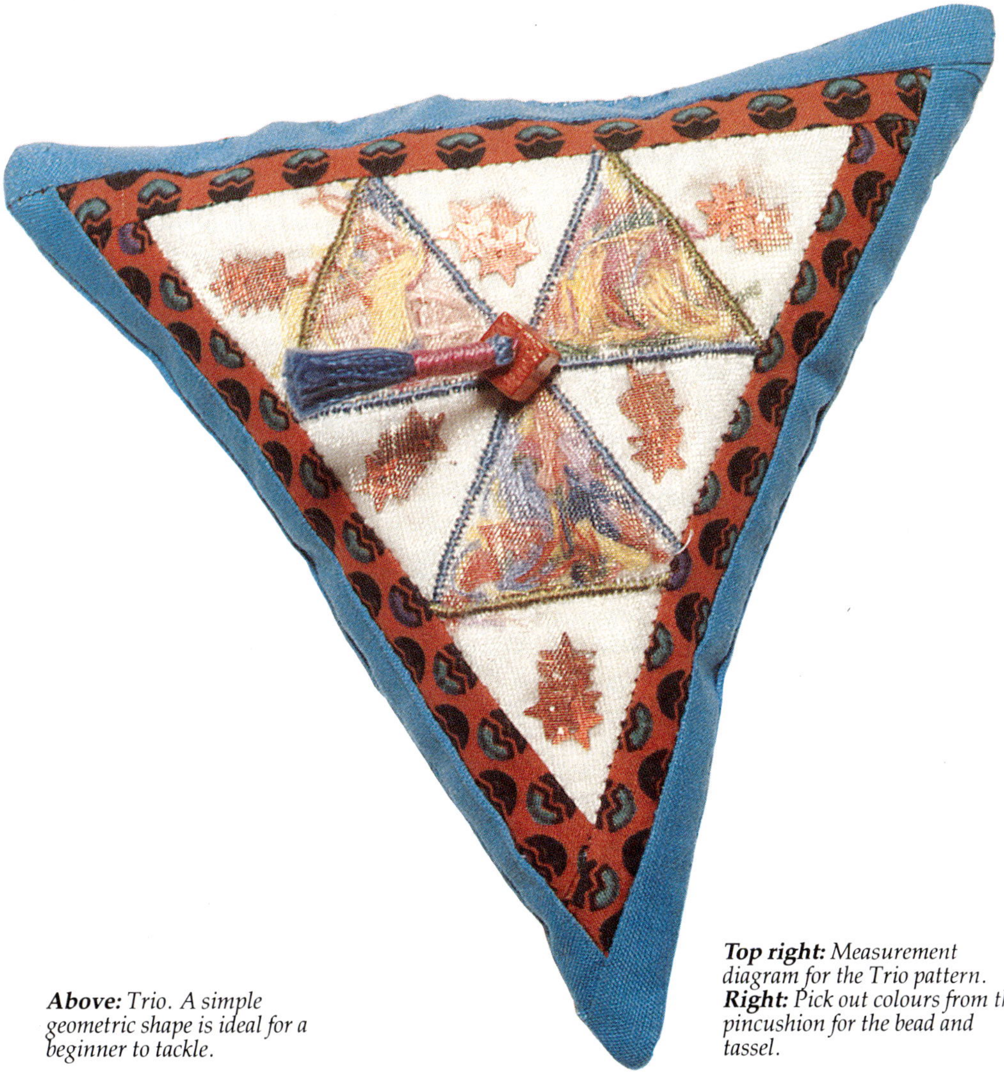

Above: ***Trio.*** *A simple geometric shape is ideal for a beginner to tackle.*

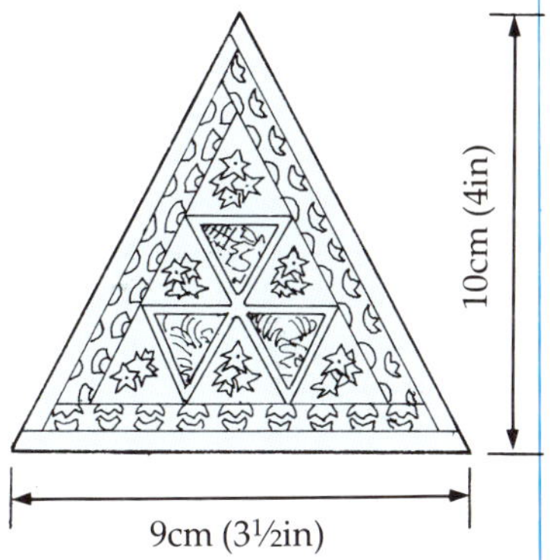

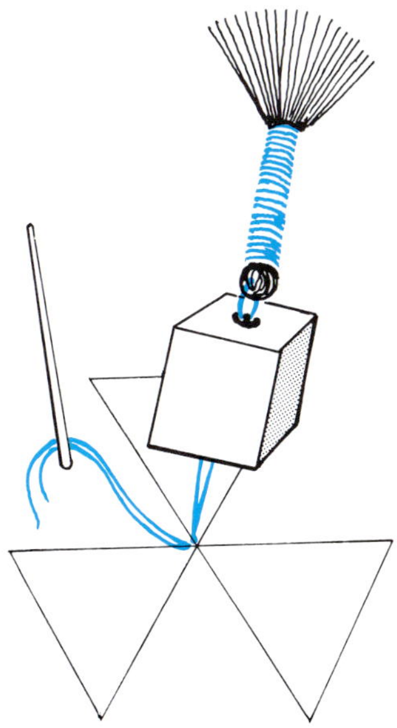

Top right: *Measurement diagram for the Trio pattern.*
Right: *Pick out colours from the pincushion for the bead and tassel.*

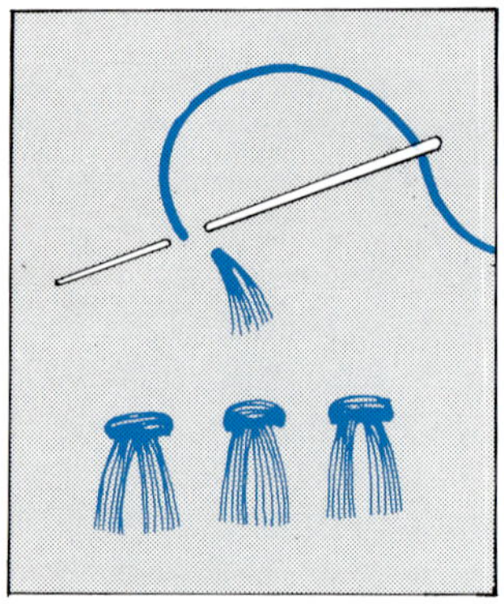

***Left:** Early Morning.*
Flower detail showing areas of French knots, fabric shadows, the padded centre surrounded by knot stitch, plus veined leaves.
***Above:** To work knot stitch, first make a small diagonal stitch to the left. Pull needle through, make a similar stitch in the opposite direction and bring out at starting point holding thread downwards. Pull to tighten knot, cut threads and repeat from the beginning.*

EARLY MORNING

Quite inspired and innovative designs are achieved by boldly combining contemporary shadow work techniques with wadded and padded quilting and surface embroidery. In this delightful cushion, the outlines of summer flowers are stitched through a synthetic sheer placed over a printed curtaining fabric. The flower centres are padded from behind with mixed-fibre threads and sequins, and outlined on the right side with tufts of coloured threads worked in knot stitch. Certain petals are padded with slivers of toning fabrics before the sheer is placed on top.

The entire surface is freely stitched picking out areas of flowers and foliage to balance the design, as the particular print dictates. French knots are scattered over petals and running stitch is worked along the veins of leaves. The finished shadowy effect gently diffuses the printed design with subtle colours.

For the background fabric, choose furnishing (curtain, upholstery) fabrics with large printed flower motifs avoiding very small designs and 'busy' repeat patterns. Good quality cotton prints, chintz or glazed fabrics are ideal. Synthetic sheers, nets or more expensive organza and georgette would make an excellent top layer. You will also need a thin layer of wadding, and muslin scrim underneath the wadding, plus fabric for the cushion back, piping or binding, as preferred. Use such shadowy flower designs for extra special quilts, covers and cushions.

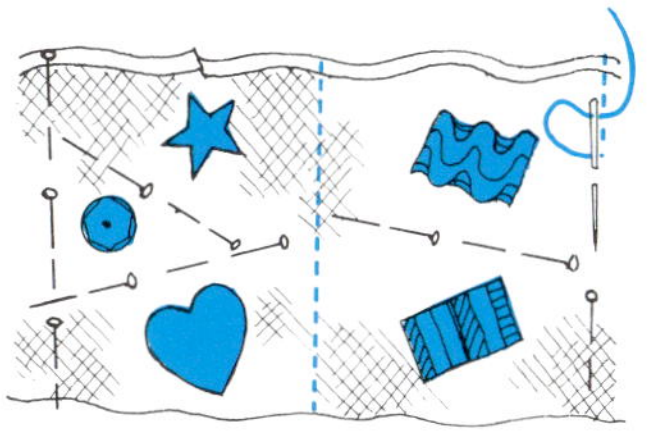

***Above:** Feeling Good. **Left:** Stitch the pockets holding the sequins and beads as invisibly as possible following broadly geometric lines for best results.*

For the project prepare the layers as for wadded quilting, padding certain petals with loosely cut shapes of fabric as you tack the layers together. Stretch the work in a hoop (*see* page 22). Machine zigzag stitch around each flower loosely suggesting the contours of the petals with different coloured threads. Change to a fine straight stitch and outline the background foliage, also in different colours. Remove the hoop, and pad the flower centres from behind with mixed threads and sequins as shown. Using knot stitch on the right side work around the flower middles in brighter coloured threads, and add French knots to the petals. Suggest veins in the leaves with running stitch to finish. Make up the cushion (*see* page 97), adding a border or piping as preferred.

FEELING GOOD

Dazzling fabric jewelry like this necklace isn't meant to compete with a string of diamonds, but it is great to wear and fun to make. You can use this twinkling, jewel-like effect for frills on a party dress, cocktail hat, bracelet, or on a detachable shirt tie or dickie bow.

For keepsake collectors, this is the perfect technique for showing off precious stones and trinkets—providing they are fairly lightweight. However for a spangled necklace you will need a double layer of fine net, a collection of sequins, both large and small, stars, crescents, shells, hearts and flowers, for example; several gaudy snippets of ribbon and shiny fabrics; plus a length of soft ribbon for tying.

For the project the two pieces of net should be roughly twice the neck measurement and 8–10cm (3–4in) deep. Arrange the sequins and fabric snips on the bottom layer, place the second layer on top, and pin in between the sequins to form pockets. Stitch the compartments as invisibly as possible with fine, matching coloured thread to hold the sequins and fabric snips safely in place. Finish the bottom edge loosely zigzagging over the raw edges. Pleat the neck edge to fit comfortably, and bind with ribbon leaving long ends for tying.

CHAPTER FOUR

PATCHWORK TECHNIQUES

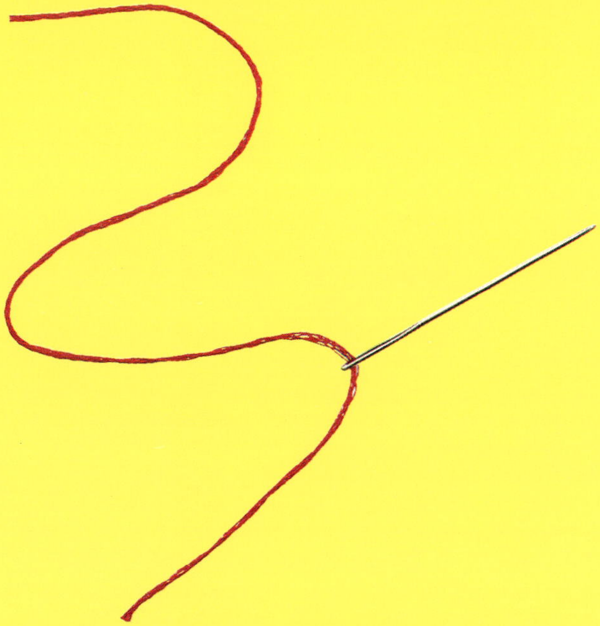

WHETHER PATCHWORK is made following traditional disciplines or as an innovative fabric art, it involves cutting materials into different shapes and sizes and stitching them together to create a whole new fabric. It is the making of an entirely new fabric that sets patchwork apart from any other textile craft.

Traditional construction methods can generally be divided into all-over mosaic designs or 'block' patterns. A block is a complete pattern and a number of blocks are stitched together to make the finished work. Patterns can be extended or reduced to fit any size requirements. Borders can be added, lattice strips (borders) inserted between blocks, fabrics pinched and pleated, painted, frayed, folded and embroidered before and after being stitched together and fashioned into all kinds of objects from patchwork quilts to floor rugs.

• TYPES OF PATCHWORK •

ALTHOUGH THERE are several styles of patchwork, the sewing methods used fall generally into two categories—pieced patchwork, where either single patches are pieced together, as in hexagon or shell designs or as in block patterns, or applied patchwork, where the patches are applied to a backing fabric, as in Log Cabin or Folded patchwork.

Pieced patchwork is traditionally sub-divided into English and American methods, although hand-sewn piecing (without backing papers) is the traditional technique used almost universally. The English method uses backing papers to make the patches—mostly of small geometric shapes such as hexagons and diamonds—which are sewn together by hand. The American block method is much quicker and tends to use larger units to make the block, which is secured with running stitch or machine stitch. Frequently the blocks are joined with lattice strips between. These are 5cm (2in) wide borders set around a 30cm (12in) block, for example—a method devised by pioneer American quiltmakers to speed up the piecing process.

Applied patchwork can be sub-divided into Log Cabin, Strip (sometimes called Random), Crazy and Folded patchwork, including Folded star and Mayflower, where each style is applied to the backing in a completely different way. Certain strip patchwork is also called the 'pressed' block method.

Seminole patchwork falls somewhere between the two —being pieced in strips rather than blocks.

Pleated patchwork is another variation where fabric is pinched and tucked before being pieced together.

FABRICS

For practical items, dressweight cottons, ginghams, lawn, linens, corduroys, tweeds, velvets and silks are all well-tried favourites. Only fabrics of similar weights should be used together—mixed weights pull out of shape most unattractively. Synthetics and certain kinds of knits are really too springy and stretchy to make good patchwork shapes, and they should be kept for more decorative, experimental work.

CHOOSING A DESIGN

The most important consideration when choosing a design is that it should relate to the item you plan to make in size, style and colour. Bear in mind that a small piece of patchwork is more effective made with small patches, but not so small as to make sewing difficult. Consider the patchwork style and its suitability—a Log Cabin design made from rough tweeds and shirtings

Opposite: *Detail of a twentieth century Turkoman tent hanging showing a rich patchwork of fabrics including woven ikat, felt, braid and velvet.* ***Right:*** *One-patch block, A Thousand Pyramids; Four-patch block, Crosses and Losses (**centre right**); Nine-patch block, Variable Star (**far right**).* ***Below right:*** *Lattice strips.*

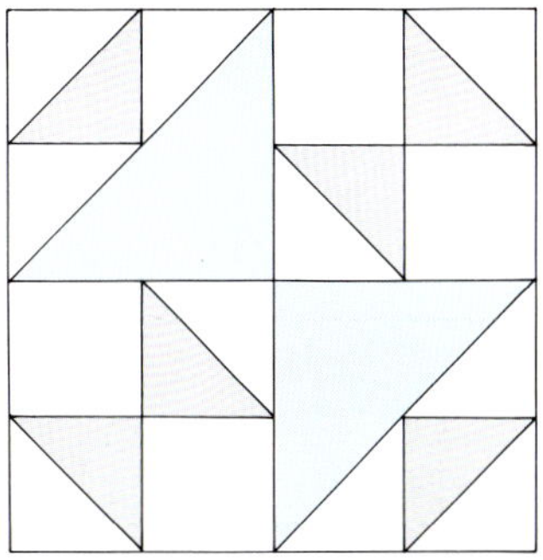

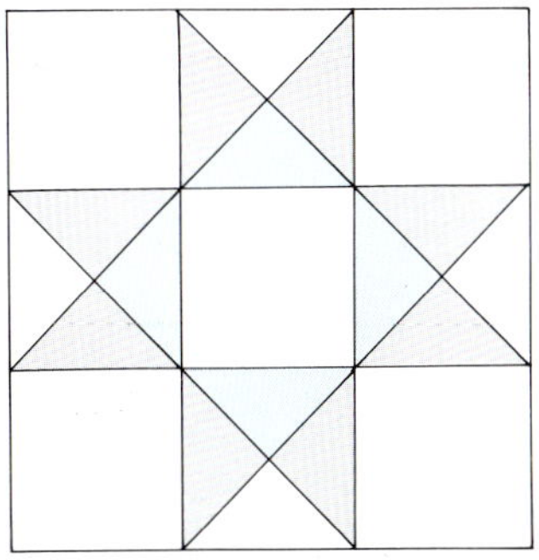

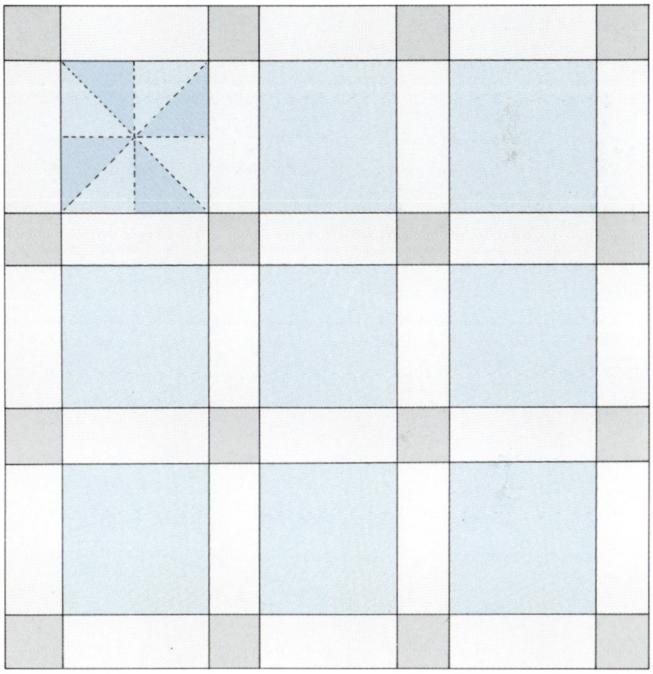

may not be the ideal choice for a nursery, for example, whereas pretty cottons in a hexagon design might be. If you are designing a major piece of patchwork to fit in with an existing colour scheme, there are several considerations to make. Look first at all the colours in the room beginning with the actual colour of the wood in furniture, floors and woodwork. Notice the wide difference in local colours such as buff-coloured pine and dark red mahogany. Then check the walls, carpets, curtains and upholstery. Your choice of colour can serve either as an accent to a colourful scheme by choosing one or two of the main colours and using similar tones, or it can highlight a restrained colour scheme by choosing more striking colours to make a strong focal point.

SIZE OF BLOCK

This need not be a random guess. In order to calculate the size, measure the overall area you plan to cover. For a wall hanging, measure the wall space, and, for a quilt, drape a sheet over the bed to get the right effect and then divide the total measurement into smaller units.

Blocks of 30–38cm (12–15in) are popular for large quilts and 15cm (6in) for cot quilts. For a cushion, use one large block or four smaller blocks. Plain or patterned borders can be invaluable for increasing overall dimensions. Patchwork for clothes is generally best pieced together and treated as any other fabric—positioning the paper pattern according to the cutting layout.

CONSTRUCTION

Although the traditional methods of joining patches and blocks into over-all repeat patterns are often the easiest, many contemporary designers, while still using standard geometric shapes, are creating new ways of putting them together—perhaps radiating from a base point, or asymmetrically—most certainly with great mathematical dexterity.

The simplest way to work is the one patch, or single unit, repeated in an all-over design. Most traditional pieced blocks are based on the four-, five-, seven- or nine-patch grid systems. Each grid has the same basic number of units which can be sub-divided in any number of ways. Pieced blocks can be joined edge to edge in an all-over repeat pattern, but, if the effect is too 'busy', they can be alternated with plain blocks of fabric or have lattice strips (borders) stitched between. These borders tend to give a design strength and unity. Another way to position the patches is to alternate plain and patterned blocks diagonally with half blocks at the edges. Whatever your choice, it is important to plan a scaled design on graph paper using colours to indicate the patches. Keep this by you as a guide for estimating fabric and piecing together the finished work.

TEMPLATES

Metal or plastic templates can be bought in several shapes and sizes, usually in pairs. The smaller solid template is used for cutting backing papers and the larger window template for cutting the fabric. The latter is also useful for judging patterned patches and includes a 6mm ($\frac{1}{4}$in) seam allowance.

If you cannot buy the correct size template for your design, then you will need accurately cut templates. Where possible, use graph paper for making precise measurements. The paper can always be cut and glued on to card, as for quilting templates (*see* page 20).

***Left:** A selection of straight-sided and curved geometric templates. Note that the shapes are not all interchangeable.*

***Right:** Plastic window and metal templates. Templates drawn on graph paper (**centre**) and templates drawn on isometric graph paper (**far right**).*

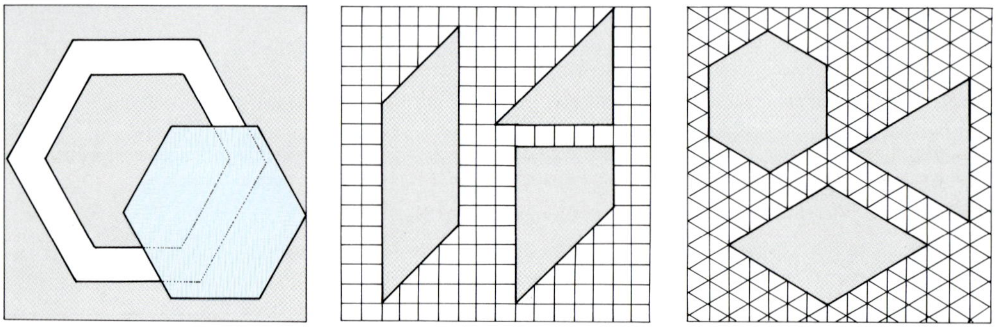

Isometric graph paper is ideal for constructing hexagons, equilateral triangles and the lozenge. Incidentally, as these shapes share a common angle, they will interlock and mix well together.

THE LONG DIAMOND

This is used to make the basic eight-pointed star, which can be further extended into other stars, including the splendid Star of Bethlehem.

To construct the diamond you will need compasses and set square (right-angle triangle). Decide the length of the sides (all four sides are the same length) and draw a line A B to this length. Using a set square or protractor, draw A C at 45° to A B. Set the compasses to the same length as A B, place the point on C and describe an arc at D. Then place the point on B and describe another arc at D. Join C D and B D.

TEMPLATES FOR MACHINE SEWING

These should include 6mm (¼in) seam allowances for fine to medium fabrics and 9mm (⅜in) allowances for heavier fabrics.

ESTIMATING FABRIC QUANTITY

This is not always easy, especially if oddments are included, but an approximate calculation can be made once you have cut the templates to size and counted how many different patches are needed.

Using a fabric width of 90cm (36in) and a 10cm (4in) square template, for example, calculate how many shapes can be cut from one width (90 ÷ 10 = 9). If you require 80 blocks, for example, calculate the length needed by dividing this number by the number of times the template fits across the fabric and multiply the figure by the depth of the template (80 ÷ 9 = 9 [rounded up] × 10cm = 90cm). You will need 90cm (36in) of 90cm (36in) wide fabric. Bear in mind that certain templates, such as the hexagon and the triangle, can be more economically placed than others. Calculate border strips in the same way.

MARKING AND CUTTING FABRIC

Position the templates and lightly mark all cutting lines on the wrong side of the fabric, using an appropriately coloured pencil. Make sure you place the templates on

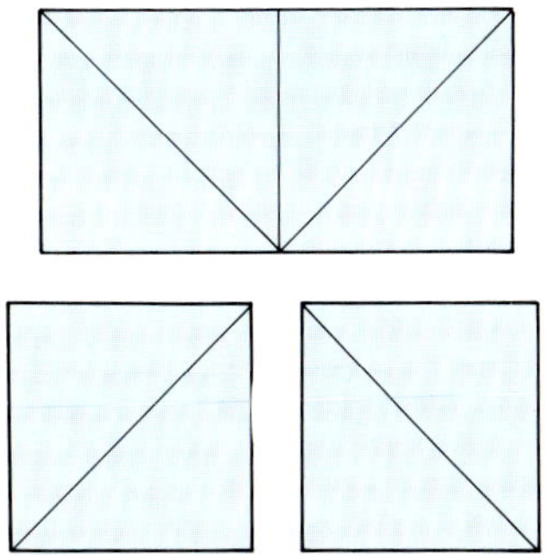

Above: *A block is pieced by first joining the smaller units such as triangles to make squares, and then joining the squares to form larger blocks.*

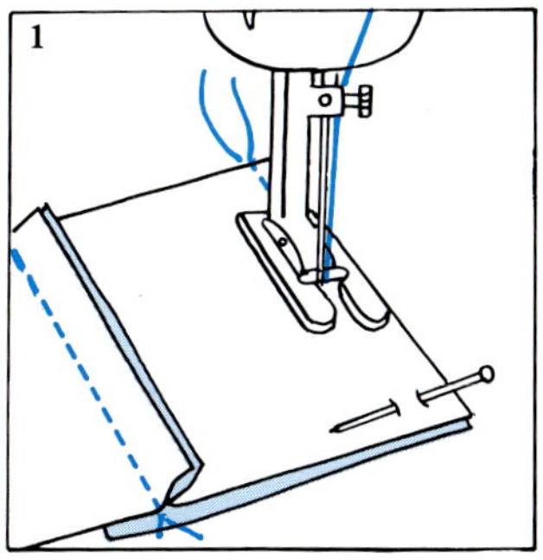

Machine sewing 1 *Place the patches rights sides together and stitch on the marked seamline or use the inside width of the presser foot as a guide, stitching 6mm (¼in) in from the edge. Reverse stitch at both ends. If your presser foot is narrower than 6mm (¼in), and the plate below is not marked, use a strip of masking tape as a guide.*

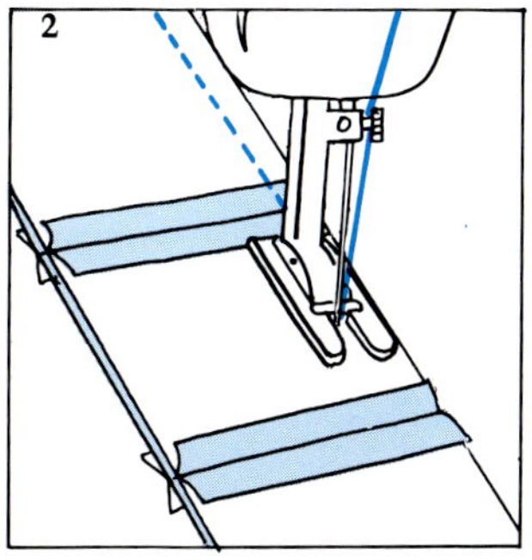

2 Having joined the small units together, press the seams open, or to one side, whichever you prefer. Then join the rows together accurately matching the seams. It is a good idea to pin through the two seams to hold them firmly in place while stitching.

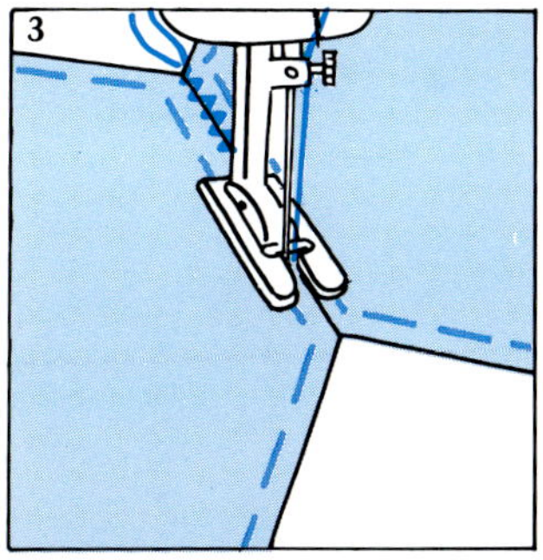

3 Hexagons and other more complicated shapes can be joined very quickly. Simply butt the edges together and join on the right side with zigzag stitching. Use a stitch width of 1½–2 and a medium stitch length.

the straight grain of the fabric, avoiding the bias grain. Reverse asymmetric shapes, such as the trapezoid, so that they appear the correct way round when stitched together. Cut out the patches separately using very sharp scissors.

SEWING PIECED BLOCKS TOGETHER

Before sewing, lay out your patches to check the overall design. Certain hand-sewn patterns may vary slightly, but in general it is good practice first to join small units, such as triangles, to form squares (and then join the squares progressively into bigger blocks, and so on). Finally, assemble the larger units to form rows across and then stitch the rows together. Add strips between or borders as needed. Once you have established the sequence for making a block, continue with it for all the blocks in the same pattern.

MACHINE SEWING

While most patterns involving simple triangles, squares and rectangles can be pieced quite successfully by machine, curves and some complicated geometric shapes are better stitched by hand.

HAND-SEWN PATCHWORK (WITH PAPERS)

The term hand-sewn patchwork usually implies the English method of sewing geometric patches together. Here both plain and multi-coloured fabrics are used to give a colourful, mosaic-like effect. The patches are sewn over paper patterns. This means that smaller, more intricate shapes can be made, and includes the hexagon, diamond, pentagon and octagon.

Each fabric patch is first tacked over a backing paper (to give sharp edges) and then the patches are overcast

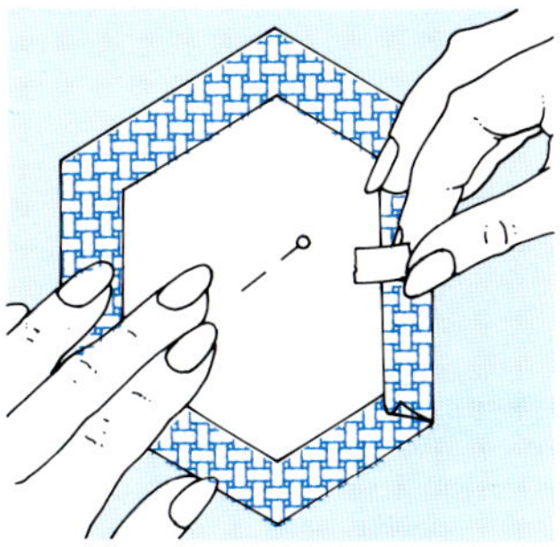

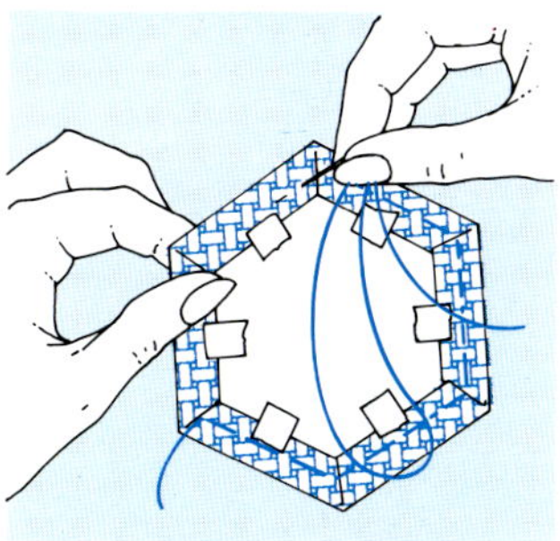

Hand-sewn patchwork 1 *Cut sufficient papers to the finished patch size. Then pin a paper to the wrong side of a fabric patch. Fold over the edges and secure to the paper with masking tape. (On silk or other fine fabrics, where pins may leave permanent marks, use tape only.) Take care with corners as you fold the double overlap. Tack one side, securing both layers. Trim the excess fabric at the point, and fold down the point.*
2 Tack the second side. Make a stitch at each corner to keep down the fold. Repeat the process on the other sides.

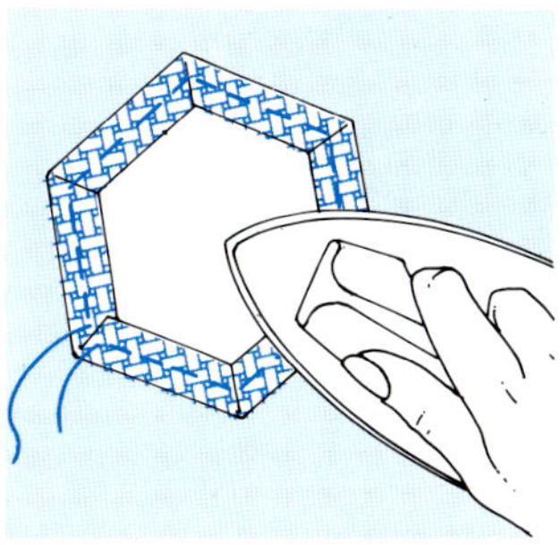

3 Remove the masking tape and press the edges.

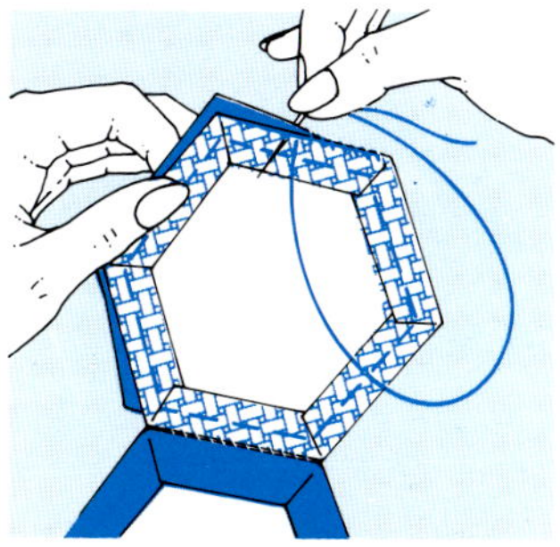

4 Lay out all the prepared patches to check the pattern, then position them in rows across. Place two patches right sides together and oversew the edges

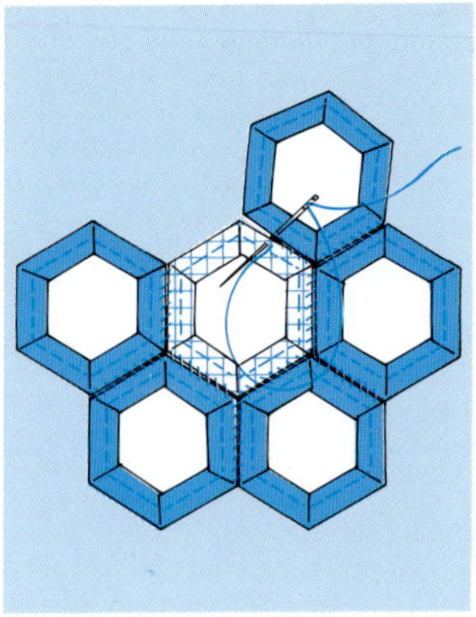

To make a rosette *which is the basic unit for many hexagon designs, join the centre patch to six adjacent patches of a contrast colour or pattern. A second row may be added in a third colour. The units are then linked together surrounded by a contrast border.*

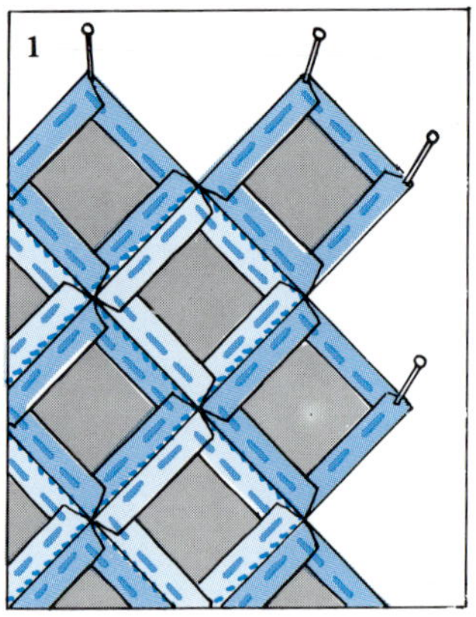

Pressing patchwork
1 *Working on a padded surface, place the patchwork right side down and pin through the patches on each side.*

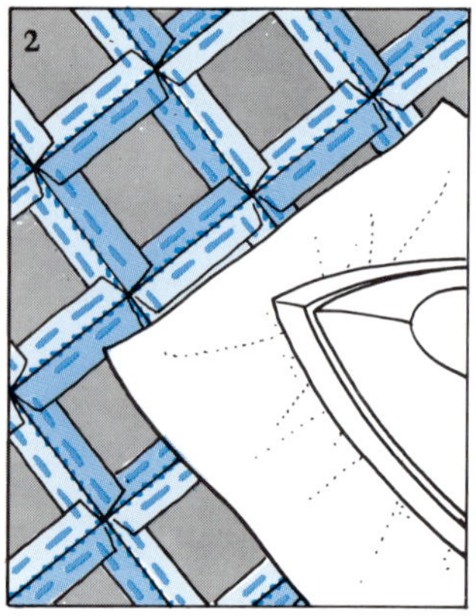

2 *Press under a cloth to prevent glazing the fabric, first on the wrong side and then on the right side, having previously removed all tacking threads to avoid marking.*

3 *Remove the backing papers—these can be used again if they are not damaged. Add any half patches to straighten the edges before making up the finished item.*

together in pattern. Rows are formed first and then the rows are stitched together to complete the patchwork.

PRESSING PATCHWORK

When all the patches have been joined together, press the entire patchwork ready for the final stages of making up. Choose a large work surface so you can spread the work flat. A folded blanket placed on the floor with a shelf on top will solve the problem of size. If the patchwork is pieced in blocks, the blocks will have been pressed as they were being made so too much intricate pressing should not be necessary.

• SHELL PATCHWORK •

THE SHELL (or clamshell) is one of the oldest motifs used in quilting and patchwork. This single shape forms a classic, all-over repeating pattern known in many countries as Fishscale or simply as Fish.

The technique involves hand sewing rows of overlapping shells in pattern or in a random way, either with or without a foundation fabric. Each shell is carefully cut out using a template and made with a backing paper to ensure a perfectly curved outline. As the patches are stitched from the right side, it is crucial that the edges are accurately curved since there is no other seaming to help disguise any imperfections. If you have a sewing machine with a swing needle, you may prefer to experiment by zigzag stitching the patches together.

Smooth-textured, fine cottons in patterned or plain colours are best for making the patches. You will need contrasting colours for designs such as chevrons, diagonal stripes and diamonds; mixed plain and patterned prints for random placing; graduated toning fabrics for shaded effects.

Shell patchwork works particularly well on small items like tea- and coffee-pot cosies, bags, bolsters and cushions, as well as on larger quilts and coverlets. Larger items should be lined and tied to keep the layers together.

HOW TO MAKE SHELL PATCHES

As an alternative to the traditional method of using a backing paper inside each patch, the following technique uses one slightly stiffer backing paper (template) for making many patches.

Shell patches 1 *To make the template, draw a circle on heavy paper or ticket card (thin cardboard) using a pair of compasses, and mark the centre both ways. Then draw two arcs at each side of the bottom section just inside the centre line. Cut out the template as shown in the diagram.*

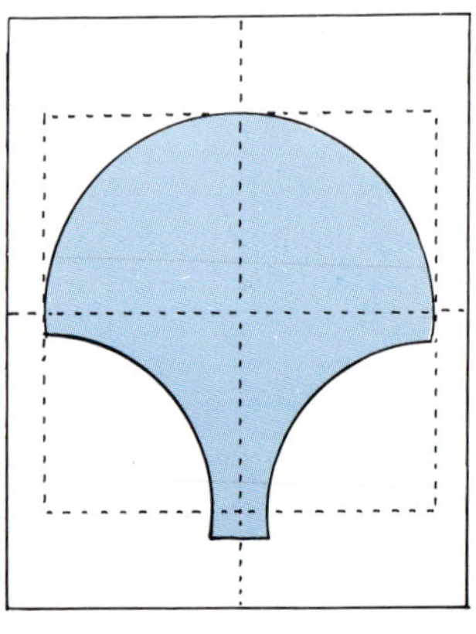

2 *Cut out the fabric patches, adding 6mm (¼in) seam allowances all round. Pin the template to the right side of the fabric. Snip into the curved edge and fold it to the wrong side. Tack through the fabric only, easing the fullness around the curve. Remove the template ready to make the next patch.*

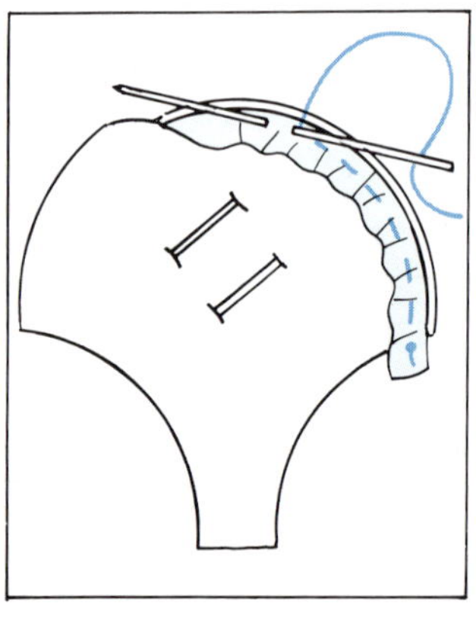

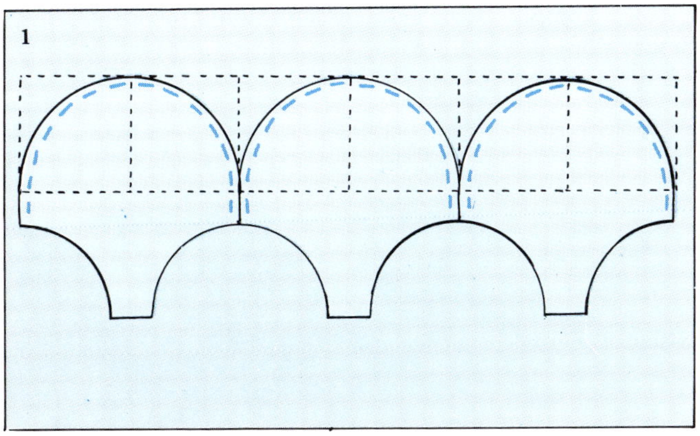

***3** To join the patches, lay them out to check the pattern. Place the top row right side up on a soft surface—an ironing board or clean floor space is ideal—and pin through. Make sure the top edges are level and the edges touching. The bottom edges can be overcast with one or two stitches, if preferred.*

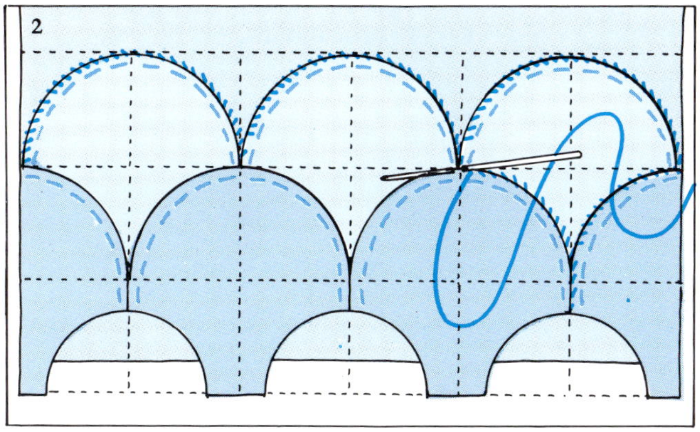

***4** Position the next row on top overlapping the bottom half of the shells, and tack in place. Hem around the curves joining the two rows together. Continue in this way to finish the patchwork. Work half shells at the side edges on every other row.*

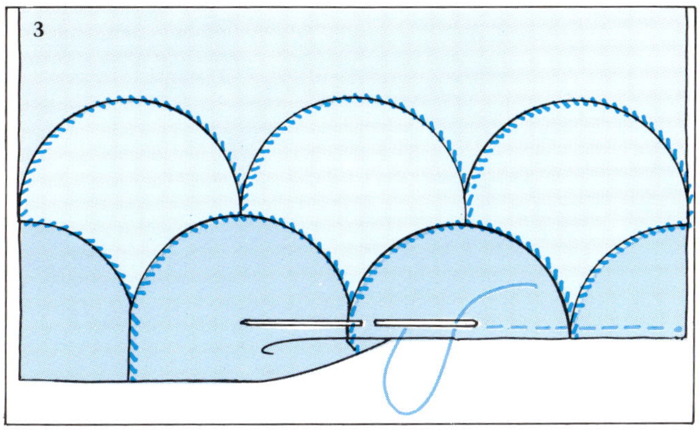

***5** On the last row, trim the bottom half of the shells and turn under the seam allowance. Tack across ready for finishing the project. Remove all visible tacking stitches.*

• CRAZY PATCHWORK •

CRAZY PATCHWORK (or Puzzle patchwork) was a favourite pastime devised by the Victorians as a means of using small scraps of the rich and beautiful fabrics then in fashion—from silks, satins, velvets and brocades to many brightly coloured and inexpensive printed cottons and chintzes.

The patchwork was made with an all-over design where patches were overlapped and stitched to a foundation fabric almost regardless of size and colour. Typical colours included many dark reds and blues, bright golden yellows and black. The raw edges were then lavishly embroidered with herringbone or feather stitches in a twisted thread, usually in the same rich, golden yellow. Quite frequently, the patches were also embroidered with strong, vibrant colours, beads, metallic threads and sequins. Throws, pelmets, cushions and cosies were made, and the edges scalloped, satin frilled, fringed or corded to give a colourful and energetic form of Victorian over-decoration. The work was always lined and tied randomly.

This is the perfect technique for indulging sentiment. If, for example, you have a collection of old fabrics, oddments of real lace, embroidered motifs, ribbons, mottoes, woven labels, even pretty buttons and braids, they can all be worked into a keepsake patchwork, in true Victorian style. Alternatively, much contemporary patchwork is made with the sewing machine, using zigzag stitch to cover the edges or straight stitch for turned-in edges.

A colourful variation with a stained-glass window quality can be made by covering the seams with 1.5cm (½in) wide black tape (or any other dark colour). In crazy patchwork, colour and pattern play a very important part, so be selective when choosing and positioning the patches. Although at first it may not be apparent, a good kaleidoscopic effect needs careful

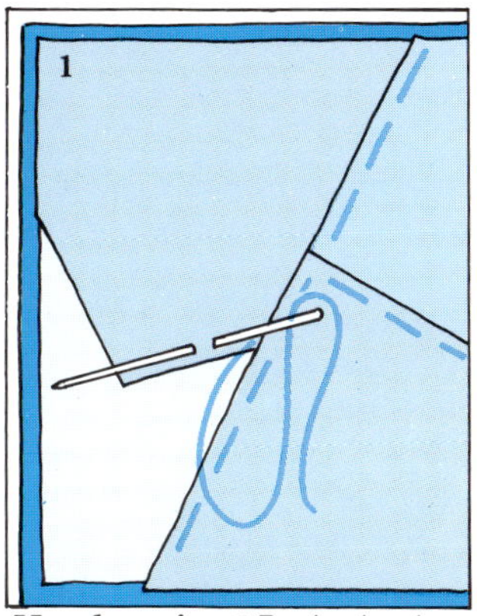

***Hand sewing 1** Beginning in one corner, arrange the unfinished patches on the foundation fabric overlapping the edges, and secure with small running stitches.*

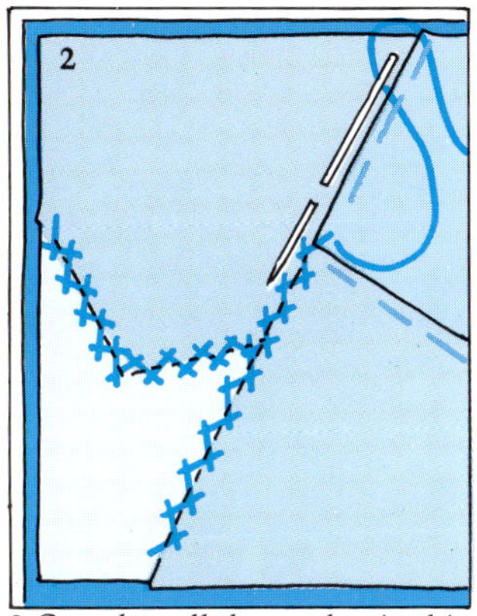

***2** Complete all the patches in this way, and then cover the edges with either herringbone, double or triple feather, blanket stitch or couching.*

planning. The use of a predominant colour randomly interspersed helps to strengthen and unify a design.

For making larger patchwork, you may find it easier to make blocks first and then piece them together, either herringbone stitching over the seams or top stitching, as you prefer.

Plain and printed fabrics—silks, cottons, lightweight wools and velvets, leather and suede—can all be used but, when planning a project, bear in mind their cleaning requirements. Mixed fabric patchwork, wool, silk or leather, for example, will need dry cleaning, but all cotton may be hand laundered.

Crazy patchwork is most effective for covers of all kinds—crib, pram, duvet, car blanket, sofa throw, cushions—for garments and curtains, for abstract 'painting with fabric' pictures or hangings.

MACHINE SEWING

Arrange the patches as for hand sewing and tack them in place. Then work either close zigzag stitch over the edges for a plain finish or make narrow turnings on the patches and secure with straight stitch. If your sewing machine also does a variety of embroidery stitches, you could simply sew them down with a pretty stitch in a complementary colour.

• LOG CABIN PATCHWORK •

LOG CABIN (or Canadian patchwork) is a famous American design using contrasting light and darker strips of fabric, which represent the construction of the north American log cabins. The same design is also found in Britain, other European countries, the Middle East and Afghanistan.

The narrow strips of varying lengths are stitched on to a square of foundation fabric to make 'pressed' rather than pieced blocks. Starting from the middle, a small square, the 'fire' or 'hearth', is stitched down and then the foundation is covered with the light and darker strips of fabric, each strip in turn being stitched, turned back to the right side and pressed as the work progresses—the light and dark sides of the block representing firelight and shadows.

The advantage of this design is that all kinds of left-over scraps can be put to good use. Traditionally, dress and shirt cottons, wool, worsted and tweeds were used. Later, the Victorians used shiny silk and satin ribbons transforming the finished effect from a homespun textile born of thrift and ingenuity into a smart, multi-coloured fabric. While all cottons are easy to handle and thoroughly reliable for patchwork, other contemporary fabrics offer a fantastic range of textures and finishes to experiment with, including novelty synthetics, sheer metallic fabrics and a vast choice of ribbons. Plaids, spots, checks, flecks, stripes and many other patterns may all be used to give new optical effects.

Using the basic square, an amazing variety of patterns can be constructed, depending on how the light

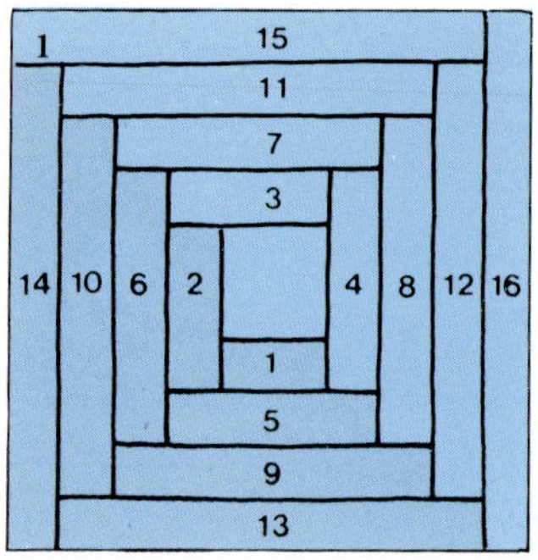

Making the block 1 *Cut a square of backing fabric to size plus 15mm (1/2in) seam allowances all round. Mark it diagonally both ways either by tacking (basting) stitches or with a light pencil line.*

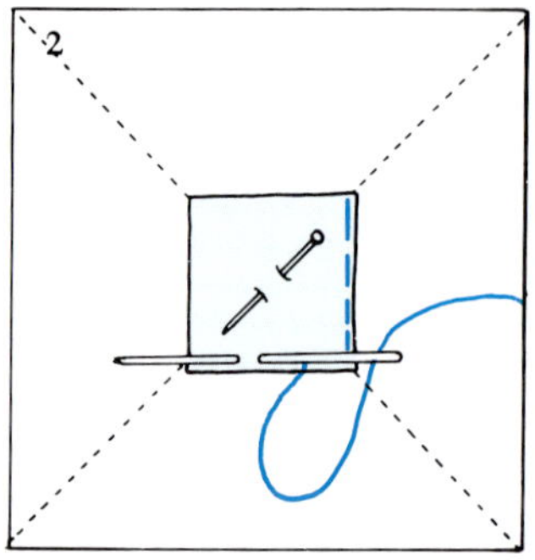

2 *Pin a 5cm (2in) square in the middle and secure with small running stitches, or by machine.*

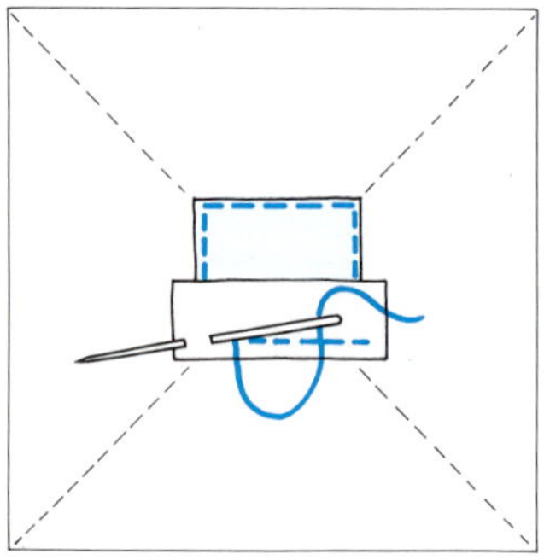

3 *Cut a light strip 6mm (1/4in) longer at each end than the central square by 6.5cm (2 1/2in) wide, and fold lengthways in half. With right sides together, place the fold over the edge of the central square and stitch across.*

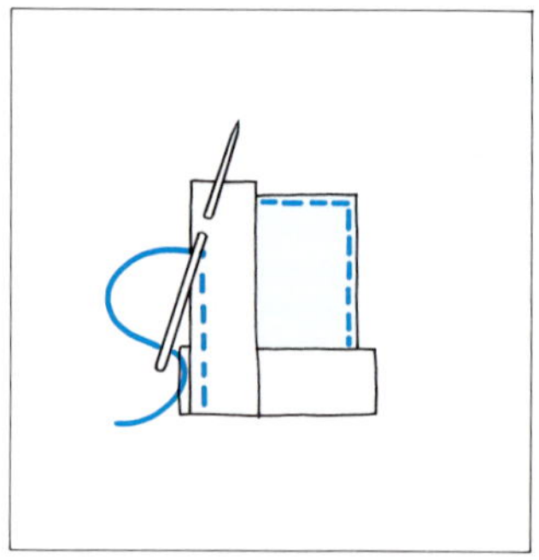

4 *Press the strip back to the right side. Apply a second light strip 6mm (1/4in) longer at each end than the length of the central square and strip, stitch and press back.*

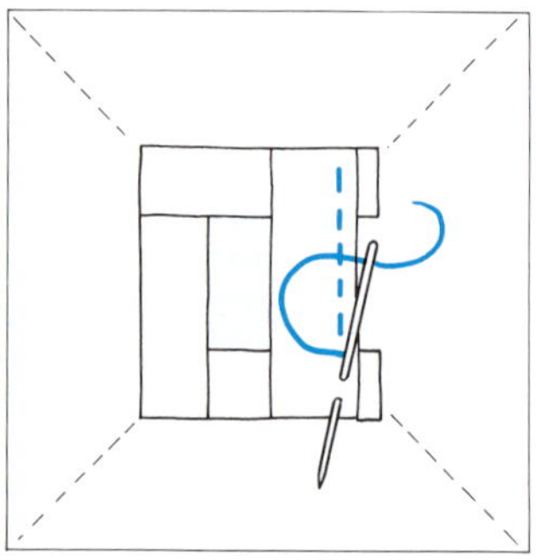

5 *Apply dark strips in the same way working around the square stitching and pressing them back to the right side.*

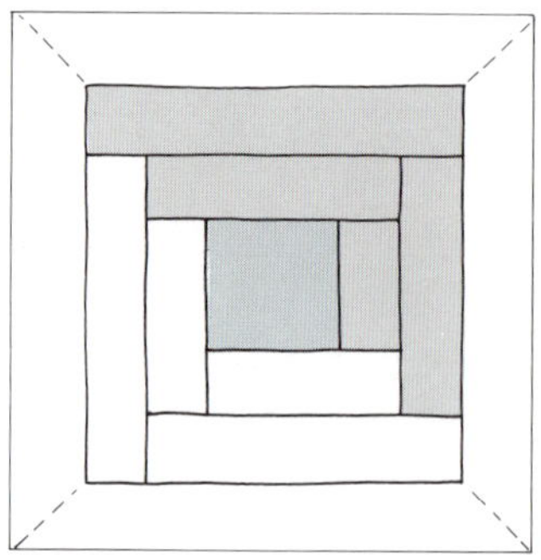

6 *Repeat the sequence adding light and dark strips to complete the block.*

and dark sections are arranged within the block, and on how the blocks are finally put together. In America each part has its own name; Log Cabin, Courthouse steps and Pineapple, for example, are three variations of the individual block while Straight furrow, Stepping stones, Flight of stairs, Barn raising and Chequerboard are names of the arrangements.

The patchwork is not usually bordered but it should be lined and top stitched between the seams of the blocks. A 30cm square (12in) block is a popular size for making quilts and 15cm (6in) square for cushions or smaller projects. The strips are usually 2.5cm (1in) wide plus 6mm (¼in) seam allowances, but, on fine fabrics, they may be cut twice the width and used double. You will need equal amounts of light and dark fabrics for the patchwork, plus foundation and lining fabric the size of the project, excluding seam allowances.

Log cabin is eminently suitable for cushions, using one large or four smaller blocks, crib covers with 12 smaller blocks, cot quilts, full-size quilts and wall hangings.

• FOLDED STAR PATCHWORK •

FOLDED STAR patchwork (sometimes called Quill patchwork) is made by attaching folded triangles of fabric (quills) to a ground fabric. The present technique, which was developed in Canada, is traditionally worked in patterns based on an eight-pointed star—one of the most popular motifs in American pieced patchwork.

Light- to mediumweight cottons fold and crease well and are preferable to synthetics or silks which are too springy and slippery. Fabric oddments can be used mixing patterns where necessary to give the correct tone rather than pattern. Small-scale prints, including flower sprigs, spots, checks, stripes and strong contrast plain colours, help to define the star motif. You will also need a foundation fabric which should not be too difficult to sew through—unbleached calico is ideal.

The star pattern is built up by working outwards from the middle overlapping triangles around a central point, and increasing the number in the rows as the patchwork is enlarged to the size required. The work naturally forms a circle but a design can easily be extended into a square. Each triangle needs a 5cm (2in) square of fabric, so, to get a rough idea of the overall amount needed, first make several practice triangles from fabric oddments or paper. Arrange them in pattern following the instructions, and then calculate the number of rows needed and the amounts of different fabrics for your planned design.

The finished patchwork block is the perfect shape for making cushion sets, or for piecing with alternate plain blocks, for example, into larger patchwork—and for lining the lids of laundry or sewing baskets. For a neat finish, borders and piped edges can be added, picking up the same or contrast colours, with a plain backing.

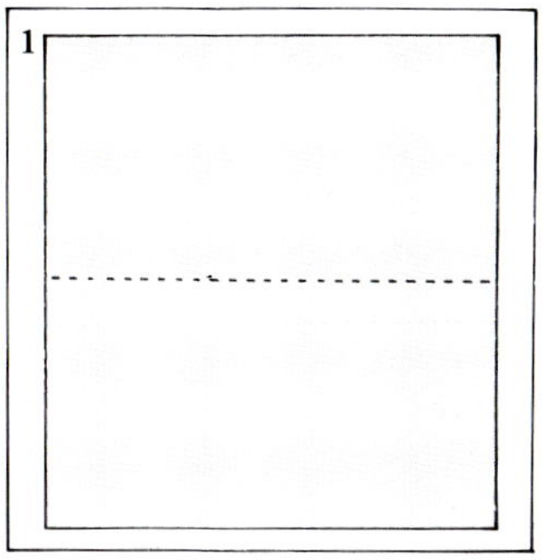

***Folded Star patchwork* 1** *Cut out the correct number of 5cm (2in) squares from your chosen fabric. Fold in half.*

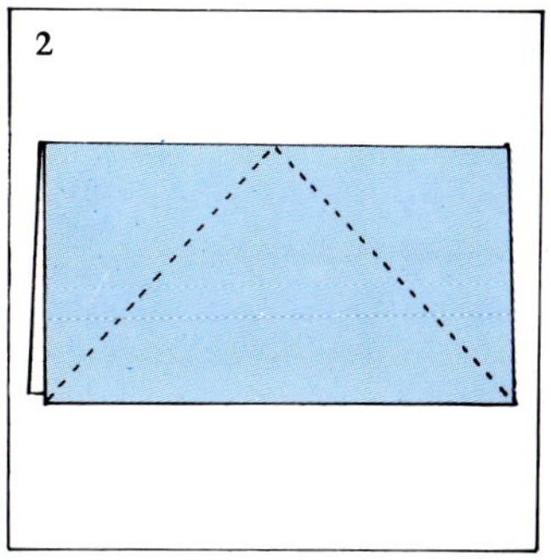

2 *Press flat. Make a triangle by folding the top corners to the centre of the base.*

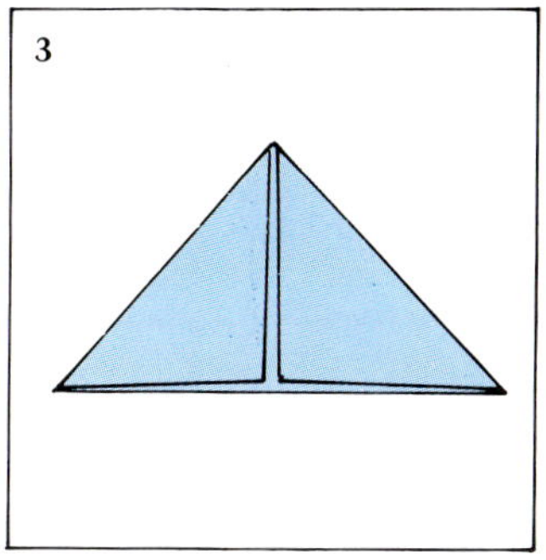

3 *Make three more triangles in the same colour. Press the edges flat.*

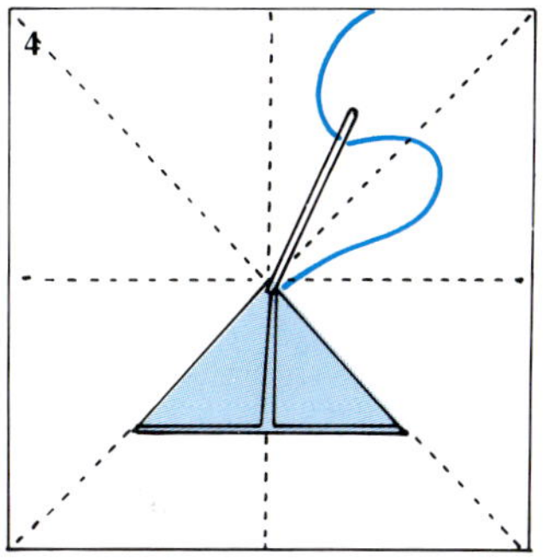

4 *Mark the foundation fabric both ways through straight and diagonal centres. Pin the first triangle in place, and secure with a short straight stitch, as shown.*

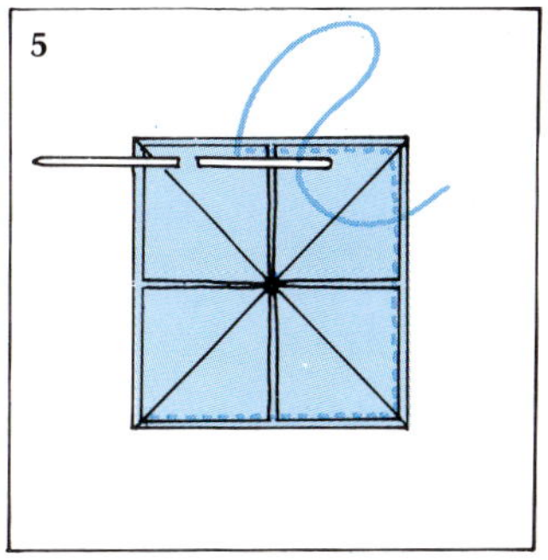

5 *Attach three more triangles catching the centre points, and then secure the outer edges with running stitch through all layers 5mm (¼in) from the edge.*

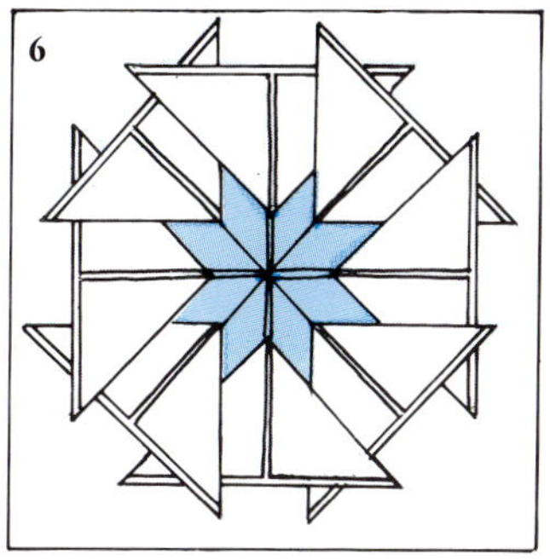

6 *Add eight triangles in colour sequence placing the points about 1cm (½in) from the centre, overlapping the corners. Sew as before. Add eight more triangles on the next row placing the points between those of the last row, and continue in this way adding 16 on subsequent rows as the size increases, and so on, to finish your planned design.*

• MAYFLOWER PATCHWORK •

MAYFLOWER OR Cathedral window patchwork combines simple appliqué with folded patchwork. This ingenious technique is thought to have originated on the *Mayflower* carrying pilgrims to America, where the women used flour sacking to make the folded foundation blocks on which they stitched their precious pieces of printed and coloured fabrics in such a way as to be sparing (without making hems) and yet, give a bright overall effect of colourful patchwork.

Essentially, the work involves folding and refolding squares of the foundation fabric so that the finished patchwork is several layers thick and makes a light, warm covering suitable for throws. Also, as the outer edges are self-finishing, additional borders are not needed.

The method of preparing the foundation reduces the size of the original square by just over half, so allow about two and a quarter times the finished size for the foundation fabric. Although the squares may be larger or smaller, 15cm (6in) is a popular size. To help calculate the amount of fabric needed, a square this size will need a contrast square patch of about 5cm (2in).

Mediumweight cottons such as calico and poplin work well for the foundation and dressweight cottons for the patches. Plain fabrics inset with multi-coloured patches can look quite stunning and give dramatic cathedral window effects. Alternatively, multi-coloured backgrounds with plain patches can be equally attractive reversing the effect to give a series of four-petalled flowers on a mixed ground.

Mayflower patchwork adapts well for cushions, bags, crib covers, quilts, throws and wall hangings.

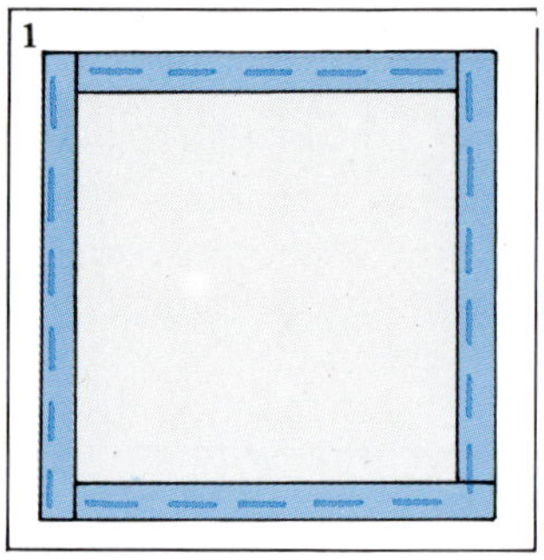

Mayflower patchwork 1 *Cut out sufficient squares from the foundation fabric. Make single 6mm (¼in) turnings all round, tack and press flat.*

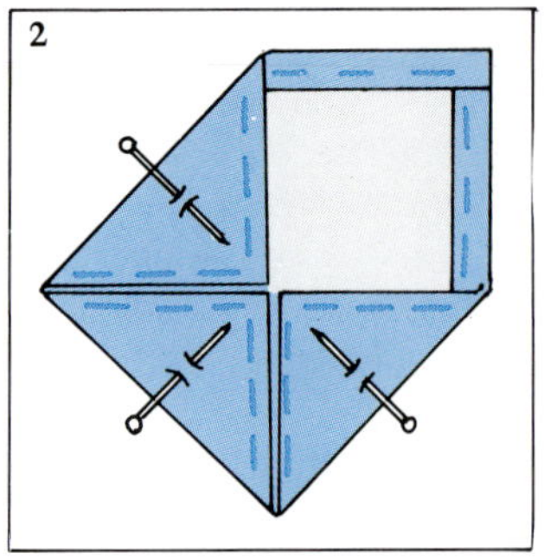

2 *Fold the four corners to the middle, pin each one down and press the edges to give a good sharp crease.*

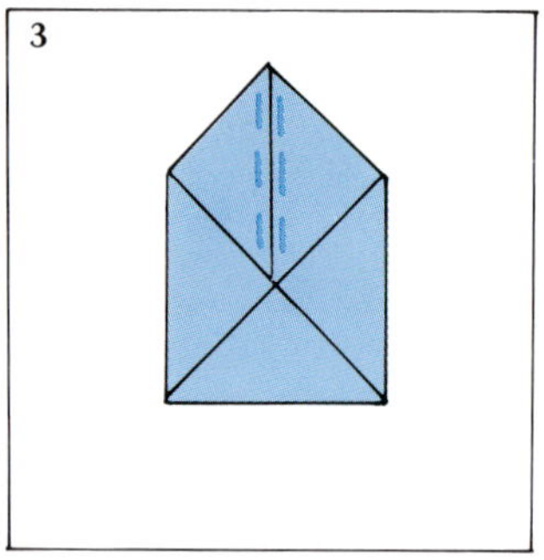

3 *Repeat, folding the corners of the smaller square to the middle and pressing the edges flat, as before.*

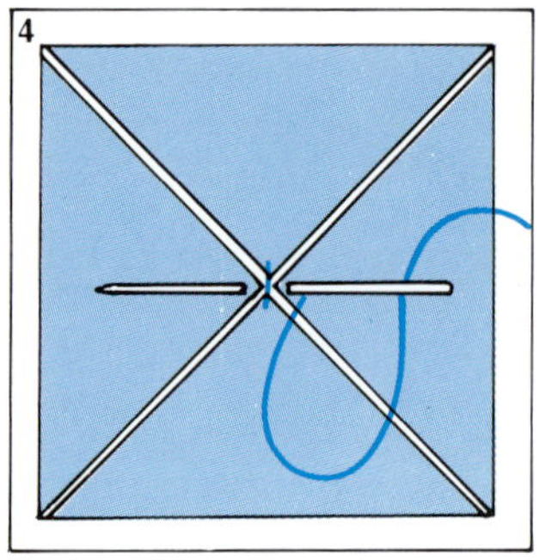

4 *Secure the points in the middle with one or two small cross stitches through all layers.*

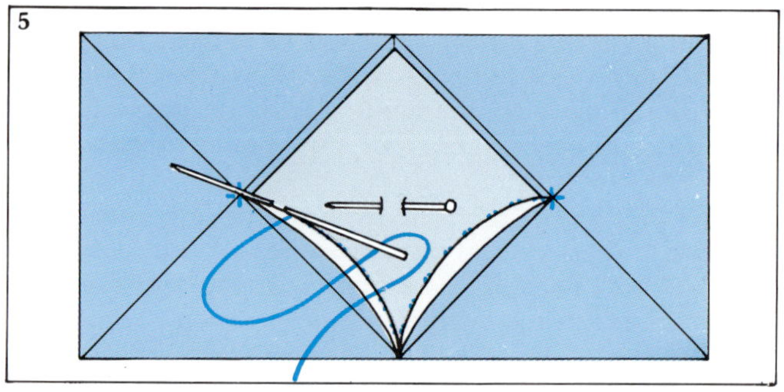

5 *Complete all the foundation squares and then join them together first to form rows across. Begin by placing two squares wrong sides together and then oversewing the edges. Cut out sufficient small square patches 6mm (¼in) smaller than the diamond formed between the two squares. Pin a small contrast patch over the seam between the joined squares. Turn the folded edges of the squares over the raw edges of the patch to form gently curved lines, and hem in place through the layers.*

6 *Repeat, and continue in this way to complete all the rows across. Then join the rows together in the same way. The remaining triangles left at the edges can either be left plain or filled with triangular patches, turning in the outer edge and hemming in the usual way.*

• SEMINOLE PATCHWORK •

THIS FORM OF strip patchwork developed by the Seminole Indians uses thin strips of coloured fabrics which are first stitched together, cut up and then re-arranged into brilliant coloured patterns—often with tiny mosaic-like patches much smaller in size than in ordinary patchwork.

The development of this simple, yet ingenious method of creating complex-looking designs was directly influenced by the introduction of the sewing machine. Closely-woven cottons or silks in plain, primary or subtle colours work well but patterned fabrics should be chosen with care. Certain patterns do not always give the right amount of contrast and the finished effect may be disappointing. Also, since there are so many seams involved, heavier fabrics are best avoided. These would be bulky and unattractive. Although the width of the strips can be varied, more intricate effects are achieved with narrower strips, but they should not be less than 2cm (¾in), including seams.

The small-scale effect of the patchwork makes it ideal for children's clothes—inserted dress panels and borders, for example; shirt yokes, pockets, bags, cushions and wall hangings.

Either make a scaled plan of your design, or, if you are not sure how your shapes will work out, experiment, using fabric oddments, by cutting and stitching several different strip patterns to find the most pleasing arrangements, and then plan your design.

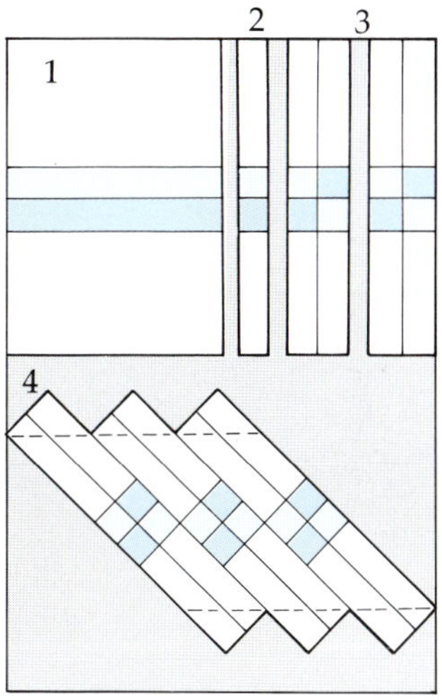

***Straight-cup strips* 1** *Sew together a selection of strips (always cut on the straight grain—four in this case.*
2 *Then cut them into equal strips.*
3 *Reverse and join the strips together in pairs.*
4 *Stitch the pairs in a diagonal position. This offsets the four patch squares to give a row of diamonds. Trim the top and bottom level ready to join on the next plain or patterned band.*

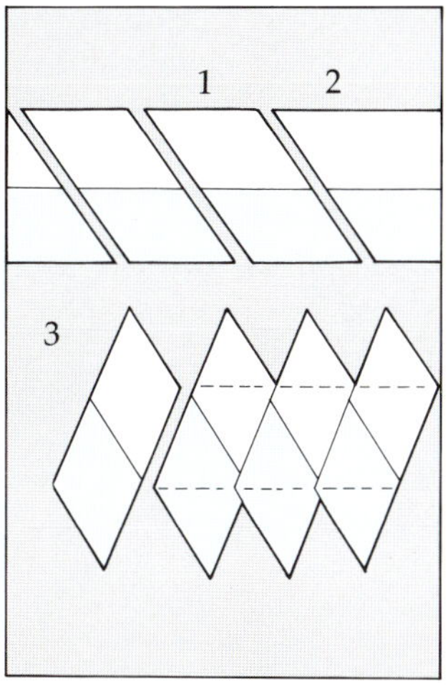

***Bias-cut strips* 1** *Sew together two coloured strips—cut on the straight grain and slightly wider than before.*
2 *Cut them diagonally into even sections.*
3 *Reposition and stitch the strips diagonally matching the corner points. Trim off the top and bottom, as shown, to give a border of triangles.*

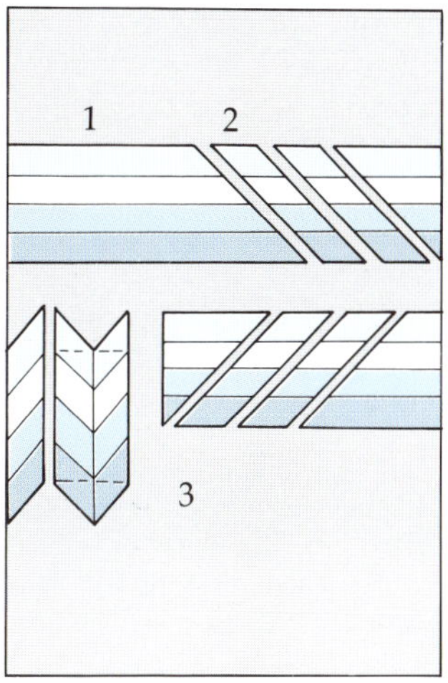

***Chevrons* 1** *Sew together the required number of coloured strips.*
2 *Cut the length in half, and then cut each one into even sections cutting diagonally in the opposite direction.*
3 *With the bias edges and right sides together, join opposite pieces. Continue in this way, adding more chevrons as needed. Press and trim the edges.*

• PLEATED PATCHWORK •

As its name suggests, pleated patchwork involves joining together blocks of pleated fabric arranged to give interesting textural and optical effects. This purely decorative patchwork, in which the surface texture of the fabric is deliberately altered before the blocks are joined, offers great scope for innovation.

Regularly formed pleats are machine stitched and can either be stitched down at each side of a block, following the direction of the folds to give a softly ridged surface, or additional lines may also be stitched diagonally across, or at right angles to the first set of folds. This alters the surface tension, and, in this way, the play of light creates quite amazing effects of movement reminiscent of drifting sand dunes.

Pin tucks can also be used. These are usually stitched quite near the folded edge of the fabric, although the depth can be varied as needed. They can be stitched in sequence either vertically or horizontally, or in both directions to form a chequered pattern. The same stitching can be used throughout, or in different sequences of straight stitch and satin stitch worked over the edge in matching, contrast or variegated coloured threads. Pin tucks combined with pleating and 'movement stitching' offer a whole new range of visual effects.

The prepared fabric is then cut into the correct size blocks and arranged to suit the design. Rectangular blocks can be joined together either following a simple square grid, in vertical or horizontal bands across, or cut into block-size geometric shapes such as triangles, parallelograms and diamonds, for example, before being stitched in pattern.

As most of the interest in pleated patchwork relies on the undulating surfaces created and the way in which the blocks are put together, plain, pastel coloured fabrics will give best results. Voile, cotton, cotton/polyester, silk, gingham, fine velvet, chiffon, lace and certain nets are ideal. However, simple, spotted, striped and shaded fabrics might also be exploited. By obscuring and distorting the design with pleats and tucks, areas of solid colour, or increased density of pattern, can be produced and used in imaginative piecing.

The finished work should be lined to hide the seaming.

PLEATS

Pleating and tucking reduces the fabric depending on the depth of the folds used. For full pleating, allow at least three times the finished size.

As an alternative to using regularly spaced pleats of an equal size throughout a patchwork, you can ring the changes by mixing areas of both deep and shallower pleats in a design. This will give a more undulating and sculptural effect to the surface, which can also be further emphasized by stitching with shaded threads. Take extra care when estimating the amount of fabric needed.

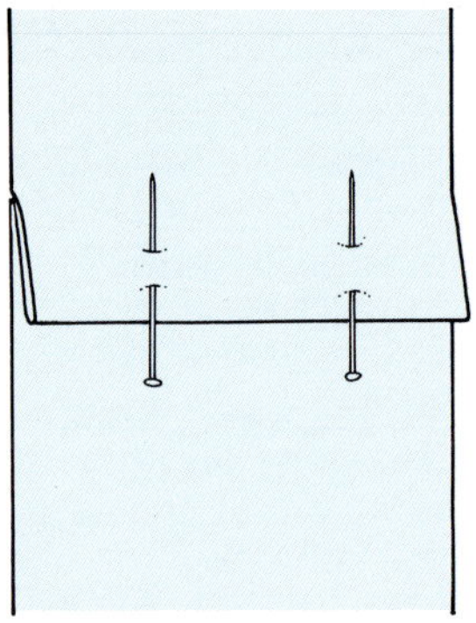

***Pleats* 1** *Decide the depth of the pleat—15mm (½in) is a popular size. Working on the right side, and along the straight grain of the fabric, pin the first fold across and press.*

2 *For the next and subsequent pleats, release the first fold, measure the depth and the distance between and then, using pins, mark the foldlines and positioning lines along both edges. Complete each pleat stitching 15mm (½in) in from the edge. Press and stitch the pleats down each side in the direction of the folds.*

For 'movement stitching' *either machine the outer edges of a block with the folds in opposite directions, or repeat over the entire surface stitching the folds up and down, or diagonally, in alternate directions. Hold the fabric with both hands as you feed it through the machine, using pins as a guideline for stitching.*

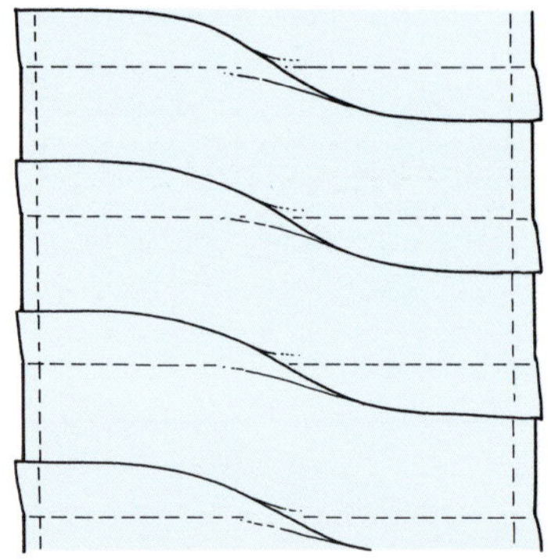

***Tucks* 1** *To make simple tucks, fold the fabric along the straight grain and, using matching or contrast coloured threads, machine between 3–6mm (⅛–¼in) in from the edge. Press the tuck to one side and repeat as needed. Accurate straight stitching is essential.*

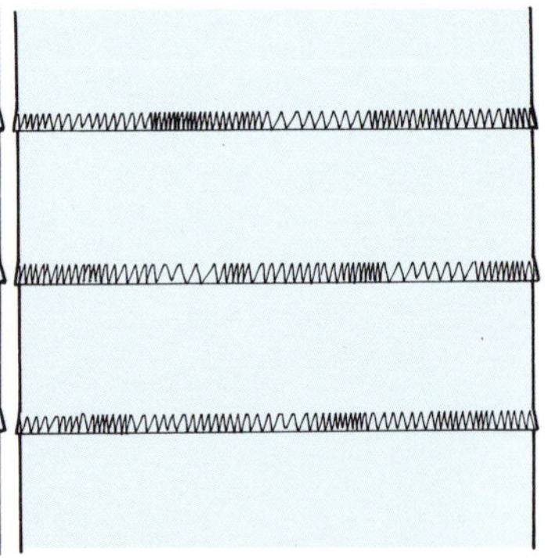

2 *Alternatively, zigzag stitch the edges, using a variegated thread.*

For a combined effect of tucks and pleats *stitch the pleats as far as setting the folds, as previously described, and then stitch the creased lines as described for tucks. Use matching or contrast colours, changing them to emphasize the effects of movement.*

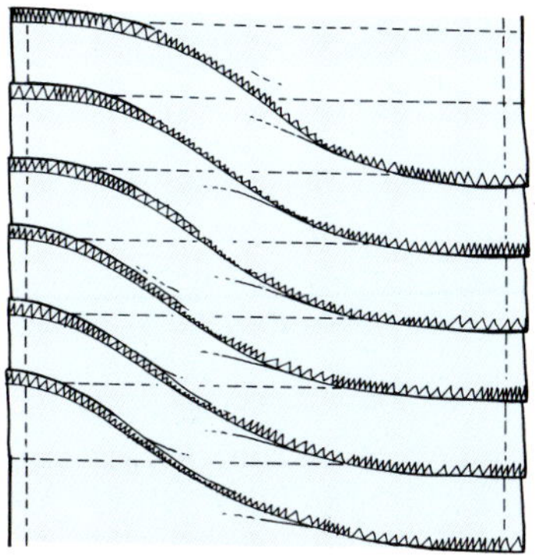

TUCKS

For a combined effect of tucks and pleats stitch the pleats as far as setting the folds, as previously described, and then stitch the creased lines as described for tucks. Use matching or contrast colours, changing them to emphasize the effects of movement.

Being much finer than pleats, tucks can be stitched quite close together over an entire area in regular or random designs, to give a gently ridged surface. They can also be spaced apart and worked in both directions to produce checks, and with a little more effort, checks can be varied to create a tartan effect. As with pleats, take care in estimating the amount of fabric needed, remembering with tartan-type designs, to calculate both directions accurately.

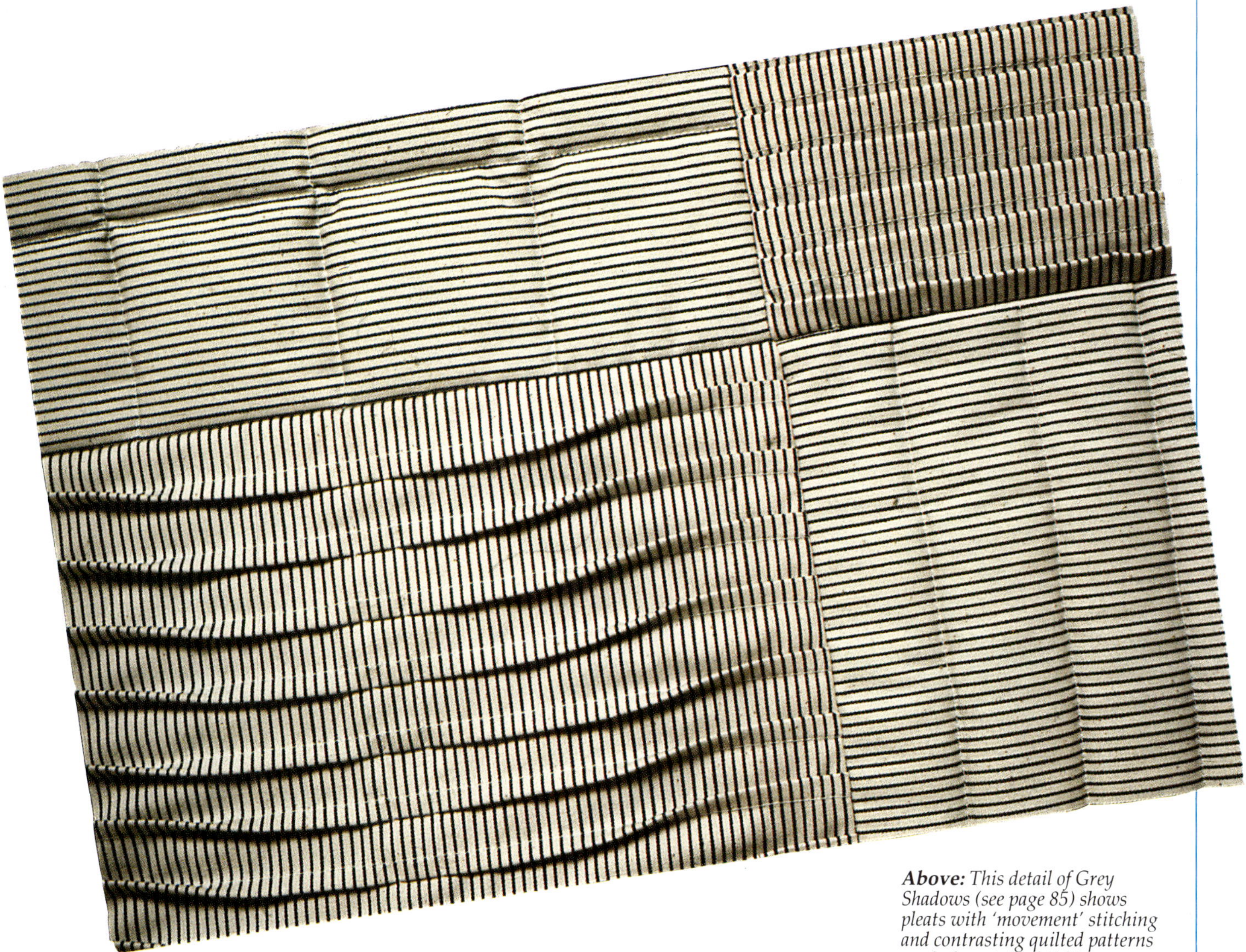

Above: *This detail of Grey Shadows (see page 85) shows pleats with 'movement' stitching and contrasting quilted patterns worked on striped ticking.*

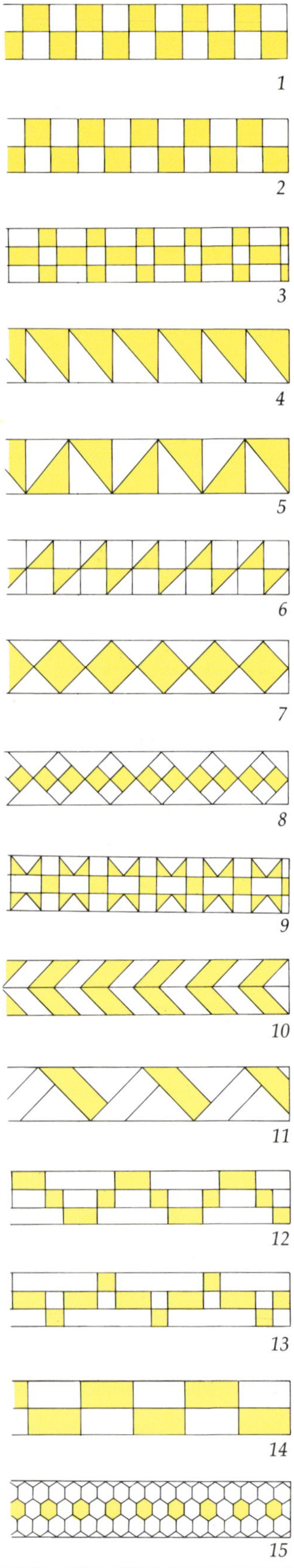

Choose an appropriate border design to complement your patchwork.
***1** Check border, **2** Victory border, **3** Paris border, **4** Sawtooth border, **5** Cascade border, **6** Hourglass border, **7** Diamond border, **8** Target border, **9** Navajo border, **10** Arrow border, **11** Zigzag border, **12** Plains border, **13** Scallop border, **14** Brick border, **15** Rosette border.*

• FINISHING PATCHWORK •

IDEALLY, THE WAY a piece of patchwork is finished should be an integral part of the overall design and be considered at the beginning. Items such as garments, cushions and other soft furnishings will have their raw edges neatened in the making-up process whereas the edges of quilts and wall hangings are treated individually. This might be a decorative border, piping, binding, or simply a self-neatened edge, as for quilts (see page 26). Notice that styles such as Mayflower and Shell patchwork have their own built-in edgings. Most patchwork is then lined and, in some cases, quilted.

Below left: *This colourful detail of the patchwork quilt Sunburst shows the contrasting quilted pattern running diagonally through the patches.*

Straight corners *Apply the two long sides of the border cut to the length of the patchwork. Cut the two shorter sides to include the patchwork and the width of the two borders, as shown, plus seam allowances, and stitch in place. Hand stitch the outer corner seams.*

Block corners *Apply the two long sides as for straight borders. Cut out the four corners to size, or piece blocks to fit, and then join each corner to its respective border to form two long strips. Stitch the top and bottom borders in place finishing the outer corner seams as for straight borders.*

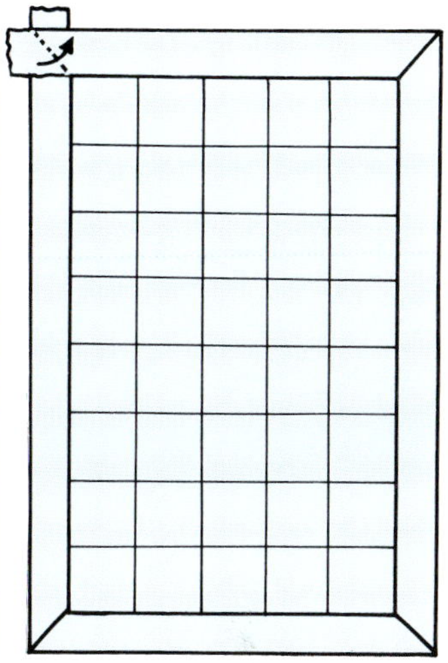

Mitred corners *Cut all four borders the required width and depth. Position them on the patchwork with the corners overlapping, and fold back the fabric diagonally across each corner. Use the creases as a guide for stitching.*

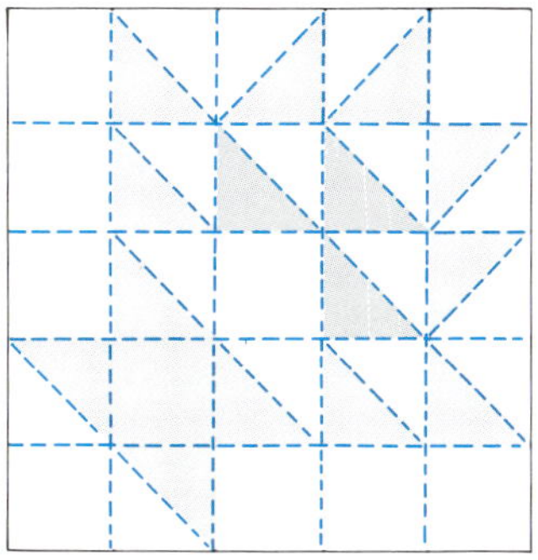

Flower basket: *shows the block quilted within each seam (sink stitch).*

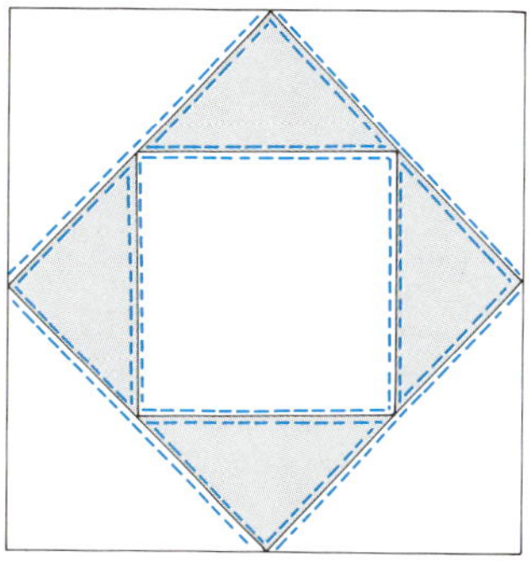

Paving stones: *shows the block quilted along both sides of the seams.*

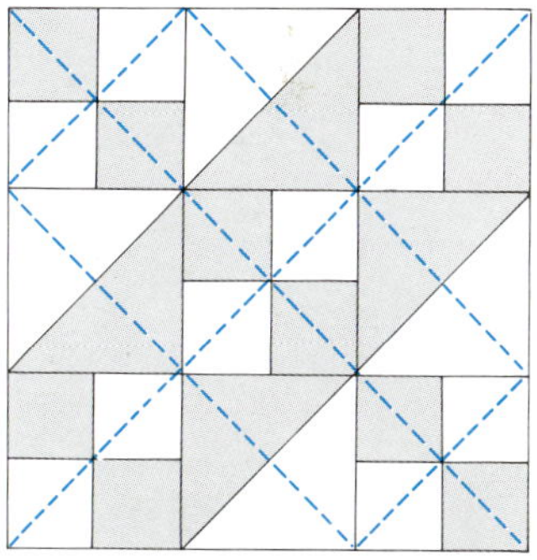

Jacob's ladder: *here the block is quilted diagonally through the patches to make a contrasting pattern.*

LINING

The finished patchwork (with or without interlining) should be lined to neaten and strengthen the seams, and large pieces quilted to hold the layers together.

For added strength, you may prefer to back some cushions and other soft furnishings and unquilted wall hangings with a pelmetweight bonded interfacing before lining.

As lining and finishing the edges are worked in exactly the same way as for quilted items, refer to the quilting section for full instructions.

CHAPTER FIVE

PATCHWORK PROJECTS

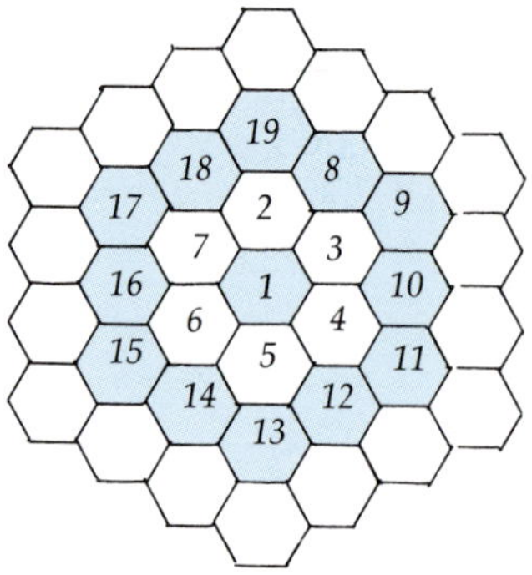

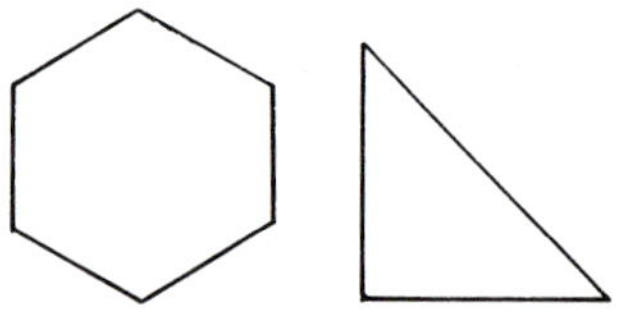

Left: *Grandmother's Flower Garden.* ***Above:*** *For the rosette, begin with the central patch 1, join patches 2–7, and then 8–19.*

• PIECED PATCHWORK •

GRANDMOHER'S FLOWER GARDEN

THIS DELIGHTFUL quilt made in Maryland, USA, during the 1840s is typical of English hand-sewn patchwork using the one-patch method. The border fabric is a beautiful flowery chintz manufactured in England earlier in the century, and the hexagons of the 'flower gardens' are made from English furnishing fabrics.

Hexagon patches can be made from a variety of colours and sewn together in either a random way or in several variations of the Grandmother's Flower Garden pattern. Here the hexagons are grouped into rosettes and joined with a linking border so that the rosettes give the appearance of a repeat pattern. Traditionally, the flower garden is made with a central yellow patch followed by two rows in either pinks, blues or yellows in mixed prints, and surrounded by a row of toning green hexagons to represent foliage, with a linking border of white patches to form the path between the flower beds. However, this can be varied to suit smaller projects and more restricted colour schemes.

Smooth, dressweight cottons or lightweight furnishing (curtain) fabrics are best for hand sewing patches with backing papers. Hexagon patchwork is ideal for large or small items from crib and pram covers to cushions, quilts, curtains, bags and pincushions.

For the project choose a mixture of prints and plain fabrics for the hexagons and both borders. Make up the patches using backing papers (*see* page 10), according to your design. For large items, 6cm (2½in) wide units are recommended with an appropriately wide outer border.

Assemble the hexagons into rosettes and stitch them together in rows across before linking them with the plain 'path' hexagons. Either oversew the seams by hand (*see* page 53), or if the patches are reasonably large, use zigzag stitch (*see* page 93).

Make the inner border from triangles stitched first into squares and then into long border strips. Add the outer border, mitring the corners (*see* page 61). Quilt through the seams to secure the layers and finish as required (*see* page 26).

DIAGONAL

Many impressive mosaic patchwork designs, created by repeating a single unit (one-patch) over the entire area, depend a great deal for their success on skilful cutting and piecing, and on some well-chosen colours. These may be simply bright and cheerful but, for the greatest impact, they should include a wide range of tonal values.

Above: *Diagonal. For the most striking effect, choose a wide range of toning colours shading from light to dark.*

In this contemporary wall hanging with its dramatic diagonal stripes, eight different colours are used, ranging in tone from very light to very dark. The design is worked in rows across, where the patches are arranged in colour sequence, and repeated in reverse to make the repeat 14 patches wide. The same sequence is repeated below, moving one patch to the right on each row to form diagonal lines.

Plain fabrics or those with very small prints or fine shirtings in dressweight cottons, lawn, brushed cotton, wool mixes, mediumweight silks or very fine wool work well with square patches.

Patches can either be made with backing papers or by machine providing they are not too small. A 6cm (2½in) square is a popular size for wall hangings, cot or crib quilts, cushions and other soft furnishings, but it can be adjusted to suit other items, as required. Fabric games-boards are fun to make using alternate light and dark square patches.

For the project make a scaled drawing on graph paper and indicate the colours. Keep this at hand for cutting the fabric and piecing the design.

Using the darker colours in the top left corner, join the patches in rows across, repeating the colour sequence. Join the rows to form the diagonal pattern and to complete the patchwork.

Make up the patchwork as needed with or without interlining, and quilt diagonally through each square. Add a plain border, between 10–15cm (4–6in) wide, to finish (*see* page 60).

SUGAR BOWL

The Sugar Bowl design is a favourite old American pattern, and one of many variations each with its own evocative name such as Drunkard's Path, Fool's Puzzle, Falling Timbers and Wonder of the World. This is a four-patch pattern where each patch is made up of two units: a small square with a quarter circle set in one corner—the curved seam being best hand sewn. The patches are pieced together so that the four corners form a circle within a larger square block.

Traditionally, two colours are used but mixed colours arranged as in this contemporary quilt can be very attractive—an excellent scrap-bag design. Here pretty prints salvaged from discarded dresses have been cleverly designed and pieced into a large symmetrical pattern with a random effect. Similar designs could be planned with mixed colours but using fewer prints; spots with sprig prints and plain colours; stripes with spots and plains; plaids with tiny checks and plain colours would all give interesting results. This kind of imposed restriction often helps in planning a design.

Dressweight cotton, cotton/wool mixes and fine silks are ideal for Sugar Bowl patchwork. Its reasonably large repeat is suitable for soft furnishings—curtains, cushions, floor seating, sofa throws and table covers.

For the project make a scale plan of your design, indicating the different colour patches, and use this for estimating fabric and piecing the design. Tones or near tones of a particular colour can be used and often add liveliness to a patchwork pattern.

To make the patch, clip the convex curve on the quarter circle, and assemble the two units right sides inside and curves together, with the quarter circle unit below. Pin the corners first and then ease the fabric as you pin around the curve. Sew the curve by hand and the straight seams by machine, if preferred.

Make up the four patches of each block and join them together. Lay them out in pattern and join the blocks into rows across and then into a complete patchwork. Quilt and finish the back as required. Add a light-coloured print binding around the edges to finish (*see* page 26).

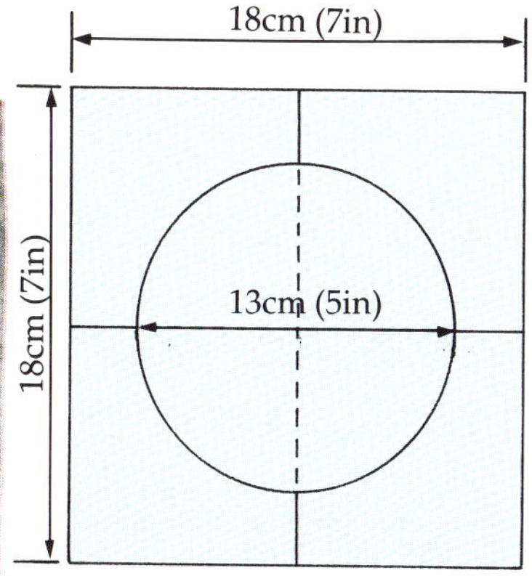

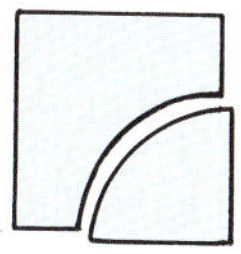

Left: *Sugar Bowl. A fascinating scrap-bag design showing mixed prints arranged in a random way. Make up each of the two units before assembling them into a four-patch block as shown (**above**).*

***Left:** Double Irish Chain. Five-patch block (**top**) and appliqué block (**above**).*

DOUBLE IRISH CHAIN

This late nineteenth-century quilt is worked in a popular American pattern known as Double Irish chain. The pattern forms a large repeat, which is traditionally made into quilts and coverlets of all sizes, using crisp cottons in plain-coloured or small patterned fabrics.

The design uses two blocks—a five-patch block, and a plain block wth a small square cleverly appliquéd to each corner. When pieced together, this gives a most intricate effect. The pieced blocks (the 'chain') can be arranged diagonally, as shown, or in a square repeat, and either machine or hand sewn. Traditionally, the plain blocks are quilted all over following the lines of the pieced square to give the over-all effect of a solidly pieced quilt.

For the project choose either two tones or two harmonizing colours for the piecing, or, for a different effect, try a random multi-coloured selection, and white or a light colour for the plain block. You will find designing and piecing easier if you make a colour plan on graph paper first. A 4cm (1½in) square patch is a popular size for the pieced block.

For the five-patch block, sew patches in colour sequence to form rows across, stitching 1–5, 2–10 and so on, and then join the rows together.

For the appliqué block, apply four patches of the correct colour to each corner. Join the blocks alternately in pattern, quilt and finish as preferred (*see* page 26).

GRANDMOTHER'S CHOICE

This Amish quilt made in Milton, Iowa, in the 1920s is a striking example of an old American pattern called Grandmother's Choice. Here, rather sombre colours are boldly contrasted with black to give an overall effect of a twinkling, faceted pattern.

The Amish, or Plain People, who belong to the Mennonite church do not believe in decoration and, although their patchwork is essentially plain and simple, the results are often powerful geometric designs with great dignity and beauty.

The design uses two blocks—a pieced four-patch block, and a plain block—stitched alternately together in a diagonal repeat pattern. As the blocks are set diagonally, the edges are filled in with half plain blocks and quarter blocks in the corners. The pattern forms a fairly large repeat and is ideal for beginners working by hand or machine. It is most suitable for coverlets, and quilts and larger soft furnishing items. Single pieced blocks are good for cushion sets and groups of four or more for floor cushions.

For the project make a colour plan of your design on graph paper. A 25cm (10in) block works well for larger items.

To make the pieced block, join the pieces into three separate rows across, and then piece the rows to form the blocks. If needed, press the seams towards the darker fabric to prevent them showing through. Make

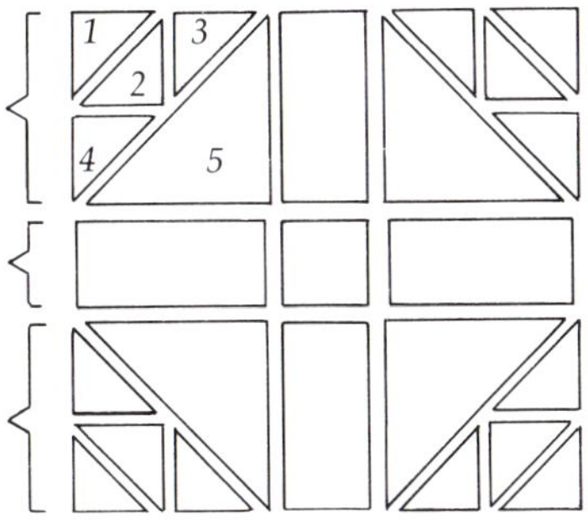

Above: *There are several ways of piecing this block for Grandmother's Choice (**right**). The simplest is to sew the small units first and join them into three horizontal rows. Then stitch the rows together to form one block.*

up the patchwork, setting the blocks alternately in pattern. Add half and quarter blocks as needed, and finish with two plain borders (*see* page 60).

FLOATING TRIANGLES

Triangular pieced blocks combining bright primary colours with grey and black are used in this stunning wall hanging to create a three-dimensional effect of shapes suspended in space.

The design, worked in silk, uses a single triangular block throughout, which is repeated in several colour combinations and joined together diagonally and vertically by narrow bands of grey to form larger diamonds. These grey bands along with black not only form the background but give the optical effect of space. Half triangles are used at the top and bottom to complete the rectangle and the finished work is quilted in such a way as to further emphasize the depth of each triangle.

Mediumweight silks and cottons in well-defined plain colours are recommended for best results. For the block, a triangle measuring 20cm (8in) from base to apex is an ideal size with 15mm (½in) wide bands between. Large repeats such as these are most suitable for wall coverings, quilts, sofa throws or bedroom rugs, where the full effect of the design can be appreciated—although smaller areas such as hexagons using six

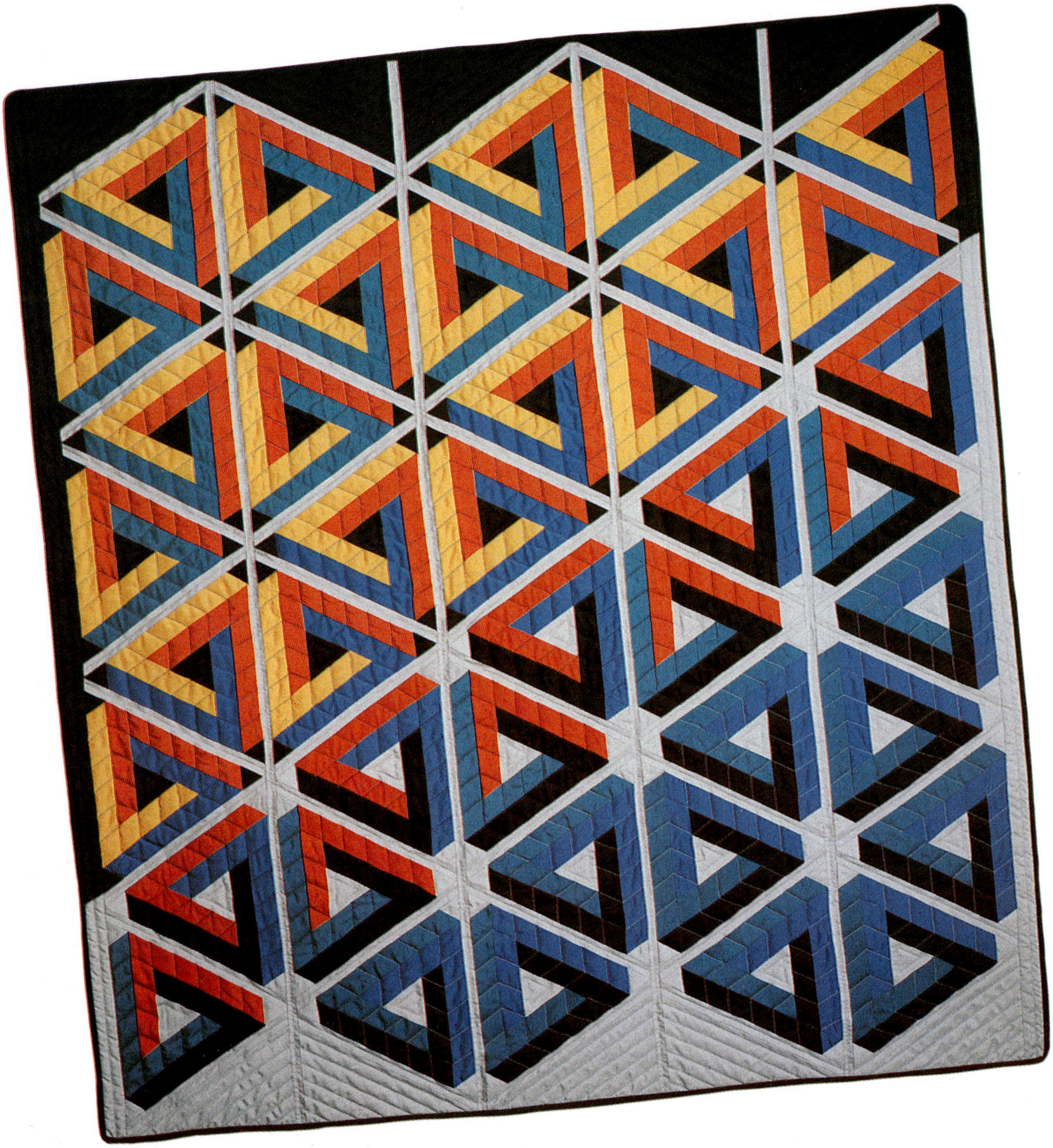

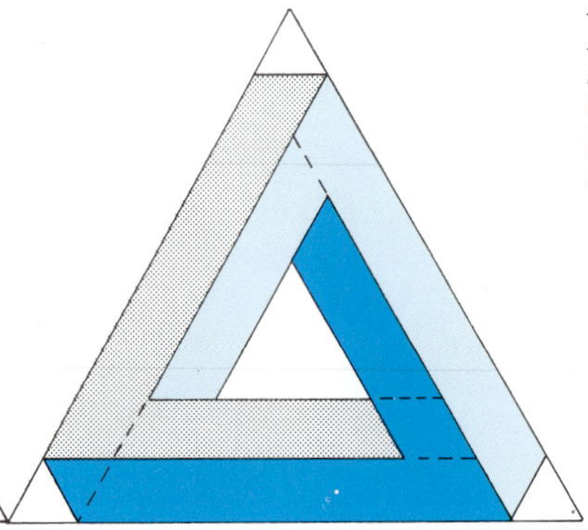

Above: *Floating Triangles. Assemble the patches in the order shown (**far left**). Then join the blocks together using narrow bands of contrast coloured fabric, and quilt as in the diagram (**left**).*

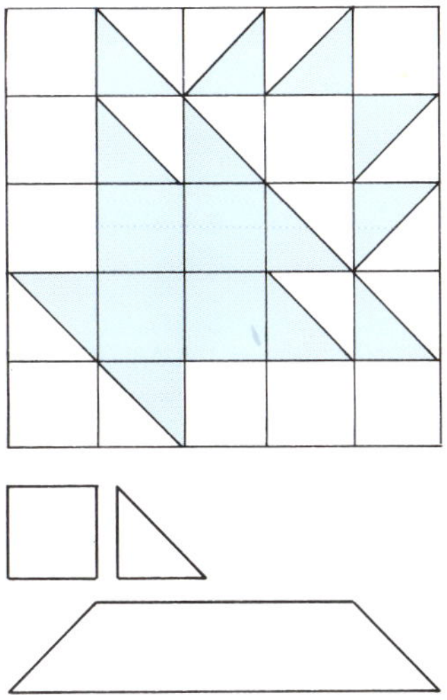

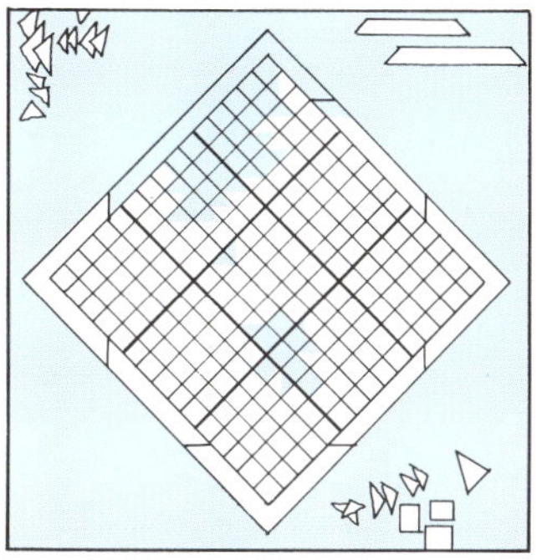

Above: *Several 'fruit basket' patches are substituted with the background colour and arranged in the corners of November Morning (**right**).*

triangles, or diamonds using eight, could be utilized to make sets of unusual shaped cushions.

For the project use isometric graph paper. Make a scaled drawing of the design indicating the colour areas, and then make the full-size templates. Use the drawing to estimate the amount of fabric needed, and keep it by you for piecing the finished work.

Make up the pieced triangles by hand or machine in the order shown, and join them together with 2.5cm (1in) wide bands cut on the straight grain. Add separate borders in colour pattern to the two side edges and assemble the patchwork ready for quilting (*see* page 49). Cotton wadding (batting) has been used for a flatter effect and to give slight additional weight to the finished work. Use a plain silk backing and quilt the design following the diagram, filling the half triangles with straight lines about 1.5cm (½in) apart. Finally, bind the outer edges with bias-cut fabric, cut twice the width, 5cm (2in), to give a double thickness and a well-padded effect. For hanging by rod, add a fabric sleeve to the back just inside the top edge and about 2.5cm (1in) from the outer edges.

NOVEMBER MORNING

The designer of this contemporary wall hanging has used traditional patterns and block repeats simply as the starting point for a most striking design. The large central diamond with several incomplete fruit basket blocks, beautifully picked out in subtle pinks and greys, combines with the pitch-black background to simulate the effect of a shattered window and falling glass.

The design uses a single-pieced block, repeated, and set diagonally to form a central diamond. This is surrounded with a narrow pieced border, four plain corners are added to complete the patchwork. Several units from the blocks are applied to the three corners to give the 'shattered window' look, and the originals substituted with the background colour. A finished block of about 25cm (10in) square works well on this design, and the whole patchwork can easily be machine pieced.

Designs on this scale are eminently suited for hangings, quilts and covers of all kinds. However, the same idea can easily be modified for smaller items—rather like a section of an unfinished jigsaw puzzle.

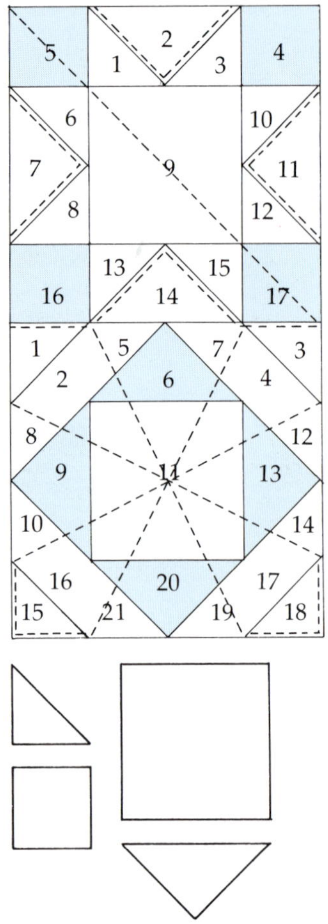

Left: Sunburst. *Make the templates shown* (**above**) *and assemble them in the numbered sequence. Quilt along the dotted lines.*

For the project and to recreate this effect, plan your design on graph paper carefully, plotting the shattered glass effect and indicating the colours. Make up the pieced block, first stitching the triangles to form squares in each row across. Then join them into whole patchwork. Make up and apply the border strips and add the four corners. Arrange the 'shattered' units to finish. Quilt and finish the outer edges as you prefer (*see* page 26).

SUNBURST

The design of this contemporary quilt, giving a dazzling effect of interlocking shapes and shaded colours, uses just two pieced blocks. The visual impact of such a design relies on skilful use of colour. Here colours are cleverly chosen and expertly arranged to give the brilliant sunburst effect. Basically, two complementary colours (in thise case, orange and turquoise blue) form the lighter area, and other closely related colours with deeper tonal values make the surrounding border.

The two blocks, each simply divided into squares and triangles, are repeated alternately on a square grid. One block is based on a star (the old American Saw Tooth), and the second has the same basic units but the corner squares are sub-divided into triangles and others reversed, so that, when they are repeated together, large diamonds are created. The finished work is quilted diagonally through the patterns to give the appearance of a superimposed texture. Light- to medium-weight cottons and silks—preferably in plain colours—work best for this kaleidoscopic effect. If prints are used, the motifs should be really tiny and inconspicuous to pre-

Left: *This delightful patchwork camel cover from Uzbekistan, Russia, has openwork bands decorated with sawtooth edgings, and uses an amazing variety of fabrics including cotton, velvet, felt, embroidered braids, and woven ikat.*

Above: *Straight Furrow log cabin patchwork.*

vent conflicting images occurring.

Patchworks based on the sunburst theme need to be fairly large such as wall hangings and sofa throws, but the idea can easily be adapted to smaller items such as jackets, padded seating, cushions or a play mat.

For the project this type of design must be worked out quite accurately on graph paper first—dressmaker's pattern paper with bigger squares is easier for planning larger works. Keep the coloured design by you as reference for checking fabric requirements and especially for putting the finished patchwork together.

The finished design has a separate border added and can be sewn by hand or machine, as preferred. Assemble each block in the same way. First join the units to make three rows across, and then piece the whole block. Arrange the finished blocks in pattern, and then join them first in rows across before piecing the whole patchwork.

Quilt the design following the dotted lines suggested in the diagram below, and finish as needed.

• LOG CABIN PATCHWORK • STRAIGHT FURROW

LOG CABIN PATCHWORK is the most widely known American pattern. Originally, it must surely have been devised as the most economical means of using up oddments of fabric too small and narrow to be useful for anything else.

The individual blocks, made by adding thin strips of fabric around a central square are divided diagonally into light and dark sections, and, when pieced together, can be constructed into varying patterns depending on how the strips and blocks are arranged.

This nineteenth-century quilt shows the Straight Furrow pattern—one of the simplest and most striking arrangements. This kind of diagonal striping is, incidentally, most effective on any narrow quilt (single bed), or crib cover or duvet, whereas wider arrangements such as Barn Raising require a broader expanse for the full effect and are obviously better for wider quilts. The block is reasonably large at 30cm (12in) square and uses strips of 2.5cm (1in) wide (finished size) in both plain and printed cottons.

For the project draft a colour plan and then divide your fabrics into groups of definite light and dark tones. Make up the blocks (*see* page 54). Lay them out in the pattern you want and then assemble them as shown. Quilt along the seams between the blocks and add a border, if preferred.

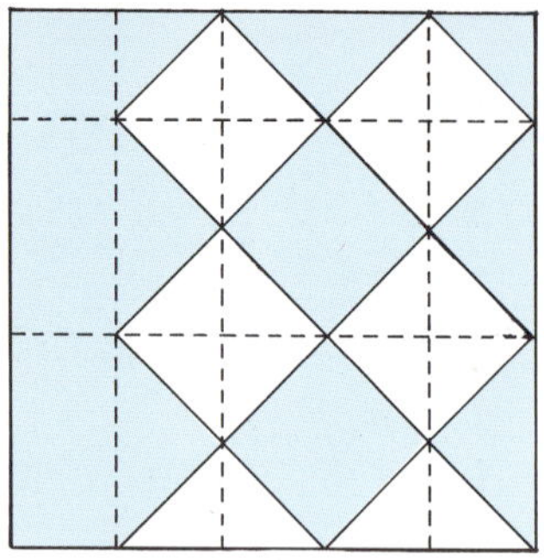

Top, above and left: *Starry Night.*
Above: *A corner detail showing the 'all dark' border.*

STARRY NIGHT

Most fabrics can be used for the Log Cabin design but for a really pretty effect nothing beats a selection of mixed prints, sprigs and spots, in fine crisp cottons. This contemporary quilt uses a dazzling mixture including satin fabrics to add extra twinkle to the starry effect. The block uses narrow strips of fabric—about 2.5cm (1in) wide including 6mm (¼in) seam allowances—which must be accurately cut for even results. A template is used for the central square and should be roughly twice the strip width.

The designer has offset the whole patchwork with an interesting border of all-dark blocks. This kind of patchwork, where large pattern repeats are created, is ideally suited for coverlets, curtains, double and king-size quilts and all types of wall coverings.

For the project make up the blocks following the instructions for Log Cabin patchwork on page 54.

Some contemporary designers prefer to make blocks without the foundation fabric, stitching directly to the central square. Whatever you choose, lay the finished blocks out in the correct pattern before sewing them together. Finally, quilt the patchwork as shown by the dotted lines in the diagram above, add the lining and self-finish the outer edges (*see* page 26).

CRAZY LOG

When an idea catches the imagination, tradition is often disregarded, but perhaps, not entirely. In this contemporary Crazy Log pattern, basic principles have been 'stood on their heads' as it were. Instead of smart, diagonal dividing lines, tones are mixed up and strips freely stitched around a central point. The blocks conform to a standard size but some strips are longer and some narrower than others, which tends to give the blocks a rather abstract appearance of Chinese letters. The choice of colours is imaginative and restrained at the same time making the whole effect jolly, bright and lively.

The Crazy Log idea is excellent for livening up any room as a wall covering, floor covering, play mat, bed-side rug, sleeping bag or a jacket.

For the project and to recreate the idea, first familiarize yourself with the approach by making one or two sample blocks. With a little experience, you will soon be able to create blocks without repeating exactly the same combinations of colour, strip width, and placement.

Notice that the centre of the block is not always necessarily a square. Sometimes it is a rectangle placed off-centre, which completely changes the image. Arrange the finished blocks in a pleasing way before sewing them together, quilt as preferred, and add a bright coloured binding to finish the edges.

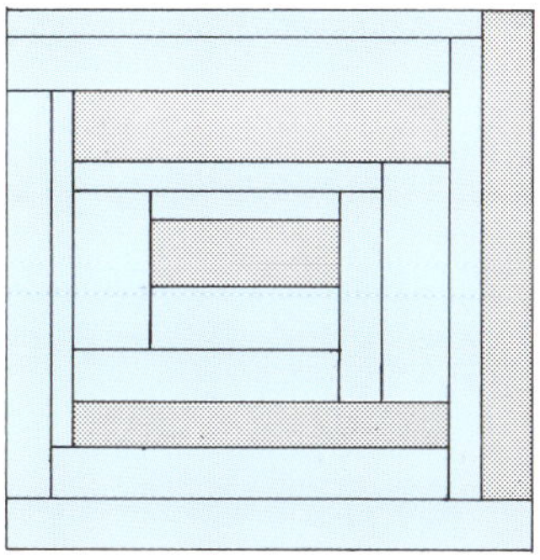

Above: *A typical example of a Crazy Log Cabin block.*

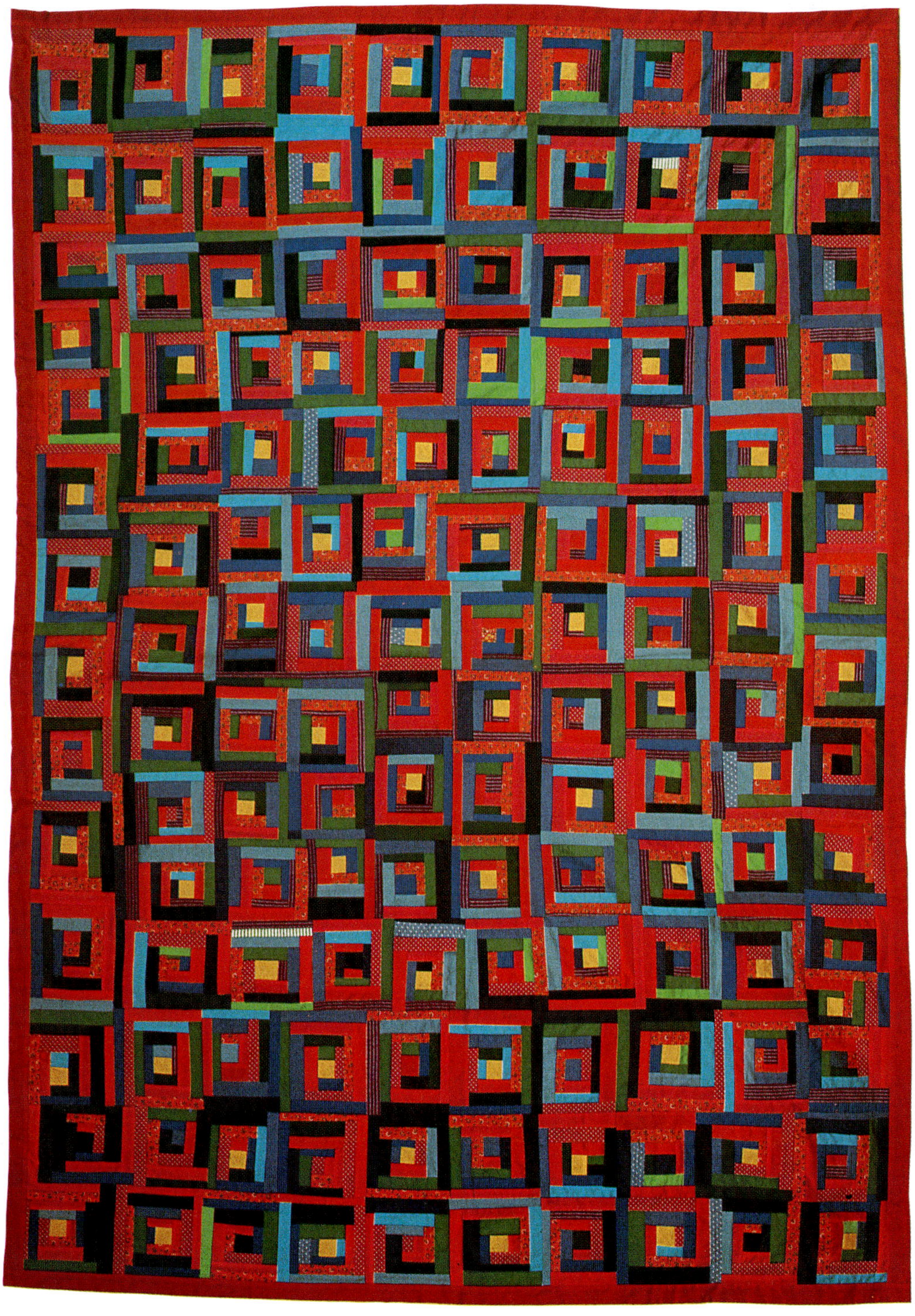

Above: *Crazy Log. The lively, haphazard effect of the quilt is emphasized by an imaginative choice of colours, including strong primaries, and clear greens and purples.*

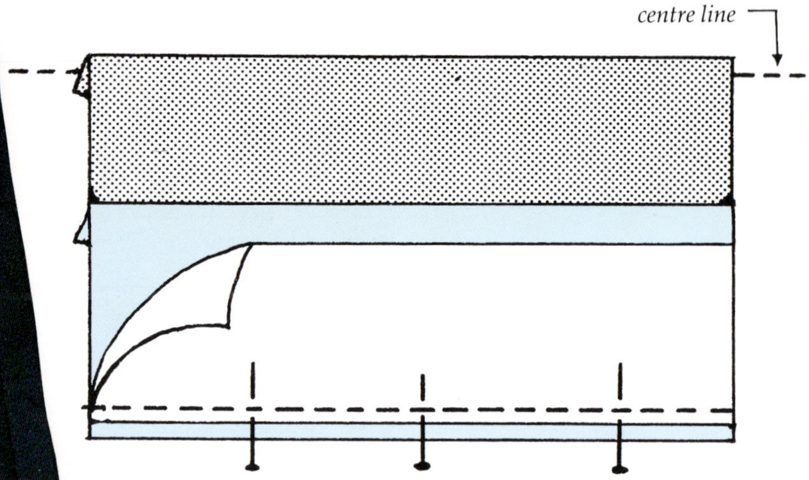

Above: *Starting in the middle of the quilt, apply the strips for the first half as shown above. Turn the work round and complete the second half working in the same way, taking care to place any motifs or letters the correct way up.*

• STRIP PATCHWORK •

STRIPEY II

LIKE LOG CABIN, strip patchwork involves stitching together long strips of fabric in pattern. This is one of the easiest methods of making patchwork. Templates are not used and the whole patchwork can be quickly stitched by machine without a foundation fabric. Strips can either be joined and quilted in one operation, or quilted in the usual way as for wadded quilting. This contemporary quilt shows a typical striped pattern using strips varying in width, 1.5–15cm (½–6in), in strong contrasting colours, with just one lively print.

Simple designs like this can be adapted quite imaginatively for floor rugs, sleeping bags, crib or cot covers and play mats. Made up and quilted without a wadded interlining, the patchwork would make stunning duvet and pillow covers—teaming the colours but varying the stripes. Any fabric can be used from wool, tweeds and suitings (for rugs) to silks, satins, cottons, cotton/wool mixes, velvets and corduroys.

For the project make a full-scale plan. (Many people attracted to the unpredictable effect of random placing are not always aware that most successful designs are invariably worked out beforehand with such a full-scale plan.) Tear or cut the strips across the width of the fabric. Make them up to the width of your design and arrange them in pattern.

Cut wadding (batting) and backing fabric to the size of your design and tack together. Beginning in the middle, pin the first strip right side up across the centre of the wadding. Place the second strip right sides and raw edges together and stitch taking a 6mm (¼in) seam. Keep the unworked wadding rolled up so that it will go through the machine. Turn the second strip over and press the seam flat. Continue in this way to complete the first half, and repeat for the second half.

Finish the wall hanging by adding a deep border, mitre the corners (*see* page 61), and work two rows of quilting to secure the layers together.

Right: *Kimono.*
Torn strips of silk are applied from one end of the kimono to the other, overlapping new colours where needed, until the entire background is covered.

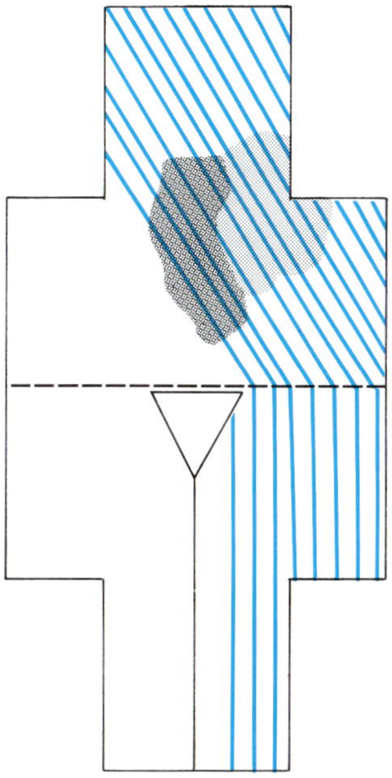

KIMONO

New ideas and traditional techniques combine to make this most spectacular garment. The garment shape, its textures and colours have all been designed and constructed like a large asymmetric painting. Strips of hand-dyed Jap silk (habutai or Chinese silk) in four colours have been torn and applied to a foundation fabric and machined down the middle leaving the raw edges to fray and give a slightly furry effect to the entire surface.

The technique works equally well with other fabrics such as loosely woven cottons, linens, taffetas and certain wools and tweeds. Similar patchwork made from softer fabrics is extremely comfortable to wear and is ideal for all kinds of garments, from amazing evening coats and wraps to part-decorated silk T-shirts. Heavier fabrics are best for floor or wall coverings and chunky-style cushions.

For the project make a scale drawing of your design with colour suggestions. Collect suitable fabrics together (dye fine silk with commercial cold-water dyes) and prepare the strips, tearing them across the fabric in mixed widths between 2–3cm (¾–1¼in). Draw the outline of the garment on the backing fabric—a medium-weight polyester/cotton provides the right amount of firmness and stability to the silk. Check your own measurements against the outline from a loose-fitting garment or a commercial pattern. Using matching coloured threads throughout, stitch evenly spaced black strips, first folding the strip at the shoulder to change its direction. Then add the remaining strips between, overlapping the ends where the colours meet. Cut out the garment and line with fine silk. Bind around the edges to finish (*see* page 27).

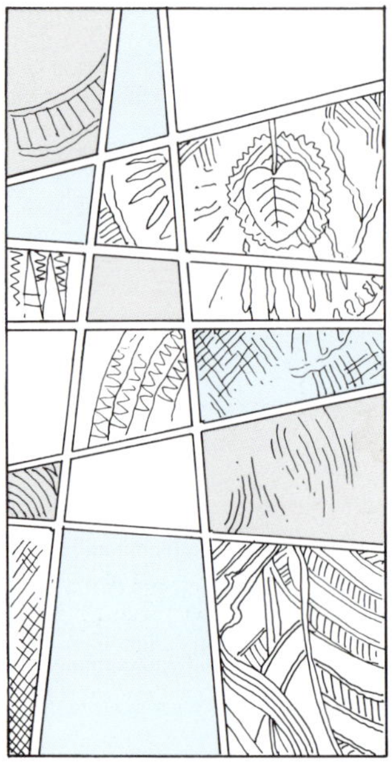

Above and left: *Landscape. Here the design can quite easily be adjusted to fit other rectangular shapes.*

• RANDOM STRIP •

LANDSCAPE

So much can be made of smaller pieces of patchwork by the way in which they are presented. An experimental sample, for example, may be mounted as a picture with a proper frame, or be given a contrasting patchwork border, as in this contemporary cushion.

Here several random patches make up an abstract landscape. Printed cotton fabrics are used to suggest foliage and some are overlaid with coloured gauze to soften the effect. The whole panel is machine stitched on to a backing fabric and surrounded with a log cabin border of natural coloured silk.

Use four or more blocks for floor cushions, or make larger patchwork by repeating blocks in different directions, for example, joined with plain lattice strips.

For the project adapt the patchwork pattern to fit any size cushion. Either make a full-scale drawing and trace off each shape as a template for cutting out the patches, or work directly on to the backing. Cut the backing fabric to the size of your cushion, lightly fold to find the centre, and position the patches butting the edges together. Tack gauze or other sheers over the correct patches and stitch as for machine crazy patchwork (*see* page 54). Add a border of Log Cabin strips (*see* page 55), and make up the cushion cover as instructed on page 97.

DANCE

In the search to find new ways of expressing abstract themes such as rhythm and movement, song and dance, modern designers are exploring random patchwork more and more. To further emphasize a personal statement, many designers also use hand-dyed cloth and painted-on images—so the finished work becomes more of a patchwork painting.

This contemporary wall hanging entitled 'Dance' conveys in simple cotton patches and fabric paint all the excitement and vitality of music and dance. Mixed coloured strips have been joined together, cut into random shapes, looking remarkably like piano keys, and restitched again into several random-shaped borders. These surround the three central images—diagonally poised like musical instruments. The multi-coloured background fabric has been painted with 'dancing' strokes to give continuity of movement and colour. Incidentally, fabric paints are easily and reliably fixed by pressing with a warm iron.

Patchwork created in this way, using all kinds of cotton sateens and poplin, develops a lively, jolly character most suitable for younger members of a family—from a baby's cot or crib cover to a teenager's wall decoration.

For the project and to recreate this effect, you will need to work from a full-scale drawing and with a similar selection of bright coloured cottons predominantly in pinks, reds, yellows and black. These should be contrasted with a lighter-toned multi-coloured fabric on which the 'dancing' strokes can be painted with fabric dye, if you wish. Follow the diagram given below, and, working from the middle, piece the centre panel and add more paint if needed. For the main inner border, experiment with varying widths of mixed coloured strips stitching, cutting and restitching the resulting patches together in different ways—in opposite directions, diagonally across and upside down. Then add the remaining pieced borders. Interline with wadding, quilt the inner border and bind the edges as shown on page 27.

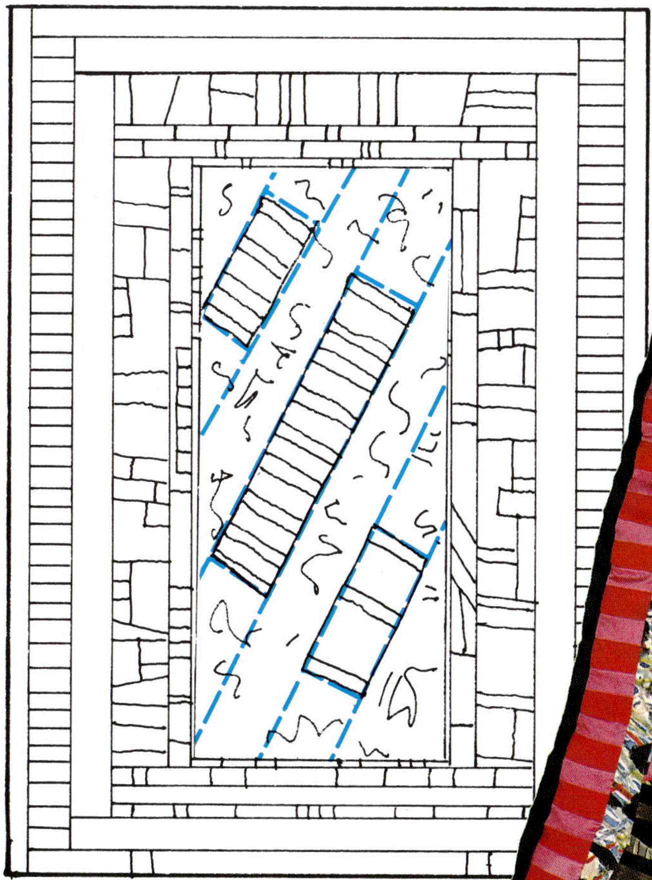

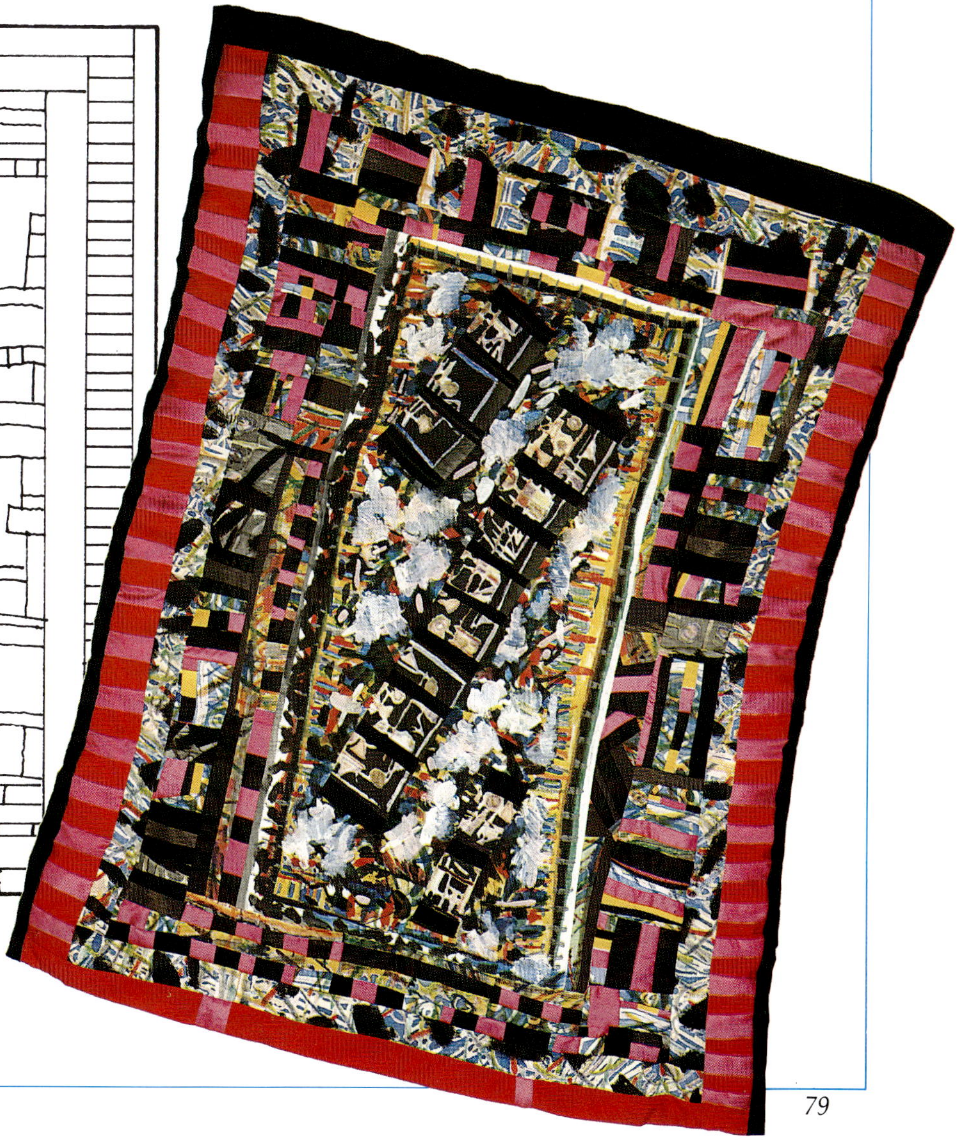

Above and right: *Dance. Using fabric and paint, follow the guidelines given above to recreate this unique effect in patchwork.*

• CRAZY PATCHWORK •

VICTORIA

THIS DELIGHTFUL crazy quilt made around the late nineteenth century shows the traditional method of scrapbag piecing. Random patches of silks and satins are sewn to a foundation fabric and made into blocks for easy piecing. One of the main features of the work, apart from its liveliness and the feeling of movement created by the diversity of the shapes, is the amount of embroidery used. Every seam and many of the patches are embroidered. Mottoes, names, dates and numerous flowers, crowns and other heraldic devices appear to have been scattered over the entire surface with great confidence and skill. All this surface activity is neatly balanced by the piecing seams and by the wide contrasting border.

All kinds of fabrics can be used but for cleaning purposes it is best to use the same type in a single piece of work. Crazy patchwork is not usually interlined and quilted. It can be used most successfully for soft furnishings including curtains, and cushions.

Patched and plain blocks can be alternated to give a less 'busy' effect and the seams machine-zigzag stitched instead of hand embroidered.

For the project cut the backing fabric into squares to suit your chosen design. Apply the patches following the instructions for Crazy patchwork and then either hand embroider over the raw edges, using feather or herringbone stitch given on the opposite page, or a bright contrast thread and double machine-zigzag stitch (*see* page 93) as preferred. Join the blocks together, decorate the seams and add a surrounding border and lining (*see* page 61) if needed.

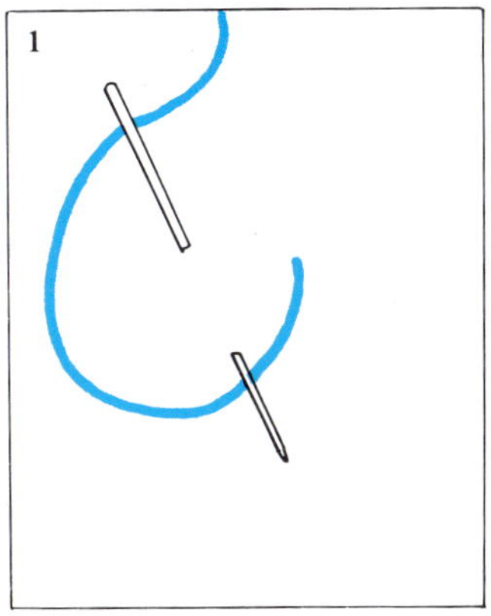

Double feather stitch ***1*** *Bring needle out, hold thread down and insert it to the left. Make a diagonal stitch towards the centre and pull needle through.*

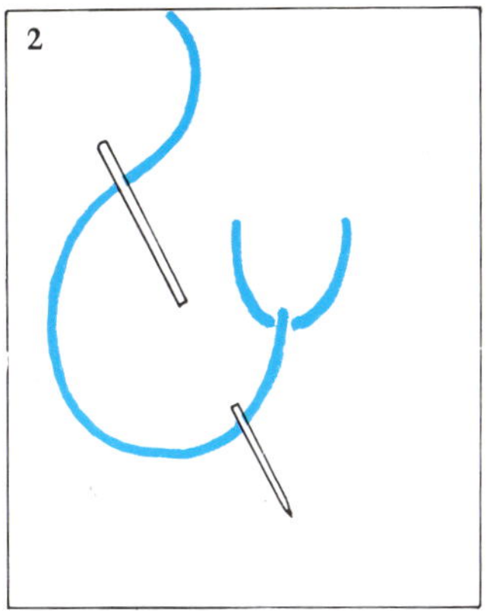

2 *Make two more similar stitches towards the left, inserting the needle on the same level opposite the point where the thread emerges.*

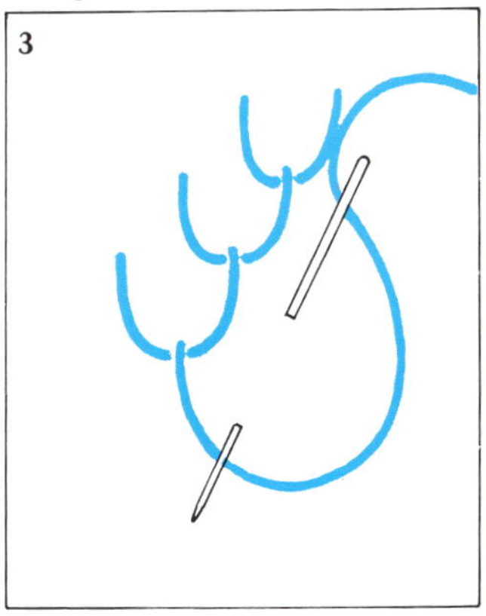

3 *Continue in this way working the last two stitches alternately in opposite directions.*

Above right: *Morning Star. A single star motif can quite easily be extended into a rectangular shape, mixing light and dark toned fabrics to give a kaleidoscopic effect.*

• FOLDED STAR PATCHWORK •

MORNING STAR

FOLDED STAR patchwork has a very attractive tactile quality. Flower prints, spots and plain cottons in strong contrasting colours have been used to make this pretty cushion cover.

Using light and dark-toned fabrics to suggest the different segments, the star is built up symmetrically working in rounds starting from the middle. Single star motifs extended with several borders are perfect for cushion sets of all kinds, sachets, and for lining circular or oval baskets such as bread and sewing baskets, even picnic baskets—in each case make the lining removable. **For the project** you will need a selection of three light and three darker-toned fabrics for the patchwork and borders, and either plain or printed fabric for the back.

Follow the instructions for Folded star patchwork (*see* page 55), and make up the central star, extending it to make a rectangle about 30cm (12in) square. Add the borders, adjusting the widths as needed to fit the dimensions of your cushion pad. Make up the cushion cover following the instructions on page 97.

Above and left: *Stained Glass. In estimating the amount of fabric needed, allow for full patches around the edges, for seams. These should be trimmed back after stitching.*

• MAYFLOWER •
STAINED GLASS

THE IRIDESCENT effect of a stained glass window created by Mayflower, or Cathedral patchwork, as it is also known, relies entirely on the choice of colours and fabrics used. Bright contrast colours can be placed at random, or shades of a single colour built up in brilliance towards the centre, as shown in this beautifully made cushion.

Here cream-coloured satin is used for the folded foundation with toning velvets for the centres—the shiny texture of the satin catches the light, adding extra dazzle to the whole effect. Mayflower patchwork can be made into handsome sofa throws and crib covers using an allover repeat pattern, or for larger bedspreads or wall hangings, blocks can be made and repeated alternately with plain sections.

For the project estimate the amount of fabric needed following the instructions for Mayflower patchwork on page 56.

Allow fabric for the cushion back and piping. It is important when making Mayflower patchwork to see that all the fabrics are well pressed beforehand, since it is almost impossible to remove stubborn creases once the patchwork is made up.

This type of patchwork can, of course, be dry-cleaned but certain fabrics, such as cottons, can also be hand-laundered. After carefully washing and rinsing, press between towels to remove excess moisture, pull into shape and leave to dry flat. Make up sufficient folded patches as shown in the diagram, and, if preferred, apply iron-on interfacing behind the appliqué squares to prevent the fold lines showing through. It is better to allow full patches around the edges to include seam allowances—and trim them back after the seams are stitched.

Make sure when stitching the curved folds over the appliqué that the thread passes through all the layers to give a pleasing quilted effect. Make up the cushion inserting a satin-covered piping around the edges.

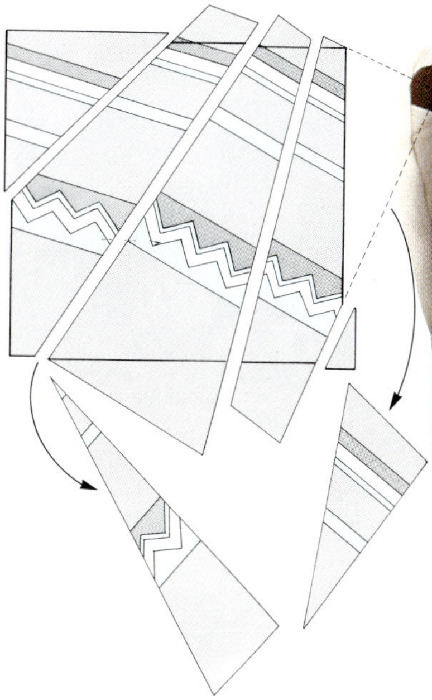

Above and right: *Florida. The diagonal cutting lines and discarded sections necessary for reshaping the patchwork strip into a square.*

• SEMINOLE PATCHWORK •

FLORIDA

THE TECHNIQUES involved in Seminole, or Cut and Stagger, patchwork produce some of the most complex-looking patterns in patchwork. The full range can be quite amazing—from tiny multi-coloured zigzags and plaids to ingenious pieces of op art.

In this contemporary cushion, strips of different coloured cottons and plain calico are first pieced into bands of chevrons and stripes. The final pieced fabric is cut and staggered into radiating diagonal shapes to create a pattern of broken borders.

Seminole patchwork is best on smallish items such as bags and bolsters—preferably in plain coloured cottons. **For the project** make a full-scale drawing, and estimate the amount of fabric needed. You will require four contrast colours including enough main fabric for the cushion front and back, plus the inset edging. Allow roughly one-third extra all round in order to make a slightly bigger piece of patchwork needed for the final reshaping. Following the instructions for Seminole patchwork on page 57, stitch together strips of the four contrasting fabrics, and make into chevrons. Make up straight bands of four colours, and then piece them in pattern with bands of the main fabric to make the finished patchwork. Cut into diagonal shapes, as shown in the diagram. Discard the pieces shown by dotted lines, rejoin in pattern and trim to size. Make up the cushion (*see* page 97) inserting an edging, as preferred.

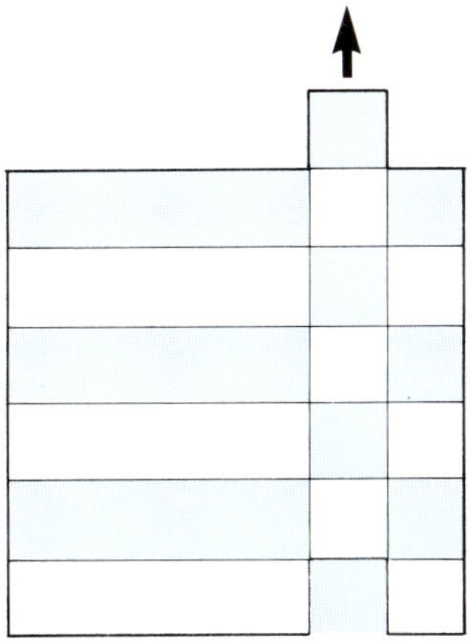

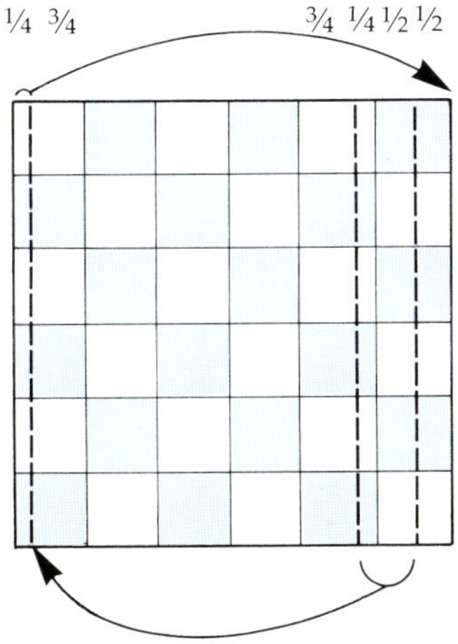

Opposite: *Op Art.* ***1*** *Alternate colours are first assembled in bands across, cut into vertical strips and adjusted to make checks before being trimmed.*

2 *From the right-hand side of the block, move the middle cut section in between the two outer cut sections at the left-hand side. Take the outer strip at the left over to the outside right. Repeat on the opposite sides.*

OP ART

Dazzling, eye-catching designs are a special feature of Seminole patchwork. Many geometric patterns designed to create optical illusions translate well into this type of patchwork. Several colours can be used for more complex effects, or just two strongly contrasting tones, as in this amazing contemporary quilt.

Here blocks of black and white checks are cut and repositioned to create a third illusory dimension of swirling movement. Fine- to lightweight cotton or cotton mixtures are excellent for designs where so many seams are involved. In order fully to appreciate the effect, optical designs usually require a fairly large expanse, such as quilts, covers, duvets and rugs. However, four blocks would make a handsome floor cushion or bolster, or a smaller wall hanging.

For the project a basic unit of 10cm (4in) is a good size for a quilt block and the blocks used in the design each contain 36 units. Estimate the amount of fabric required for your design, allowing equal amounts of both colours. Extra fabric should be allowed for each block to account for repositioning. For example, seven bands are needed to produce six when repositioned. Following the principles of Seminole patchwork on page 57, make the blocks by joining together seven strips alternately in bands across. Cut and reposition them before rejoining into checks (1).

To make the pattern, certain strips are cut into graded widths of 8cm (3in), 5cm (2in), 2.5cm (1in) and set around a nine-patch. Cut and reposition the right and left sides of the block, as shown in diagram (2), and then turn it around and repeat on the opposite sides to complete the block. Make up the required number of blocks and join them together. Add a separate backing and quilt diagonally through the squares. Edge with a chequered or plain border, as preferred.

• PLEATED PATCHWORK •

GREY SHADOWS

DESPITE THE GEOMETRIC constrictions involved in pleating and tucking, softly textured and surprisingly free-flowing patterns can be achieved, as shown by this delightful contemporary quilt. Made from striped cotton ticking, it combines quilting with pleating and tucking in a very simple way. Blocks of vertical quilting are pieced alternately with blocks of horizontal folding to suggest a large basketweave pattern. The quilt is finished with a 5cm (2in) wide bias-cut border where the diagonal stripes of the ticking make an interesting contrast.

All cottons and other light- to mediumweight fabrics that keep their creases well are perfect for pleating and tucking projects, preferably in plain or pale, coloured stripes so that the full effect of the shadowy textures can be seen. Another possibility is mediumweight silks with matt rather than shiny surfaces. A 30cm (12in) square block is an average size for a quilt and other larger works such as rugs and wall hangings. Single blocks will make handsome cushions, and four blocks are ideal for jumbo-size floor cushions, but the size can easily be adapted to fit other geometric designs.

For the project allow extra fabric for pleating and tucking (*see* page 58) and a bias-cut border, when estimating the main fabric. Following the instructions for pleated patchwork, make up the blocks in pattern, as shown in the diagram given below. Join the finished pleated blocks alternately with plain blocks. Assemble the layers as for wadded quilting and machine quilt the remaining blocks in pattern. Add a backing and a border, mitring the corners.

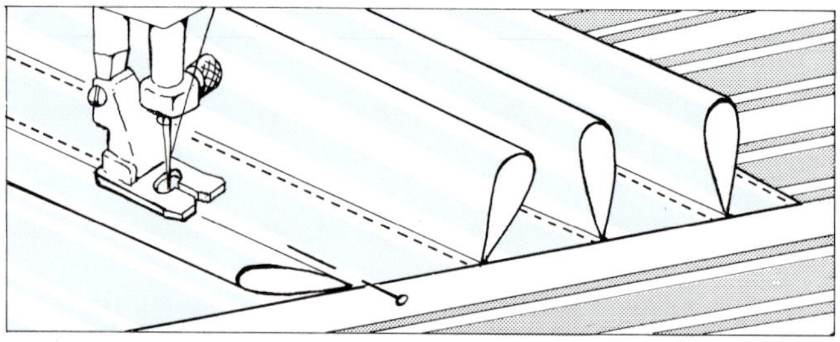

Top: *Changing Colours. Each fold is pinned in place and machine-stitched close to the lower crease line, first on one side then on the other. In this way, the double stitching helps to keep the fold in an upright position.*

Above: *This detail shows clearly the different colours created by applying the pleated bands of striped fabric in opposite directions.*

CHANGING COLOURS

Striped fabrics, with slightly wider stripes than ticking, provide the opportunity to introduce subtle colour tones to pleating and folding with some fascinating results. Simple two-colour stripes can be folded so that the two colours are made to fall on either side of the crease line, and, when pressed flat, each fold effectively blocks out the colour underneath. This works particularly well with stripes about 2cm (¾in) wide, as in this imaginatively tucked quilt.

The entire surface is softly ridged with bands of evenly-spaced tucks using just three pastel coloured cottons. Bands of two of the colours are tucked and applied in reverse to the backing fabric. By using a Regency-style stripe, each tuck shows solid colour on one side and fine stripes on the other, which gives the counter-changed effect when reversed.

Pastel coloured dressweights and sheeting will give similar effects. It is a good plan to experiment with different striped fabrics before embarking on the major project. This may lead to making a series of samples,

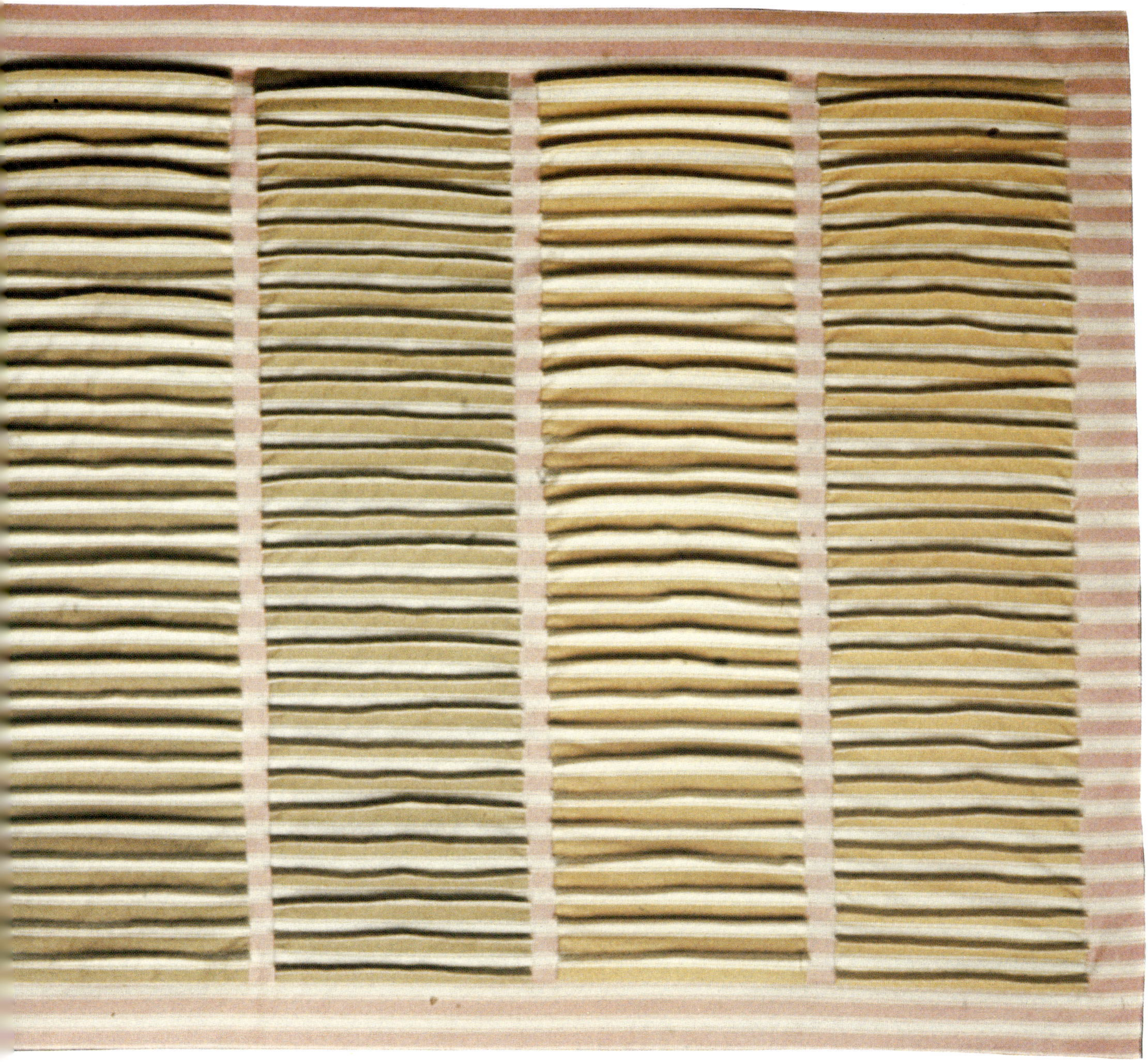

which could be framed as a collection of pleated pictures. To recreate this particular effect, the depth of the fold should be exactly the same as the distance between.

For the project, in order to estimate the amount of fabric needed, first make a rough plan of your design, and then pleat a sample of your chosen fabric (*see* page 58).

Prepare the bands by making 2cm (¾in) hems along the two long edges and press flat. Following the instructions for Pleated patchwork, make the tucks on each band. Position the first band across the width of a prepared backing, beginning in the middle and using the stripes for alignment. Pin or tack in place along the folds, turning under the short edges as needed to leave a border of backing fabric all round. Starting in the middle of the band, stitch between the folds close to the bottom crease line, through both layers. Repeat on the opposite side of the fold, and continue in this way to stitch the band in place. Return to the middle and stitch the remaining half.

Position the next and subsequent bands alternately in opposite directions before stitching in place.

CHAPTER SIX

APPLIQUE TECHNIQUES

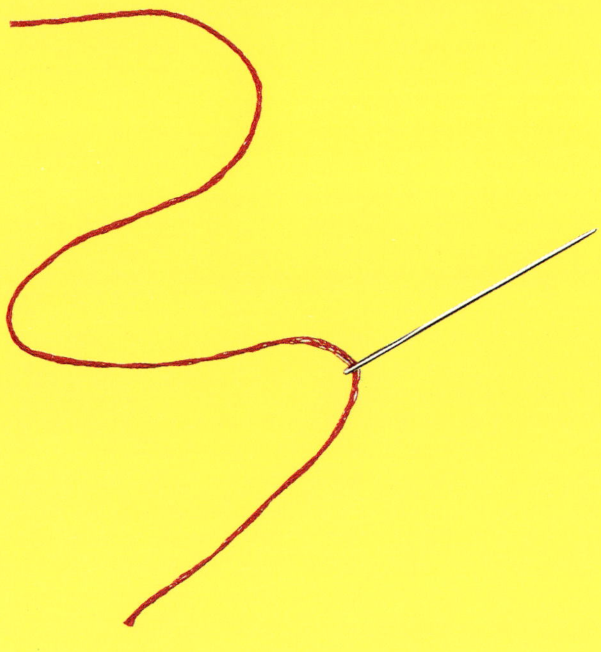

APPLIQUÉ IS the process of attaching cut-out fabric shapes to a foundation fabric by means of stitching, which may itself be plain or colourful and decorative. Essentially, appliqué is a two-dimensional technique which may be strictly functional, such as a knee patch on dungarees, or purely decorative such as a satin motif on a négligé. However, in picture making and more experimental work, it can be a vital art form in which personal statements are expressed. The play of light on surfaces, stitching, subtle modelling of fabric may all be exploited to create work with immensely tactile qualities.

There are several distinct styles of appliqué to choose from involving a number of techniques.

Standard appliqué (onlay) has plain or patterned fabric shapes cut out and stitched to a ground fabric, as in traditional English and American quilt designs.

Appliqué perse has printed birds, flowers and animals, for example, originally cut from whole cloth and applied to a ground fabric.

Reverse appliqué (inlay) has designs of two or more colours cut out to form a counterchange pattern, or has several layers cut through—a technique adopted by the Cuna Indians of Panama and Colombia to make their, famous molas (blouses) and headbands.

Padded appliqué involves stuffing certain areas of the appliqué with either whole or loose wadding to give the surface a softly sculptured effect. To take padding slightly further, and make fully stuffed shapes, a whole new area of three dimensions is possible.

Folded appliqué is a simple method of designing whereby whole fabric is folded into eighths and the pattern cut out—much like paper snowflakes are made—before being applied to a contrast coloured background.

Shadow appliqué uses sheer and semi-transparent fabrics overlapped on either the right or wrong side to give subtle changes of colour density. Combined with free machine stitching, and fabrics and threads rich in texture and colour, it offers wide scope for experiment.

Picture appliqué—where the choice of subject is wide open for innovation—combines manipulating fabric, shape, texture and technique to create unique effects.

Lace appliqué uses all kinds of lace, net, sheer and fine fabrics and trims and applies these in individually shaped motifs, doilies, edgings and whole cloth to a ground fabric in order to produce very delicate, lacy effects. The ground fabric may be cut away from behind the finished motif.

FABRICS

Almost any material can be used in appliqué, and, like patchwork, a varied selection is often a stimulating source of design inspiration. Your ultimate choice should be governed by what you plan to make, bearing cleaning requirements in mind. For practical items, the fabric needs to be easy to handle and either washable or suitable for dry cleaning. While felt and lace scraps, for example, are excellent for picture-making, they would not wear well on a child's dungarees that have to be regularly laundered.

With delicate fabrics and those that fray easily, such as some silks and satins, a lightweight iron-on interfacing is recommended for extra support. Designs are transferred (in reverse) to the interfacing, either before or after ironing it to the wrong side of the fabric. The applied fabrics should not be heavier in weight than the ground fabric, although a second (finer) supportive layer can be added to the background, if needed.

One of the main features of appliqué is making fabric 'work' not just in colour and shape but in pattern and texture. Patterned fabric, for example, can be used to suggest all kinds of images and textures such as stripes for ploughed fields, flower sprigs for gardens, pile surfaces for animal fur and checks for brickwork.

APPLIQUÉ DESIGNS

There are two essentially different approaches to appliqué design. One is to plan a design on paper and work from tracings or templates, and the other is to work spontaneously with fabric, scissors and stitches, applying the design directly to the ground fabric without pre-planning.

Inspiration for designs may come from widely different sources—traditional quilt patterns, Hawaiian appliqué, family photographs, landscape painting, a child's drawing, or simply from a colourful arrangement of fabrics. Before deciding, it is important that your design should suit the item you plan to make in both a practical and artistic sense.

TRANSFERRING DESIGNS

Whatever approach you decide, it is best to put your idea down on paper. If you prefer to work spontaneously, the drawing will be an invaluable guide as you cut and stitch through the different appliqué stages.

To work from a plan, you will need to make a full-scale drawing, preferably with colours and textures indicated, and sections that are to overlap noted. This makes sewing easier if awkward angles can be avoided. If the original design is too small, enlarge it, following the diagram opposite. Wash the ground fabric and press it flat. Then trace off the finished design and, using dressmaker's carbon paper, transfer it to the right side of the prepared ground fabric, following the straight grain.

Trace the outline of each section separately on to another sheet of paper, and cut out to use as templates. Mark the straight grain on each one, otherwise the patches will pucker if they are cut on the bias grain, and number the templates in order of application.

Above: *Templates numbered in order of application.*

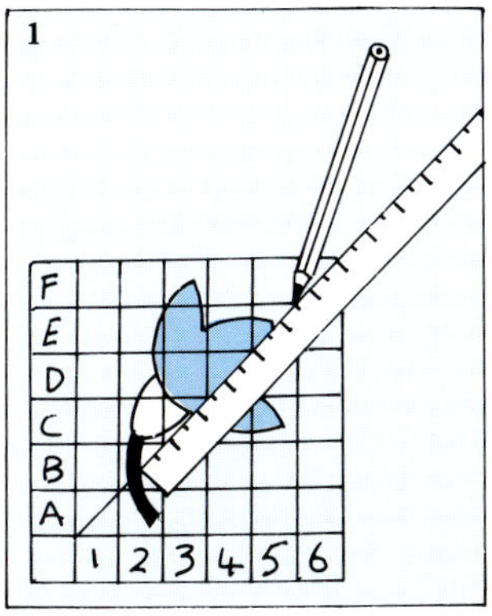

Enlarging a design 1 *Trace off the design and enclose it within a rectangle. Using numbers and letters to identify each section, divide the design into squares. (The more complicated the design, the smaller the squares should be). Draw a diagonal line through the rectangle.*

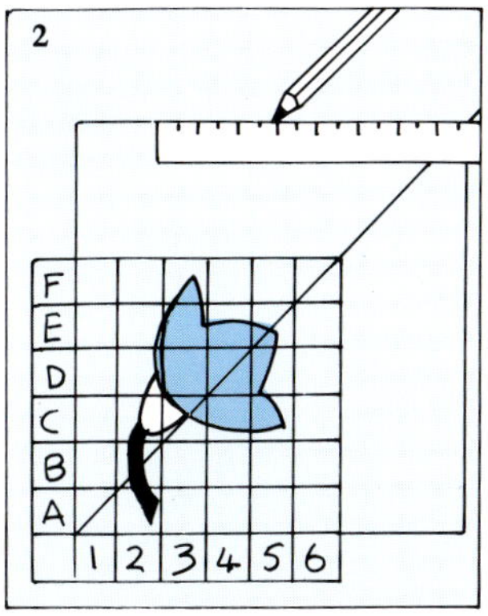

2 *Place the design on the bottom left corner of a larger piece of paper and extend the diagonal line to the height needed. Complete the rectangle and divide it into the same number of squares.*

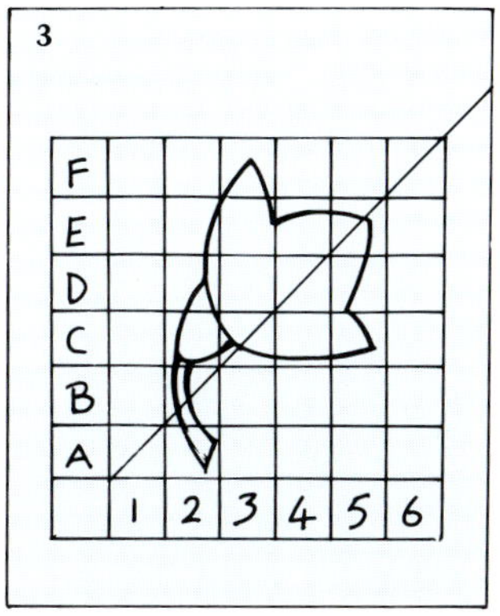

3 *Identify the squares and draw in the design free hand, copying the lines from the smaller design.*

ENLARGING A DESIGN

To enlarge an existing design, is not such a difficult matter as is often supposed.

In principle, the existing design is transferred line by line to a bigger size using the square grid method. Here the main point to bear in mind, when deciding the size of the grid, is the complexity of the original design.

PREPARING TO APPLIQUÉ

If you do not plan to turn under the edges of the patches, you can begin to sew as soon as the shapes have been cut out. Otherwise make the necessary turnings, as shown in the diagrams, leaving raw edges on the areas to be overlapped. Check with your original plan when positioning the final design.

Preparing to appliqué
1 *Position the template on the right side of the correct fabric and draw around the outline with a sharpened coloured pencil. Mark a cutting line 6mm (1/4in) outside the line.*

2 *Cut out the shape leaving a little extra fabric—about 6mm (1/4in)—all round, in case of fraying while handling and working the next stage.*

3 *Work stay stitch by hand or machine, just outside the fold line. This helps to make turning easier and gives a sharper edge to the patch.*

4 *Trim back the fabric to the outer marked line being careful not to cut into the stay stitching.*

Below: *Lisu hill-tribe embroidery from Thailand. Colourful strips of cotton are sewn onto a background fabric with rows of folded triangles inserted to form a repeat pattern.*

FRAMES

Where possible, stitching appliqué is much easier, and less likely to pucker, if it is worked in a frame. Small pieces can be stitched in a hoop and bigger pieces in the larger, rectangular slate embroidery frame.

The background fabric should be stretched evenly but not too tightly as the appliqué should be at the same tension. Hoops can also be used (upside down) with free machine appliqué, with or without engaging the presser foot.

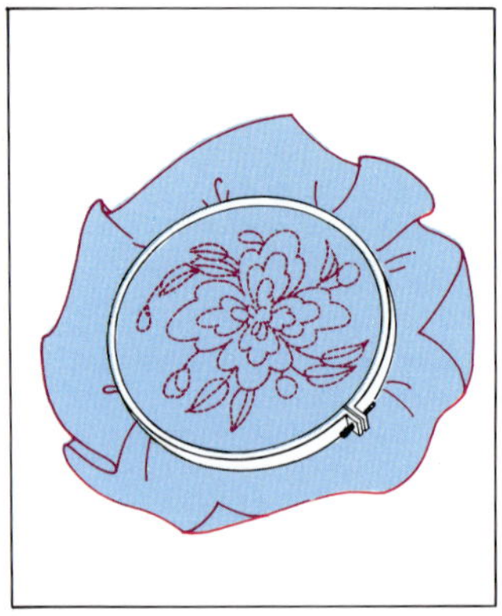

Left: *Place the ground fabric over the inner ring, cover it with the outer ring and smooth out the fabric, stretching it firmly and evenly. Then, tighten the screw attachment. Tissue paper can be placed between the ring and the embroidery so as not to mark delicate work.*

NEATENING CURVES AND CORNERS

This helps to give a really neat finish to your appliqué shapes.

Seam allowances may vary from 6mm (¼in) to 2cm (¾in) depending on the type of fabric used and the purpose required. Straight seams can be neatened in several ways, but where a seam curves or where you need to eliminate excess bulk, the resulting seam allowance must be trimmed either by clipping or notching. This helps to give a really neat finish to your appliqué shapes.

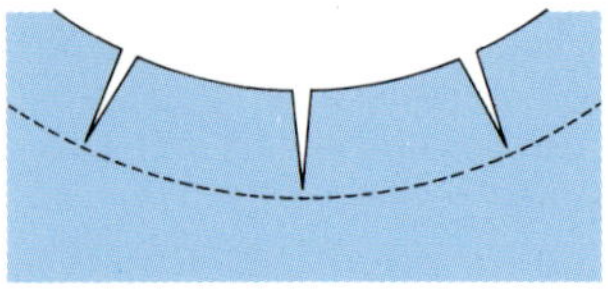

On inner curves *clip into the seam allowance as far as the stay stitching.*

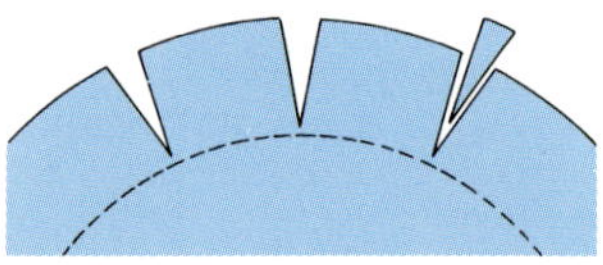

On outer curves *cut out notches to prevent bulky folds forming underneath.*

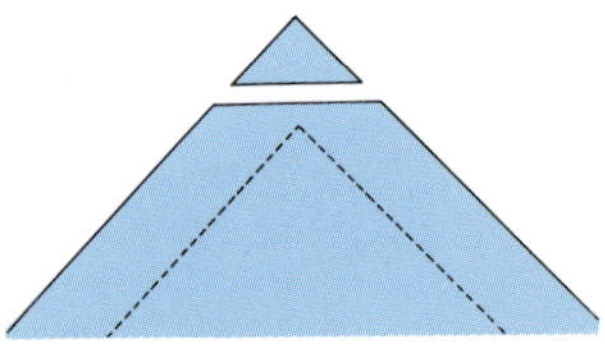

On outside corners *trim the point back to reduce the amount of fabric in the mitred corner.*

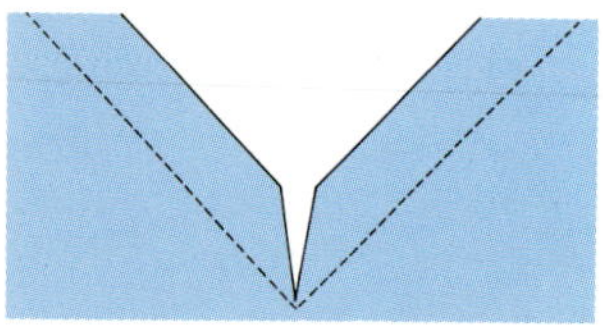

On inner corners *clip into the point as far as the stay stitching.*

• HAND SEWING •

THERE ARE SEVERAL ways of stitching appliqué by hand, the choice depending mainly on the fabric used and the effect needed. Some methods are meant to be concealed, as in plain handstitching, while others are decorative, being embroidered or couched, or they can be both as part of the whole design concept.

On fabrics that fray, where turnings are recommended, secure the patches with slip hemming, or running stitch as given on the opposite page.

On non-fraying fabrics, such as felt and leather, cut patches without seam allowances and apply them unobtrusively with stab stitch or small running stitches, using a coloured thread to match the appliqué. The edges can, of course, be decorated afterwards.

Instead of tacking or pinning, which would make permanent holes, these materials can be held in place by applying a small amount of fabric adhesive.

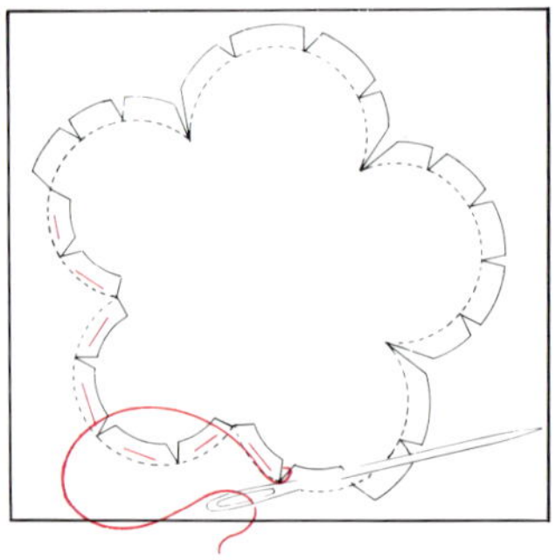

First method 1 *Clip into the curves and corners, fold the turnings to the wrong side and finger-press flat. Tack the turning to secure.*

2 *Position the patch over the traced line on the main fabric and, if needed, secure with vertical tacking stitches to prevent wrinkling. Slip hem around the edge of the patch, and remove any tacking threads.*

Second method 1 *Stay stitch around the shape. Clip into the edges and position the patch on the main fabric over the traced guidelines without turning in the raw edges. Secure with vertical tacking stitches but avoid stitching into the seam allowance.*

2 *Using the point of the needle to turn under the raw edges and the stay stitching, slip hem around the shape.*

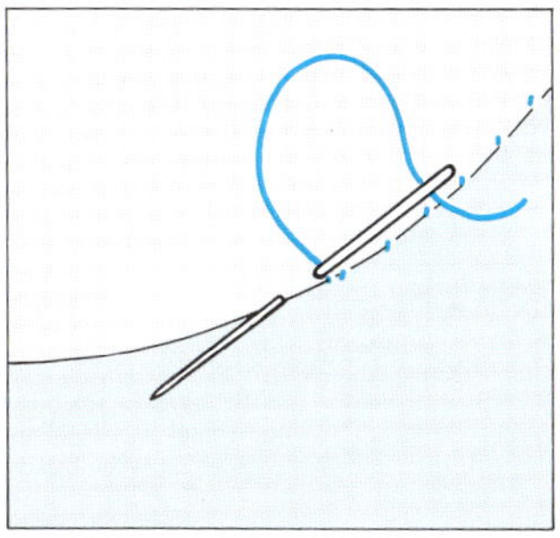

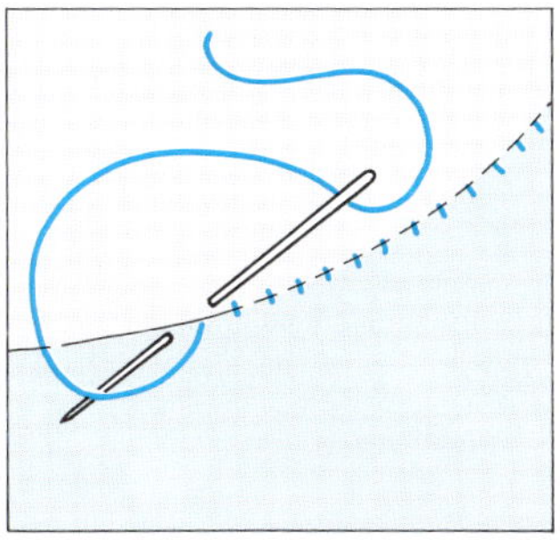

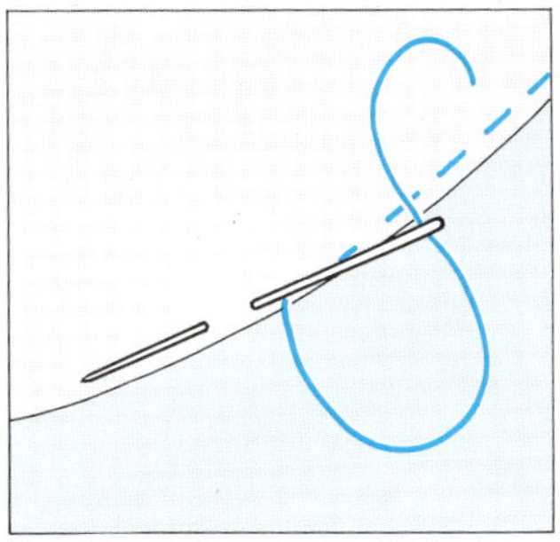

Above left: *Slip hemming. Bring out needle through seam fold of patch and take a small stitch in ground fabric below. Insert needle directly above, make next stitch through fold and repeat.*
Above: *Stab stitch. Bring needle through just outside patch. Reinsert it above close to edge and repeat.*

Above: *Running stitch. Take several evenly spacea stitches on needle before pulling through.*

• MACHINE SEWING •

MACHINE-SEWN appliqué has the advantage of being hardwearing, most suitable for practical items, and generally time saving. This is also one of the areas in appliqué where new ideas can be quickly expressed. A combination of appliqué—superimposing different layers of fabric and printed motifs, for example—with free machining can produce unconventional effects. In experimental work, the contrast between raw edges, straight stitching, and the firm lines of zigzag and satin stitch offers a wide choice of linear expression. Braids, ribbons and strips of fabric can be applied by free machine techniques.

Below: *A typical Mola blouse in reverse appliqué made by the Cuna Indians of Panama. The design of fierce-looking cats (a derivation of native body-painting) is built up from several layers of coloured fabric and patches, and the faces are embroidered.*

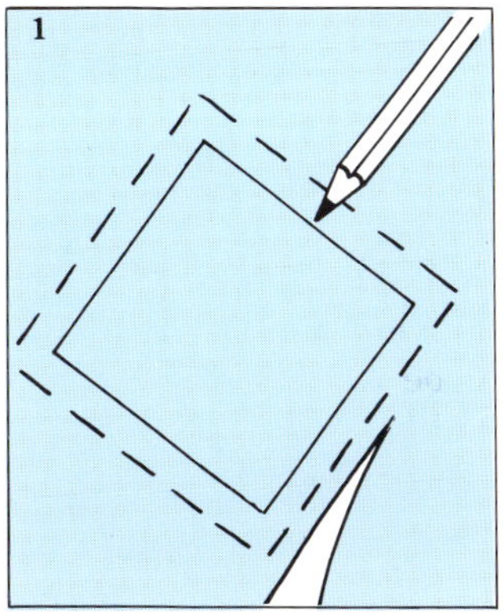

Straight stitching 1 *Pin template to right side of fabric and draw around with a sharpened coloured pencil. Mark a cutting line 6mm (¼in) outside drawn line and cut out just beyond this line.*

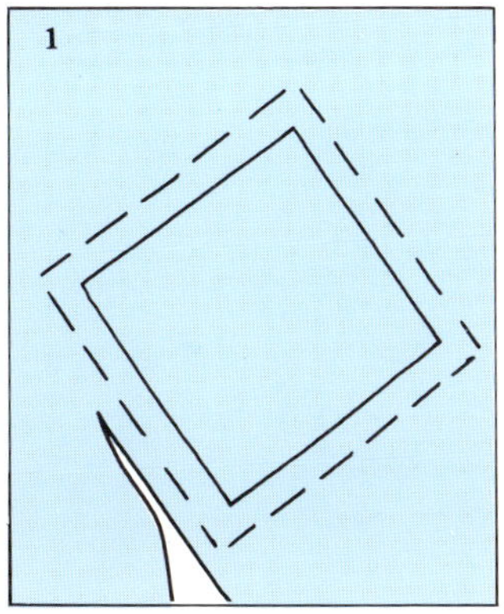

Zigzag stitching 1 *Position the template on the right side of the fabric and draw around the outline. Cut out, leaving 1.5–2cm (½–¾in) extra fabric all round.*

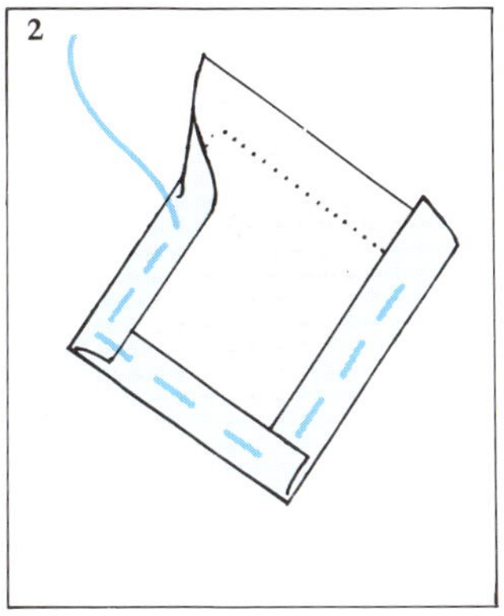

2 *Stay stitch just outside the fold line. Trim the patch back to the cutting line, and snip into curves and corners. Fold the turnings to the wrong side and tack.*

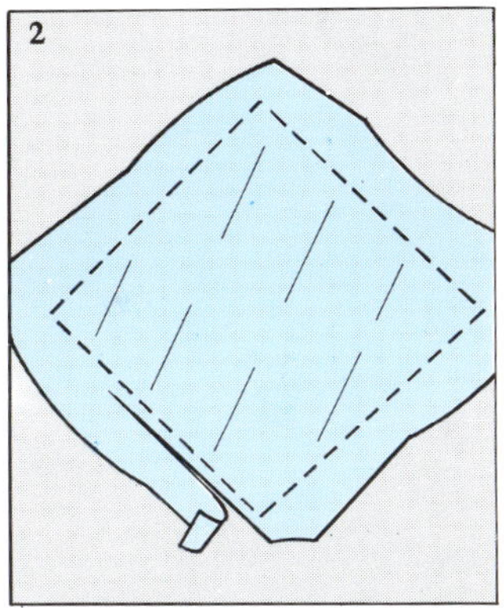

2 *Tack the patch to the main fabric with vertical stitches, avoiding stitching through the extra fabric. Machine stitch in place following the drawn line. Trim back the extra fabric to the stitching.*

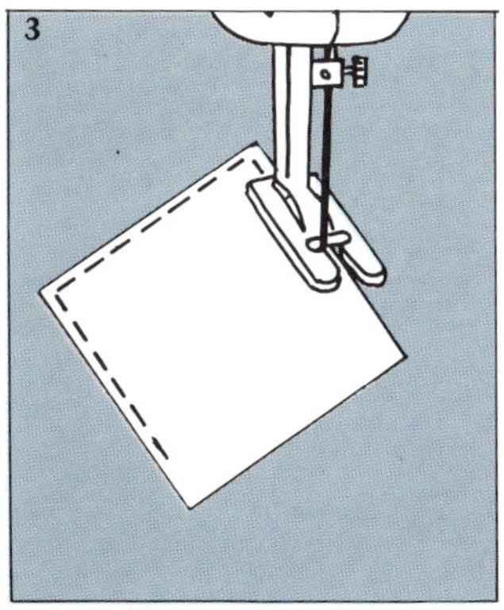

3 *Continue to make evenly spaced stitches around the appliqué shape. Finish by taking both threads through to the back*

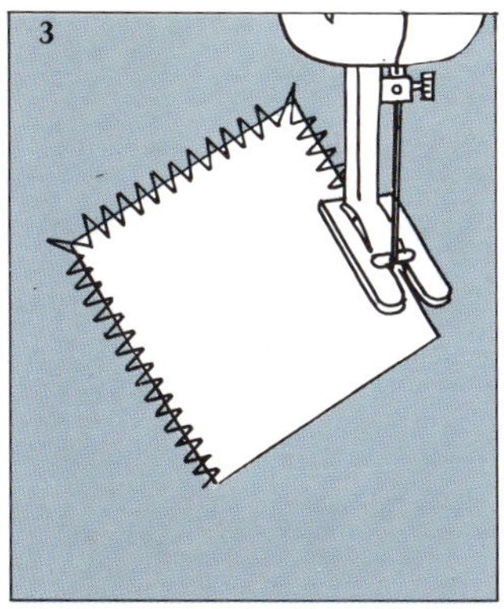

3 *Close zigzag stitch over the edge. Neaten the ends on the wrong side and remove all the tacking threads.*

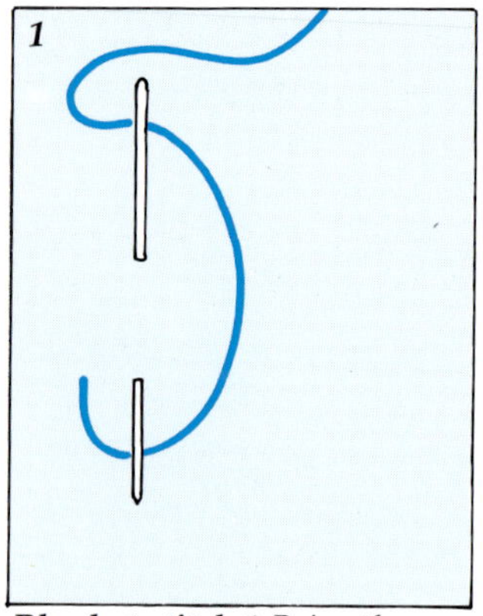

Blanket stitch 1 *Bring the needle out just below patch edge. Insert it above through the appliqué, and bring out directly below with thread under needle.*

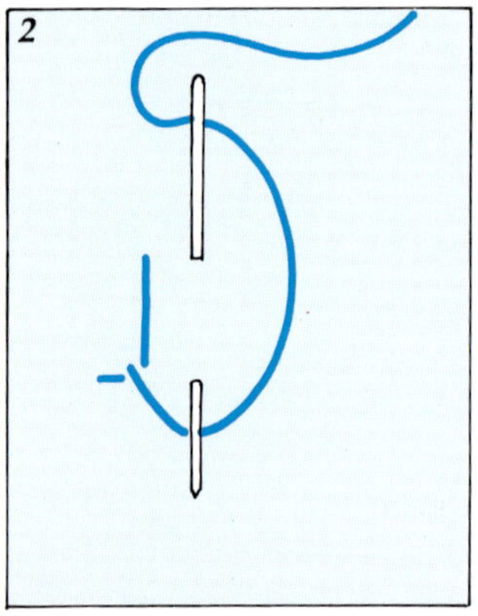

2 Repeat around the patch. Where possible, make sure that a single stitch goes into an angled corner and that the stitches are adjusted evenly around outer corners.

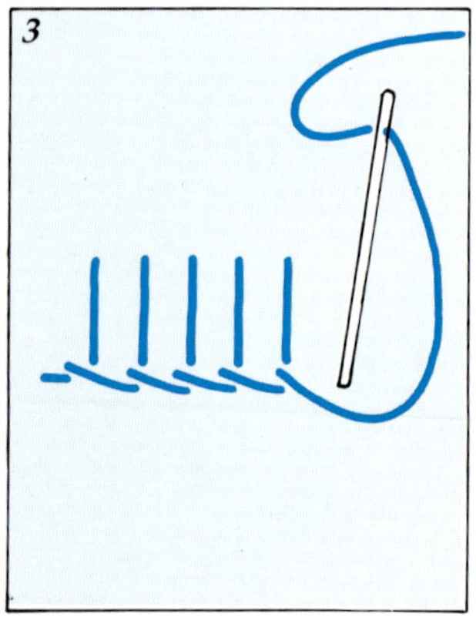

3 To ensure continuity around the edge, finish the stitching by taking the needle through to the back at the bottom of the stitch.

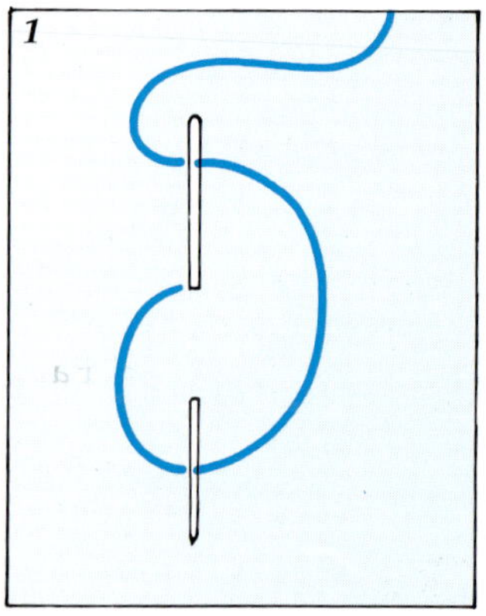

Chain stitch 1 *Bring needle out close to edge of patch. Hold work so that the edge runs vertically, and make a straight stitch downwards inserting needle at starting point.*

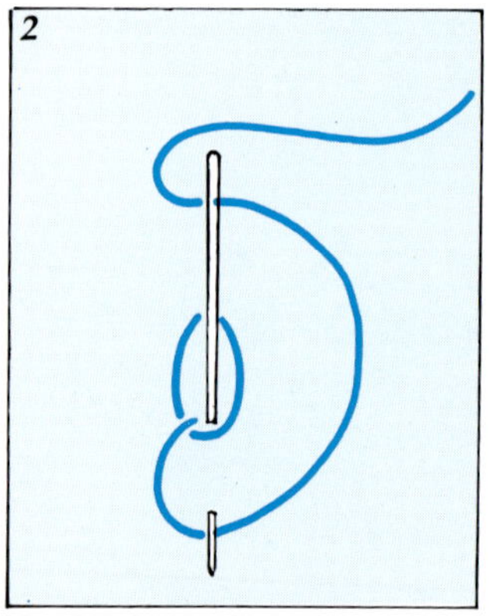

2 Repeat, inserting the needle where the thread last emerged. Bring out the needle with the thread below the point.

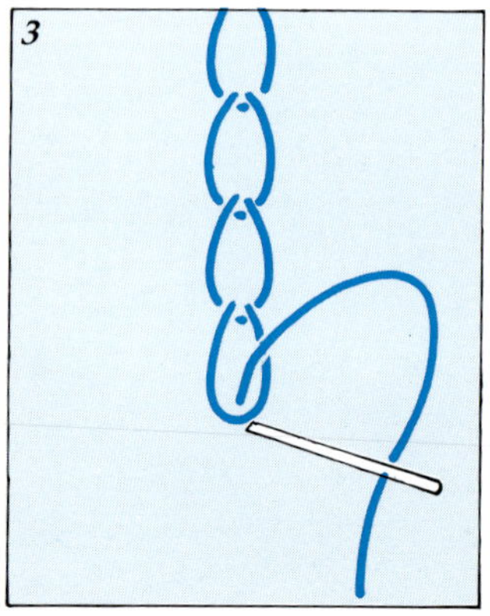

3 Continue to chain stitch around the edge of the patch, and finish by taking a small stitch over the last chain loop to hold it.

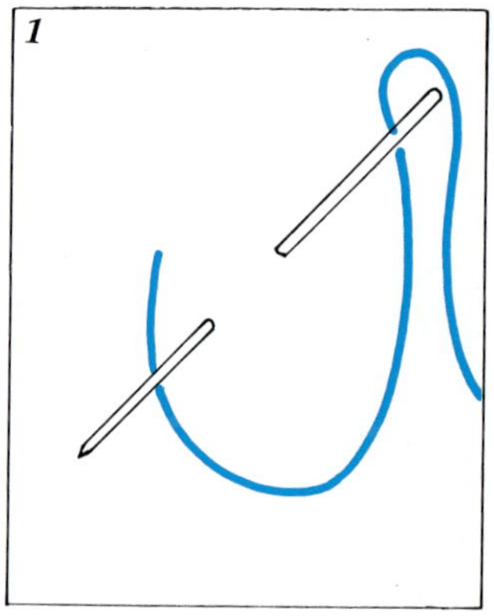

Fly stitch 1 *Bring needle out to left, and, holding the thread downwards, insert needle to right. Make a diagonal stitch to the centre and pull through.*

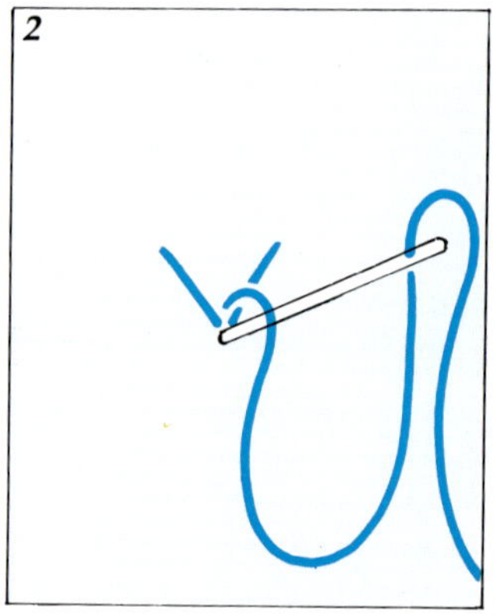

2 Hold the V-shaped loop down with a short straight stitch, and repeat as needed.

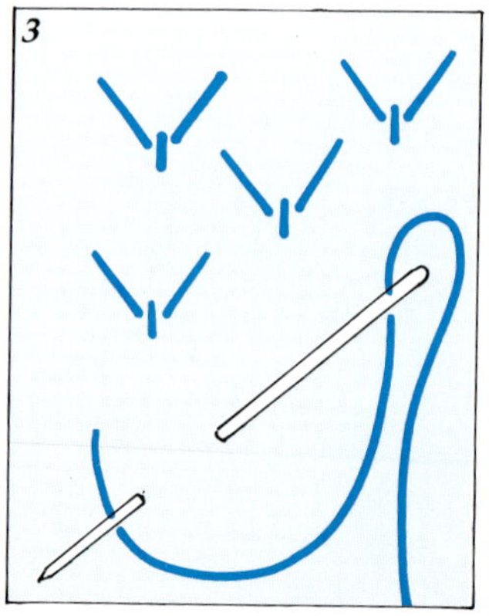

3 Work the stitches either close together around the edges of a patch or outside an embroidered line to soften the effect.

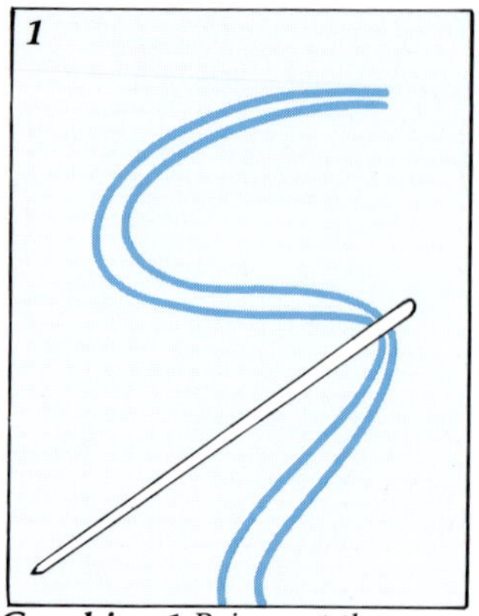

Couching 1 *Bring out the thread to be couched at the right directly over the appliqué edge you want to conceal.*

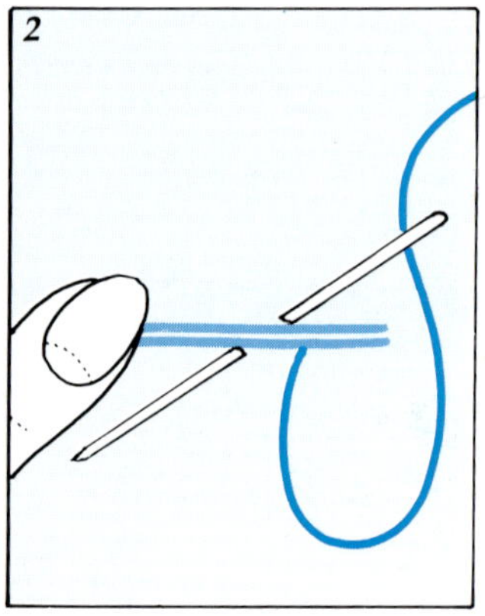

2 Hold the thread down towards the left and bring out the couching thread below. Make a short upright stitch into the patch and bring out below the threads.

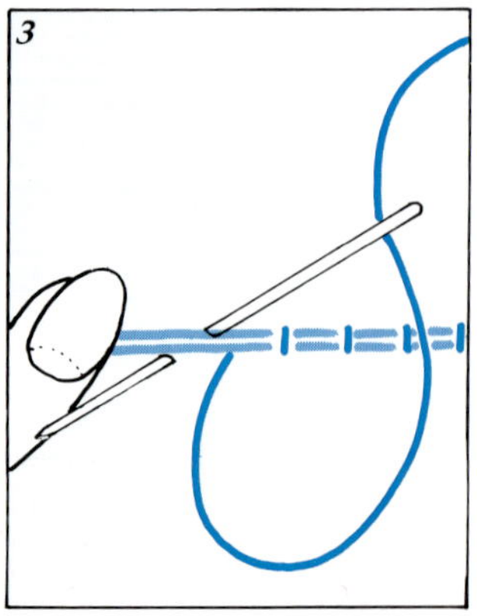

3 Continue to make evenly spaced stitches around the appliqué shape. Finish by taking both threads to the back.

EMBROIDERY STITCHES

On non-fraying woven fabrics the patches can be applied quite successfully without making turnings. The raw edges of the patch should be overcast, then tacked in place on the main fabric, and the edges covered with hand embroidery stitches or couching. Given on the opposite page is a selection of suitable stitches, which may also be used for decorating any fabric patch.

Of the many different types of stitches that can be used for edging a motif, blanket stitch is a popular choice especially for non-fraying woven fabrics, and should be worked fairly close together over the edge of the motif. On non-woven fabrics such as leather or felt, stitches such as chain stitch and couching can be worked just inside the edge. For a more decorative finish work fly stitch over the edge, adding French knots or seeding between to soften the outline.

• REVERSE APPLIQUE •

THE SIMPLEST method of reverse appliqué uses two layers of contrast coloured fabrics where shapes are cut away from the top fabric, allowing the colour beneath to show through. Other contrast patches can be sewn to the back as needed. This technique has been perfected by craftworkers in India, Pakistan, Thailand, Laos, and the Cuna Indians of Panama, who are famous for their distinctive designs.

The Cuna Indians have devised a more complicated method of working most colourful and intricate designs on their garments by applying coloured patches under second and third layers of fabric—even as many as six layers. The appliqué is worked in bright, primary-coloured cottons and the entire surface area is filled with the design, giving the finished work a well-padded, almost quilted effect.

Working reverse appliqué
__1__ This design uses four different coloured fabrics.

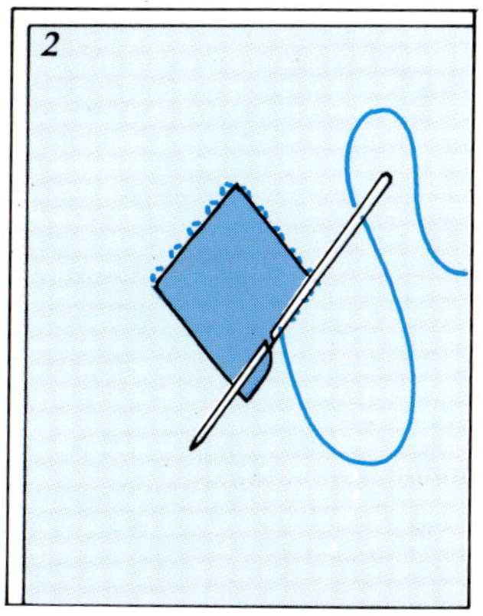

__2__ With the ground fabric right side up, apply the four small diamond-shaped patches (with the edges turned under) and slip stitch them in place.

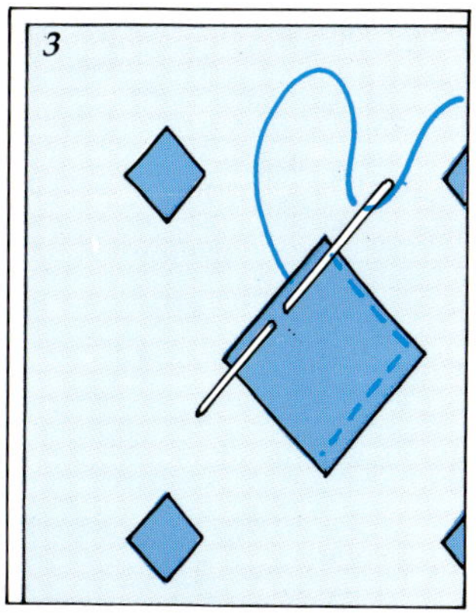

__3__ Working on the right side, apply larger diamond patches (with raw edges) in the centre and tack to secure. These raw edges will be covered by the next layer of fabric.

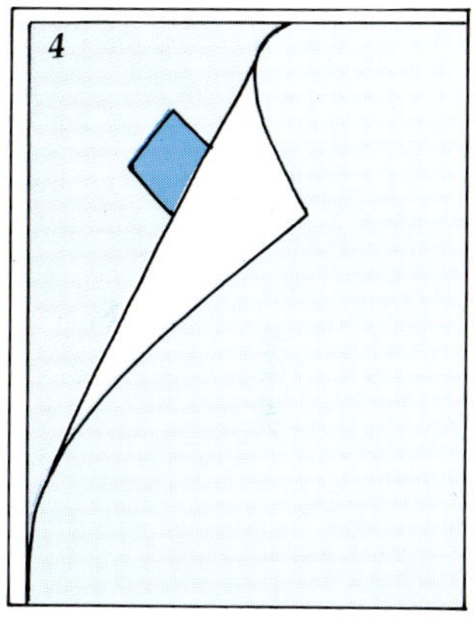

__4__ Position the second layer of fabric right side up over the appliqué and pin to hold.

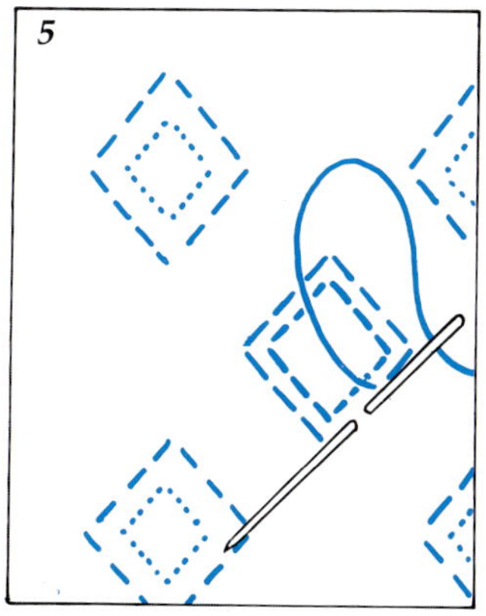

__5__ Turn the work over, and, with the wrong side facing, tack around the stitched areas, leaving a margin between of about 6mm

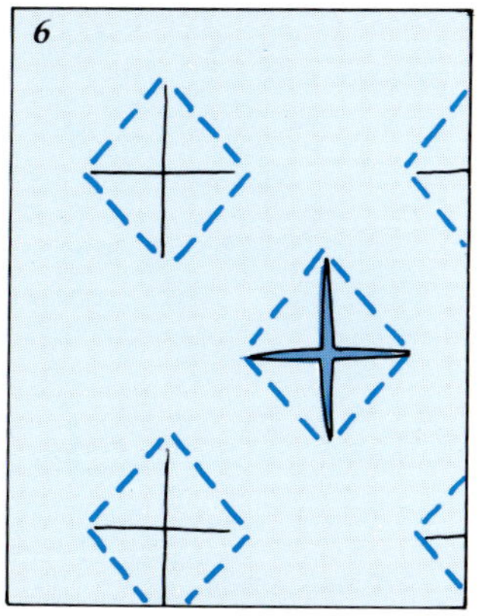

__6__ Turn the work right side up and snip into the corners as far as the tacking stitches.

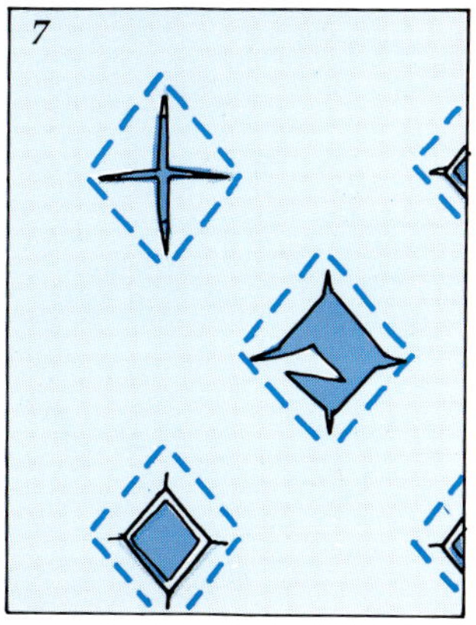

__7__ Trim the excess fabric inside the diamonds leaving a tiny seam allowance of about 3mm (1/8in).

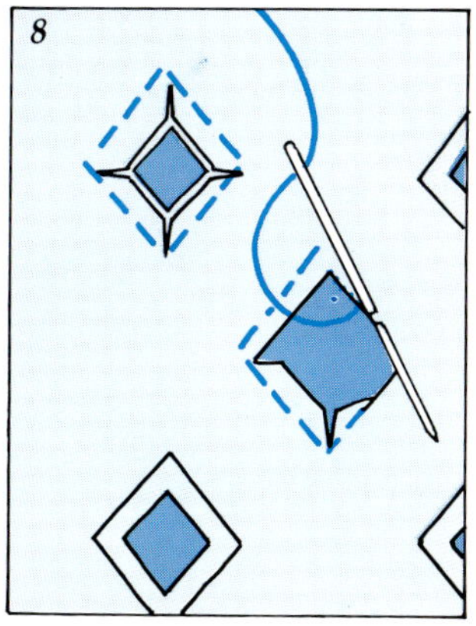

__8__ Roll under edges and slip stitch. Leave tacking threads as a guideline.

• PADDED APPLIQUE •

BEAUTIFUL RELIEF surfaces can be made by padding certain areas or individual appliqué shapes. There are two very simple methods.

In the first, the appliqué is attached in the usual way, either by machine or hand sewing using slip hemming —this stitch giving a nicely rounded edge to the padding—but an opening is left in which loose wadding is inserted and the edge is then sewn down.

The other method uses a layer of wadding cut to the same size as the appliqué patch (less turning allowances) and the two layers applied as one.

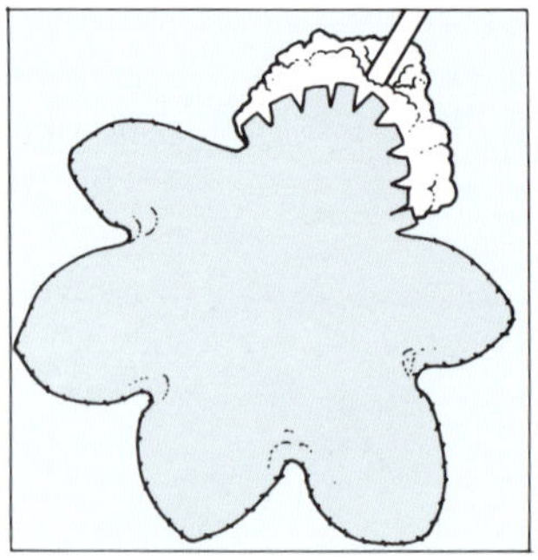

Left: *Padded appliqué. Use a fine knitting needle to ease the wadding into the corners of a motif to give a nicely rounded surface.*

FOLDED PATTERNS

THIS METHOD of designing is popular in many countries including India, Pakistan, Hungary and Hawaii

Using two squares of different coloured fabrics (the lower one cut slightly bigger to include seam allowances), press and then fold the layers separately first in half, then in quarters and finally in eighths. Pin the layers of the appliqué fabric together and transfer your design to the top section. Cut out very carefully and unfold. Position the design centrally on the ground fabric matching the fold lines. Pin and tack the appliqué in place. Working from the middle out.

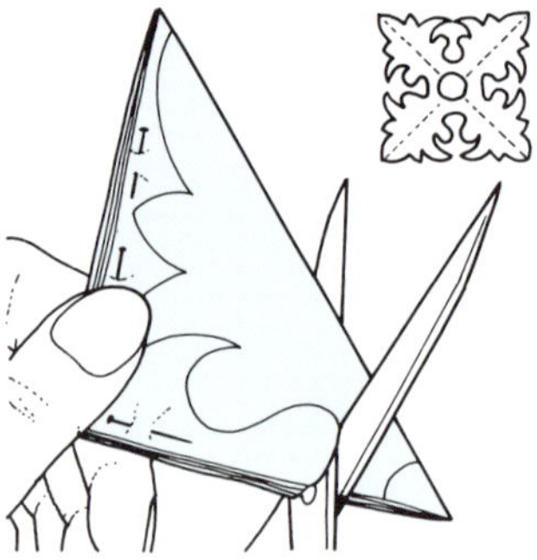

Left: *Folded patterns. Holding the folded fabric firmly, cut out the design keeping the scissors at right angles to the fabric.*

MOTIFS IN RELIEF

A more complicated way to pad appliqué shapes can provide amusement in a piece of work because the edges of motifs are not completely attached to the ground fabric—flowers and leaves, for example, treated in this way give a very pretty effect.

Pin two layers of appliqué fabric together with a layer of interfacing between to give body. Trace the motif on top, zigzag stitch around the outline and trim back the edges to the stitching. Make a small slit in the back and pad with loose wadding to give a pleasing shape. Over sew the slit. Position the motif on the ground fabric and secure either through the middle by hand or partially zigzag stitch to the ground fabric.

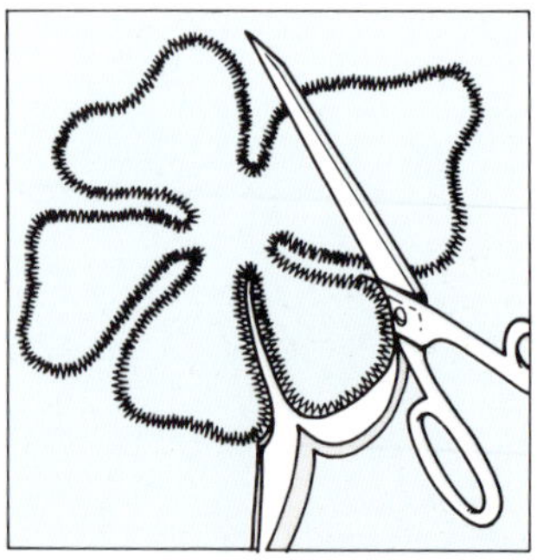

Left: *Motifs in relief. After stitching around, cut out the motif close to the stitching.*

• FINISHING •

When all the appliqué is finished, and any further decoration added, take out the tacking threads—using tweezers to hold stubborn ends—and remove the work from the frame, if used. Press on the right side, using a cloth. Avoid over-pressing so as not to flatten the appliqué.

Many people prefer to remove the backing fabric from under the appliqué patches, cutting to within 6mm (¼in) of the stitching. This usually allows the work to hang better, and dark-coloured ground fabrics are prevented from showing through lighter appliqué, although a light, iron-on interfacing will also prevent this happening. However, wall hangings do benefit from retaining the ground fabric and any other extra backing you may have added intact, as they provide support for the finished weight.

Finish your appliqué as required. Add a fabric casing along the top edge of a hanging to take a dowel rod. Refer to the Quilting and Patchwork sections for quilting, adding borders, finishing edges and lining. Instructions are given opposite for making a simple cushion cover.

CUSHION COVER

To back a cushion cover you will need fabric the same size as the top section, which should be pressed. Before cutting the fabric, check the size of the cushion pad and make the cover 2.5cm (1in) smaller, to give a well-plumped shape. Cut out the back section to size adding 1.5cm (½in) all round for seam allowances. Pin the two sections together, machine stitch around 1.5cm (½in) from the edge, leaving an opening for turning through. Trim the corners. Neaten the seams by overcasting by hand or machine zigzag stitching, turn the cover right side out, and press. Insert the pad and slipstitch the opening to close.

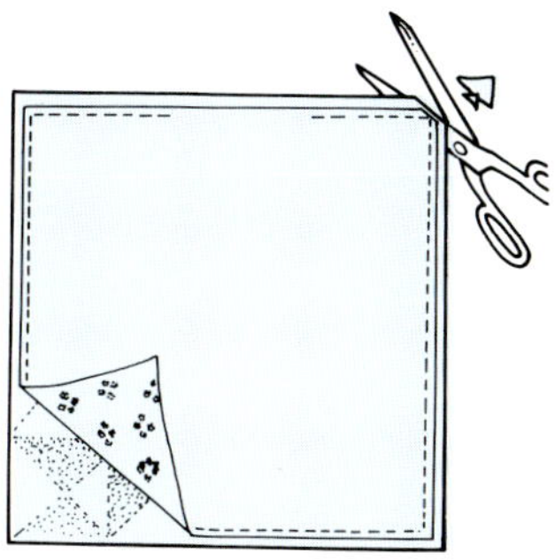

Left: *Finishing. Trim the corners across fairly close to the stitching to prevent unsightly lumps appearing on the right side.*

Below: *Summer Garden detail. This contemporary quilt combines quilting and fabric dyeing with padded appliqué and embroidery. The whole design is constructed like a 'nine-patch' block (as in patchwork). The central patch is a diamond-shaped flower-bed set between herbaceous borders with butterflies and flowers appliquéd in relief.*

CHAPTER SEVEN

APPLIQUE PROJECTS

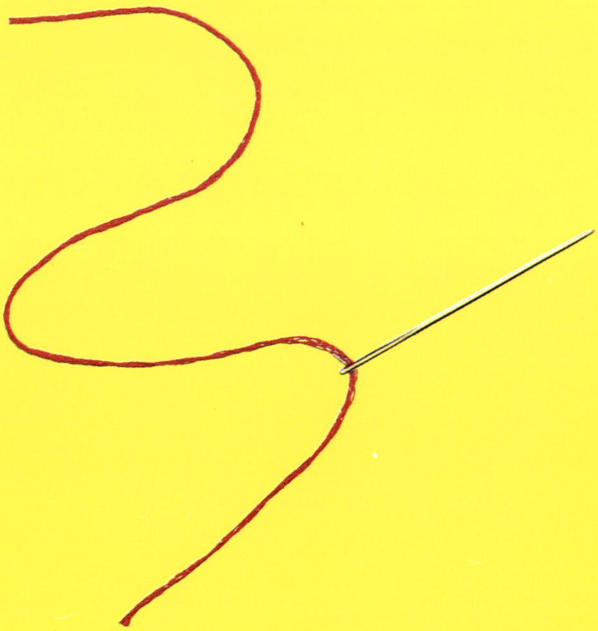

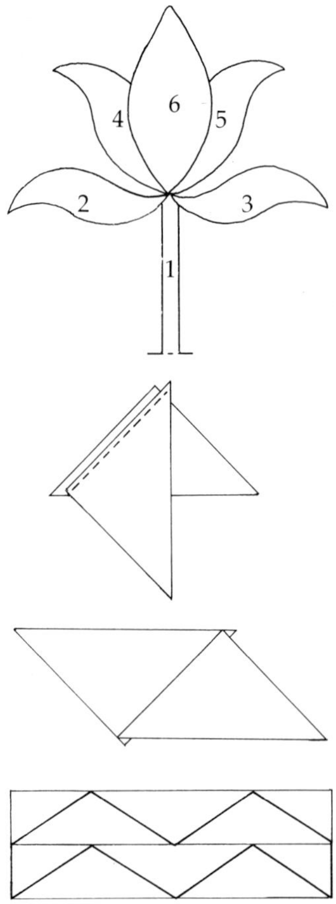

Left and above: *Variegated Tulip. The zigzag border is made quite simply from two rows of pieced triangles. Remember when sewing the triangles together to match the seam lines, as shown, and not the cutting lines.*

• STANDARD APPLIQUE (ONLAY) •

VARIEGATED TULIP

THIS PENNSYLVANIA German quilt made during the 1850s shows a typical tulip design appliquéd in bright contrast colours. Both figurative and floral motifs in fresh, primary colours are a traditional feature of Pennsylvania German design, and were used in their appliqué designs with great panache in various combinations of red, pink, yellow, green and purple.

Here, the quilt, made from plain cotton fabrics throughout, uses appliquéd blocks—about 30cm (12in) square. These are pieced together in a square grid and finished with a zigzag border pieced from triangles of a colourful flower print and the white background fabric. The appliqué motifs are fairly large shapes with smooth outlines, which makes them relatively easy to work, and ideal for beginners. A single block—which might be a practice piece—is perfect for a cushion. Larger or smaller cushions can be made into all kinds of colourful sets with some stunning results. For example, a rainbow sequence could be introduced by reversing the pattern and using a dark background with lighter coloured motifs. Alternatively, six blocks could be used to make a

Right: *A nineteenth-century American quilt known as the Garden Wreath. The quilt top is divided into a number of blocks and shows appliquéd spray and wreath patterns combined with patchwork maple leaves. Many of the American quilts of this period were made in a similar way by a combination of patchwork and appliqué.*

crib cover in similar rainbow or pastel colours, a most acceptable gift for a new baby.

For the project enlarge the design and make the templates as shown in the diagram given above, following the instructions given in appliqué techniques. For repeated use, stick the traced design to thin card (cardboard), as for patchwork templates.

Cut out the motifs as instructed in your chosen colours, with the correct number of blocks for your design. Fold each block diagonally in both directions, and lightly press with a warm iron to mark the central guideline. Apply the shapes, positioning them centrally on the block in the order indicated by numbers in the diagram. Using matching thread and slip hemming neatly secure the appliqué in place.

Join the blocks together by machine, taking 6mm (¼in) seams. Make the border by piecing together contrast triangles, as shown in the diagram, and attach to the quilt.

Assemble the layers as for Quilting (*see* page 20), and quilt around the motifs using toning thread. Fill the background with small diamonds or squares, and finish the edges as required.

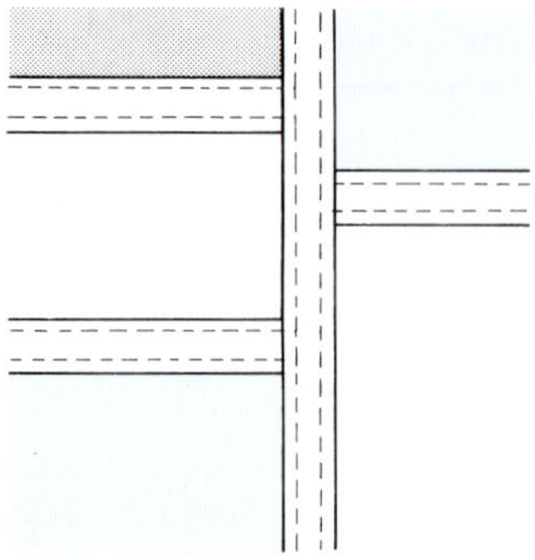

***Above and left:** Cube. There are several ways of applying the tape but the simplest is to tack and stitch in place all the horizontal pieces first, and then the vertical pieces on top, making sure they are accurately positioned, and all raw edges neatly covered.*

CUBE

The sources of inspiration for contemporary appliqué design can differ widely. It may come from stained glass windows, aerial photographs of fields, primitive art, television graphics, or modern painting. Boldly drawn shapes simply outlined with a coloured tape or ribbon can make very striking images, as in this colourful abstract 'painting'.

Here, commercial tape (which requires no turning under) was used not only to cover the seams but also to provide an integral part of the design—using it as a line to link one unit to another—by being applied directly to the background. Such a technique makes this type of appliqué easy for beginners and fun to do.

Mixed fabrics—silks, cottons, tweeds and velvets—can be combined for pictures and wall hangings of all shapes and sizes, but fabrics for practical items such as a playmat, bag or jacket, window blind or curtain, should have similar cleaning requirements. Larger appliqué shapes may tend to pucker slightly without extra stitching or quilting, but this can be helped by backing the appliqué fabric with bonded interfacing ironed on before cutting out.

For the project make a full-size drawing and prepare the background fabric as instructed in appliqué techniques and stretch in an embroidery frame, if preferred. Press on bonded interfacing to the appliqué fabrics, if needed, particularly on bigger shapes, flimsy fabrics or those that easily fray.

Cut out and position the patches on the background fabric, then pin and tack thoroughly to prevent them from slipping. Pin the tape or ribbon over the raw edges turning under the short ends or tucking them underneath adjacent edges. Machine stitch along both edges of the tape using matching coloured thread. Remove the tacking threads and mount your picture, as preferred.

***Left and right:** Adam and Eve. The diagram gives the main outlines to be embroidered and the basic shapes to be appliquéd.*
***Below:** Experimental appliqué using parcel ribbon to form a simple check pattern with random placed machine-embroidered flowers on top.*

ADAM AND EVE

This delightful contemporary-style appliqué combines mixed fabrics, machine embroidery and hand-dyeing in a very distinctive manner. Such a fantasy landscape simply twinkles with scraps of blistered satins, printed chintz, glitter fabrics and multi-coloured threads. Tiny, brushstroke-size motifs are applied to a plain cotton background and overlaid with machine embroidery. To describe the birds, foliage and figures, the designer contrasts shiny solid areas with thinly suggested lines in shaded threads that meander throughout the design to form such an essential part of the work. The central area behind the figures and as far as the horizon line is hand painted with fabric dye in a pale turquoise blue.

This type of experimental appliqué provides a great deal of freedom for the designer both in subject matter and ultimately in where and how the patches should be applied. Essentially, it is the perfect technique for expressing simple ideas in a fantasy mood.

For the project recreate this effect by making a free-style drawing and indicating the main colour areas. Select fabrics and variegated threads and arrange snippets of them on the design to check the overall effect, bearing in mind that the finished stitching will tighten up the whole design. So much of the success of this technique depends on the decisions made at the time of machining. An embroidery hoop should be used (*see* page 92).

Following the instructions in appliqué techniques, lightly transfer the main lines to the foundation fabric and position the patches. Using a light-toned variegated thread (to give a rainbow effect without changing the thread) zigzag over the raw edges to secure the patches. Fill in the central figures and add more solid areas as needed. Using fabric paint, lightly suggest the background by painting between the motifs. Change to a darker variegated thread and outline the flowers, foliage, birds and figures, and the distant horizon line. Hand sew facial details and scatter straight stitches to suggest sky. Frame the picture, as preferred.

Left: *Detail of Landscape with Otter. Delicate fabrics and ribbons are sensitively outlined in this inspirational piece of picture appliqué.*

LANDSCAPE WITH OTTER

Fantasy appliqué is perhaps a more appropriate name for this technique, which uses only the tiniest pieces of fabrics and threads to express an idea so imaginatively, as in this landscape picture. The images, suggested in fabrics such as lace for the otter, cut-out printed flowers, and velvet foliage, are delicately outlined with colourful machine stitching. Light touches of fabric paint are added to the plain cotton background, overlaid in parts with sheer muslin which gives a soft, dreamy quality to the whole design.

Similar picture appliqué could be worked for a special gift, or you may prefer to make your own collection of fairytale pictures.

For the project the design is worked in a similar way to the Adam and Eve landscape, shown on page 103. Apply suitable expressive fabrics in order, building up the design from the fabric-painted background overlaid with muslin to the velvet foliage and the lace otter.

Straight-line stitching in contrast-coloured threads is used to outline the main motifs while random stitching is worked over the entire surface in matching coloured threads. Mount or frame the finished picture as preferred.

Left and above: *Sea bathing.*

• STANDARD APPLIQUE (ONLAY) •

SEA BATHING

USED IMAGINATIVELY, hand embroidery is the perfect technique for describing the intricate and colourful details involved in pictorial appliqué, as in this charming contemporay picture.

Should you wish to work your own choice of landscape, this need not be too daunting, even for a beginner. Here, the designer made a preliminary drawing from a colour photograph—this helped to simplify the images into colour areas, textures and tone—before selecting the appropriate fabrics and threads. These were then carefully chosen, each one, where possible, with a sharply contrasting texture. The beach huts, for example, are suggested with rough tweeds and corduroys, the sky with smooth cotton, the sea with sheer net, shingle with knobbly linen, trees and shrubs with velvet and felt, and so on.

The pieces were applied by hand to a strong hessian backing and the whole landscape was gradually built up. Layers were overlapped to show perspective, and to give depth to the sea, for example, and finally the embroidered details were added with a few well-chosen stitches. Colourful blossoms and grass are suggested, pebbles on the beach, brickwork and wooden surfaces—all of which enliven the picture and sharpen the finished effect.

This kind of embroidered appliqué adapts well for wall coverings of all sizes.

For the project enlarge the drawing and select suitable fabrics, following the instructions given in appliqué techniques. Also choose some threads—six-stranded embroidery thread gives a well-raised effect.

Transfer the main design lines to the hessian background, which should be at least 10cm (4in) bigger all round than the finished size. Cut out the appliqué patches, allowing extra fabric on underlapping edges.

Position them in the correct order, and then tack thoroughly to secure. Using matching coloured thread, stab stitch around each shape adjusting the size of the stitch to suit heavier tweeds and felts. Suggest the water breakers by folding layers of net, cut the figures from felt, and hand stitch the features.

For the embroidered details, work back stitch to suggest wooden cladding on the bathing huts, French knots for the pebbly shingle, straight stitches for the grassy bank, gorse flowers and leaves, chain stitch around the window frames, and use a long chain stitch for the brickwork on the chimney stack.

Stretch the completed appliqué and then tack or staple it over a firm wooden stretcher. Frame as desired without or under non-reflecting glass, as preferred.

WEDDING PARTY

Frequently in pictorial appliqué certain details require subtle embroidery rather than showy decoration. At first glance, therefore, it may not be obvious just how much embroidery is involved, as in this delightful contemporary picture showing well-observed and quietly stated details.

Here, one of the main considerations is to choose the correct tones required to show perspective. This is, perhaps, sufficient to explain why some details are worked in toning colours and give a low-key effect. Notice the grass tussocks, the rhododendron bushes and the gravestones where interesting details are suggested in just slightly darker tones.

Like the Sea Bathing picture, shown on page 105, the designer used a colour photograph as a starting point and made a preliminary drawing before selecting appropriate fabrics and threads. Here, stranded embroidery threads can be used either singly for stitching the patches in place or in any number of strands for the embroidered details. When choosing your fabrics, notice that felt is used for a major part of the picture, including the trees, grass, gravestones, figures, wedding cars, and all the decorative ragwork on the church and window details. In contrast, slub linen is used for the church, velvet for the roof and windows, hessian (burlap) for the path, tweed for the road and

Right and bottom left:
Wedding Party. Much of the charm of this picture is its subject, which is quite realistically portrayed in a wide range of textured fabrics — all cleverly cut and embellished with embroidery stitches to show many fascinating and well-observed details.

wall, and cotton for the sky. Piece by piece the picture was built up on a hessian backing and the embroidered details finally added to highlight the whole picture.

As an alternative suggestion, the picture could be adapted to a smaller size for a personalized wedding album cover, as a very special gift.

For the project appliqué the picture in the same way as the Sea Bathing landscape. Cut out the patches from the fabrics suggested, and apply them in the correct order to give a convincing effect of perspective.

To keep a good shape around the edges of the trees that are decoratively cut, attach them with running stitch rather than stab stitch. Notice also that the church roof and clock are outlined with couching to give a smooth line. Complete all the appliqué—including the ragwork and window frames, before adding the embroidered details. For the embroidery, work straight stitch to describe the features on the figures and the grass and gravestone details, use bullion knots for the horse-chestnut tree, fly stitch for the rhododendron bush, chain stitch for the railings, car ribbons and wall, and back stitch for the trim line on the car. Stretch and mount the finished picture as preferred.

• APPLIQUE PERSE •
FLOWER GARDEN

Motifs cut from contemporary furnishing fabrics can be used to create most enchanting designs as shown here in the three cushions.

Each cushion is individually designed, taking as a starting point the cut-out motifs from printed chintz, and rearranging them in a pleasing way on a plain or patterned background. In this way, an interior scheme can be perfectly co-ordinated by appliquéing motifs from the same fabric used for the soft-furnishings—which is also an ideal way of utilizing leftover oddments. Floral, rather than formal, motifs are much easier to build up into free-flowing designs, although stylized and geometric patterns can be included. These may be used quite graphically—perhaps as a patterned background or a flower vase, or as a trellis behind a trailing plant, for example.

Surface stitching is another important element in the design. Here, the main outlines are machined using a wide satin stitch in darker and lighter tones picked out from the printed fabric. Straight stitching is used to fill the flower centres with radiating lines, the outlines of veins, shadows under petals, and the swirling tendrils and stalks that link leaves and flowers together. Alternative uses for perse motifs include the edges of table cloths and napkins, bed linen and duvet or down quilt covers: a quick and effective decoration is to break into the edge with just one or two motifs zigzag stitched around and trimmed.

For the project the same method is used for working all three design ideas. Select your motifs from firm furnishing fabrics, such as glazed chintz, and arrange them on a plain background in a pleasing design. Decide which of the flowers (or leaves) should be 'in front' and tuck the others underneath trying them in different directions until you have an interesting composition. Add contrast fabrics between the motifs to form part of the background, as in the blue and pink designs.

Place a thin layer of wadding backed with tissue paper underneath the work and then, following the instructions in appliqué techniques for machine stitching, pin and tack the motifs in place.

To prevent puckering on large flowers, stitch the centres with radiating straight lines before covering the raw edges with wide satin stitch. Using matching or contrast threads, work the leaves in a similar way, stitching the veins before the outlines. Remove the tissue paper and make up the cushion cover (*see* page 97).

Below: Flower Garden. Glazed chintz is used for both the appliqué and the ground fabric in all three 'flower garden' cushion covers. These fabrics are excellent for repelling dust, but if you prefer to use an untreated furnishing fabric, then coat the finished cover with a silicone dust preventative spray — especially where light, pastel colours are used.

Above: The diagram shows the basic outline of cut-out printed flowers arranged on a striped fabric appliquéd to a plain ground.

SALAMANDER

Selecting and cutting printed patterns and motifs and rearranging them into new appliqué designs has great potential. Small amounts of, perhaps, expensive or unusually printed fabrics can be skilfully arranged—thus maximizing their effect—as shown in this exotically styled wall hanging where unconventional flowers and animals abound.

The design uses several panels of heavy damask each bordered by one or more unusual prints. The appliqué motifs, cut from variously patterned and printed fabrics, are applied on top, and the main shapes outlined with couched braid or cord.

Here, the art of cutting a motif from a patterned fabric, as opposed to an already printed motif, is demonstrated in these lively animal shapes and flower stalks. Suitably patchy fabrics in realistic colours are used for the salamanders and the frog. Large printed flowers are appliquéd and the centres and stamen added separately, while the stalks are suggested with leafy fabrics applied to a basic earthy colour.

Individual panels can be adapted for framed pictures or cushions, or grouped into repeat patterns for quilts and other large projects.

For the project make a full-scale drawing, and select appropriate fabrics and cords. Following the instructions in appliqué techniques, cut the background fabric for each panel, the appliqué motifs and the borders, first backing them with iron-on interfacing, if needed. Apply the motifs, neatly oversewing them in place before couching over the raw edges and sewing the panels to the backing. However, notice that certain small parts of flowers, stamen and borders are applied on top afterwards, and also that borders on the lower sections of the two outer panels can be applied (by machine) at the same time as working the appliqué. Stretch the work in a hoop for couching the outlines (*see* page 93).

Tack the finished panels to the backing. Make up the borders and apply them in order, covering the raw edges of the panels. Couch cords over the edges of the borders to finish. Insert fabric loops for hanging, line and finish the edges, as preferred (*see* page 26).

Opposite: *Salamander.*

Right and far right: *Penny. You will find that where a layer of wadding is added underneath an appliqué shape, wrinkles are less likely to occur. On large unpadded shapes, it is especially important to closely tack the whole area with vertical stitches.*

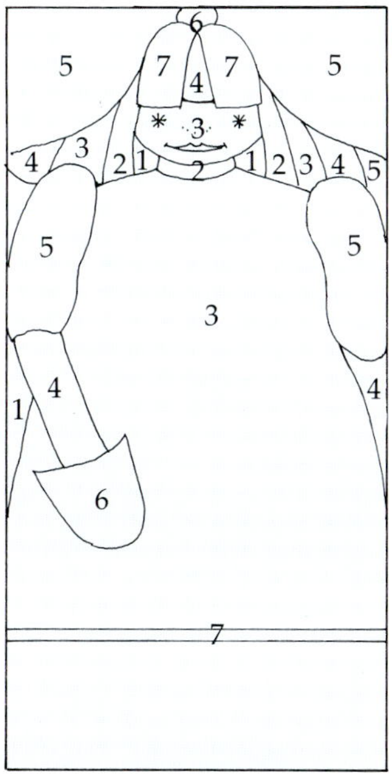

• PADDED APPLIQUE •

PENNY

PADDING NEED only be very slight to give a rounded image to features, especially on larger figurative appliqué, as in this colourfully patched cushion.

Here, the face, hair, bow, puffed sleeves and pocket are padded with a thin layer of wadding to highlight the main features and thereby give a subtle hint of a third dimension. The depth of padding can obviously be increased if a more undulating surface is preferred.

The design uses a mixture of fabrics, including furnishing linens, cotton rep, patterned prints, velvet ribbon, and gold thread, and provides ample opportunity for mixing all kinds of alternative plain cottons and prints in different colours and textures.

To give surface interest, smooth linens are used for the face, bow and pocket; slub linen for the hair, with the curls picked out in shiny gold thread; furnishing weight cotton rep for the pinafore; a colourful cotton print for the dress, with a seed pearl necklace and a velvet ribbon border, while silk threads are used for the features.

Without the cushion pad, the cover could be made into a pyjama sachet or bag as a special gift for a child.

For the project use an embroidery frame. Enlarge the design to approximately 30cm by 60cm (12in by 24in). Following the instructions in appliqué techniques, cut out the shapes from the fabrics suggested, allowing extra fabric for turnings, and apply them to iron-on interfacing. Cut out wadding for the correct shapes to be padded, and tack it to the wrong side of the corresponding appliqué fabric. Prepare each shape and apply them in order, as shown, slip hemming them to a calico backing, previously stretched in a frame.

Hems are not needed on the outer edges—these will become the seam allowances for making up the cushion. Sew on the necklace, catching each pearl with a separate stitch; apply the ribbon border to the bottom of the pinafore and the gold thread curls—couching the curls with matching thread, and embroider the features with straight stitches, using silk threads. Make up the cushion with a plain back (*see* page 97).

• PADDED QUILTING •

POSIES

THREE-DIMENSIONAL PADDING AND QUILTING COMBINE well with spray-dyeing to produce some of the prettiest effects in appliqué, as in these delightful evening bags.

Here, the front of each bag is appliquéd with a cluster of separately padded flowers and leaves which are spray-dyed and embroidered in softly shaded colours to match the dyed and quilted background. In each case, an interesting feature is made of the quilting where the outline of the individual appliqué motifs is overlapped and repeated as an all-over pattern. As a finishing touch, tiny silvery beads are dotted over the surface to highlight the design.

Both bags are constructed in the same way which involves joining together the plain back and front sections with a contrast binding. The opening is secured by narrow fabric ties and each bag has a plaited fabric shoulder strap.

Lustrous cottons and acetate satins and silks are ideal for both the main fabric and lining—these not only accept dye well but are excellent for showing off the quilting and the padded contours of the appliqué motifs. Similar motifs may be used to decorate the neckline of a dress, or they could be stitched on to a soft ribbon tie as a soft sculpture necklace or belt.

For the project for bags A and B, first enlarge the design on to tracing paper following the measurements given, and then make separate tracings of the appliqué flowers and leaves where appropriate.

Bag A Using dressmaker's carbon paper, transfer the design to the front section of the bag (back section optional) and the top section of each of the appliqué flowers, but do not cut out at this stage.

Following the photograph as a colour guide, spray-dye the background, masking out the appropriate areas with film using a fine spray to give a softly shaded effect. Suggest the flower centres in a deeper tone with fine brush strokes radiating from the middle. When thoroughly dry, permanently 'fix' the dye following the manufacturer's instructions, and press the fabric to remove any creases. Cut out the different sections leaving at least 3cm (1¼in) all round. Assemble the two bag sections as for machine quilting and, working outwards from the middle, quilt the design using a deep toning thread. Sew on the beads placing them at

Above and below: *Posies. Bag A. Enlarge the basic outline of the bag front and flowers and spray-dye before quilting through the layers.*

Below: *Bag B. Enlarge the design, place the bottom edge of the bag to a fold, and spray-dye before quilting the layers together.*

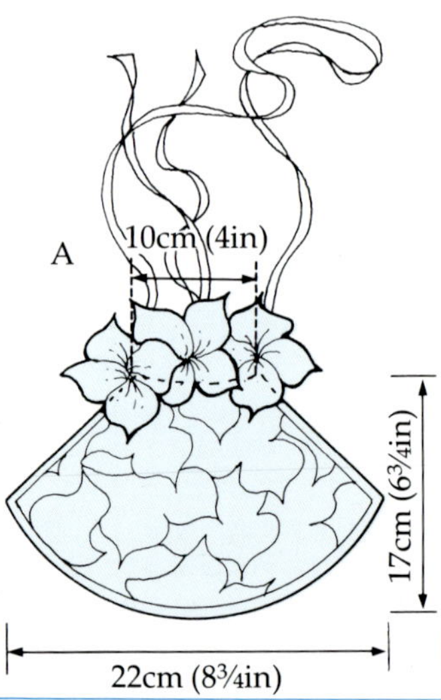

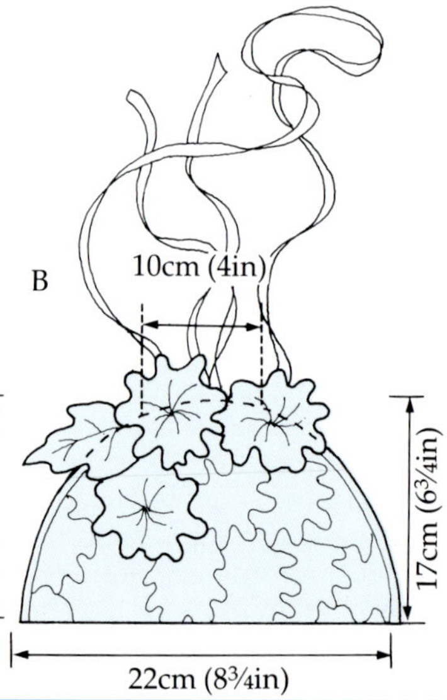

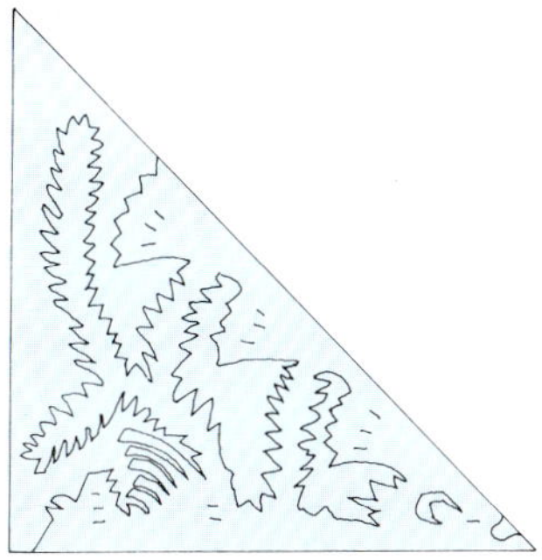

Above and left: *Kapa Lau. Transfer the design to the top section, pin and hold the eight layers securely before cutting through.*

random over the background. Bind the top edges of the two sections with either pre-dyed or commercial bias binding in the correct colour, inserting 25cm (10in) long rouleaux or narrow ribbon ties centrally under the inside seam. Plait a 1m (39in) long shoulder strap using either pre-dyed shaded fabric or narrow ribbon. Pin and baste the two bag sections wrong sides together inserting the strap, as shown, and then bind the edges to form the seam.

For each flower, tack the back and front sections wrong sides together, close zigzag stitch around the edge and trim the fabric back to the stitching. Pad each flower following the instructions for Padded quilting. Secure them to the top edge of the bag working clusters of French knots in the middle, and adding the remaining beads to finish.

Bag B Transfer the appliqué motifs and background design to the fabric as for A, placing the bottom edge of the design to a fold. Then, using fabric dye in the same way as for A, decorate the background and appliqué motifs in two softly shaded colours.

Work the remaining sequences as for A, folding the fabric in half before joining the sides of the bag together with bias-cut binding. Catch the appliqué flowers in place with a few stitches around the edge and several beads in the middle.

• FOLDED APPLIQUE •

KAPA LAU

THIS STRIKING example of a folded quilt typifies the brilliant colour and bold, formalized design of Hawaiian appliqué. The design, which is intricately cut from cotton whole cloth using the folded technique, shows traditional motifs of Hawaiian flowers and foliage on a grand scale. The appliqué is first hand stitched to a coloured background, interlined, and then quilted and the motifs outlined and filled with contour quilting so that the entire surface is covered.

Designing appliqué with ordinary paper cut-outs is amazingly simple, and it was this technique that the women quiltmakers of Hawaii were first shown by American missionaries, which they quickly developed into their own individual style.

Interestingly, the small snowflake-type design taken by the missionaries soon grew in size to the proportions of the local vegetation which the islanders used as inspiration for their magnificent designs—the Breadfruit tree and the Pineapple being the most famous. These cut-out patterns, *kapa lau*, are often so enormous that they cover a full-size quilt. Other favourite motifs, also taken from nature, include ferns, figs, paw paws, waterfalls and turtles.

Traditional colour combinations are vividly striking. They are usually limited to just two or three colours such as white on a brilliant red or green background, or vice versa, or schemes such as red, green and orange, or scarlet and white on yellow. Alternatively, a printed cotton could be appliquéd to white, or a pastel colour superimposed on a pretty print. For best results, choose fine, closely woven cotton or lawn fabrics.

Folded appliqué is most suitable for quilts of all sizes—using large or smaller repeated patterns—cushions, bolsters and floor seating.

For the project enlarge the diagram, which gives one eighth of the finished design, to the size needed for the corresponding section. Alternatively, create your own design by experimenting first with a smaller square of paper.

Trace off the design ready to transfer later on. Following the instructions in Folded appliqué, fold, cut and stitch the appliqué to the background. Assemble the three layers as for Wadded quilting—tacking along the crease lines—and stretch in a quilting hoop. Quilt following the outline of the design, repeating evenly spaced lines 1.5–2cm (½–¾in) apart over the entire surface. Finish the edges of the completed quilt as preferred.

• SHADOW QUILTING •

ELM TREE LANE

Illusions of space, colour and form can be created with great sensitivity by using just a simple collection of sheer fabrics and machine stitching, as in this delightful country landscape picture. The design uses colour and overlapping gauzes to express a wide spectrum of tonal densities, where in certain areas, such as the trees, several layers have been built up to give the impression of form. Here, as in more experimental picture-making, frayed edges are exploited and play an important part in the atmosphere and overall effect.

The whole landscape with its softly feathered edges is outlined with a fine, machine-stitched line in a slightly darker tone. The fineness and apparent random placing of the lines are key elements in the composition—an effect which may need a little preliminary practice to recreate.

Gauze, organdie, lace, net, muslin, voile and other semi-transparent fabrics in mixed colours can be used for this form of shadow appliqué–a technique best suited to experimental picture-making. You may find silk organzas and other slippery sheers difficult to control whereas matt fabrics tend to 'stick' and are easier to handle in layers.

For the project work a small sample piece to get the feel of working in this way with sheers, before embarking on the main project.

Make a full-scale drawing and indicate the colours before selecting the appropriate sheers. Choose a smooth cotton background fabric to the size required, allowing extra all around for stretching. Following the instructions given in Appliqué techniques, lightly transfer the main lines of the design to the backing, and then cut out the motifs by placing the sheer over the drawing and tracing around the shapes, allowing extra for fraying. Pin the shapes to the backing, starting with the background behind the trees, then the foreground, and stitch in place before applying the trees. Trim back or fray the fabric, as needed. Apply and stitch the bottom layers of the trees before the top layers, trimming and fraying to finish. Stretch and frame as required.

Right: *Elm Tree Lane. In addition to the increased density of colour, overlapping gauzes produce fascinating watermark effects which lend a spontaneous quality to the whole picture.*

Below left: *A contemporary piece of appliqué using shadow work, machine embroidery and copper wire to suggest a free-form landscape.*

• PICTURE APPLIQUE •

RING O' ROSES

MANY CONTEMPORARY designers are rediscovering picture appliqué to record simple daily activities in fresh, appealing styles. The subjects, as in this charming picture, frequently show lively characters in bright, colourful felt—simply stitched and unadorned.

Apart from the individual clothes of the children, and the chintz curtains at the door, the rest of the picture is cut from a range of different coloured felt. The children's clothes are cut from printed striped and patterned fabrics, corduroy, denim and cotton. Their limbs and heads are also cut from felt and have hand-stitched features.

Hand-embroidered details are used to suggest the two bay tree tubs and the wall behind.

Essentially, the whole picture is very simply constructed and would not be too difficult for a beginner to tackle. An ideal size would be about 23cm by 30cm (9in by 12in).

The picture's attractive nursery rhyme quality, with its colourful and easily recognizable figures, makes it the perfect present for a small child.

For the project make a full-scale drawing, and then choose the appropriate fabrics and felt, including a firm cotton backing fabric slightly bigger in size to allow for stretching in an embroidery frame, or, later, in a picture frame.

Following the instructions in Appliqué techniques, cut out the shapes from the fabrics suggested and apply them to the backing fabric in the correct order–stretching the backing in a frame, if preferred. Tack or apply a little fabric adhesive to hold the appliqué shapes. Using matching coloured threads, neatly stab stitch the shapes in place (*see* page 93), and add the features. Embroider the brickwork using chain stitch to make the bonding pattern, and work lines of chain stitch down the tubs. Stretch and frame the finished picture as required.

***Left and right:** Ring O'Roses. Using the main picture as a guide, first select the different fabrics for the appliqué shapes, and then number your drawing in the order of application. Keep this by you as reference when stitching.*

Above: *Cherry Tree.*
Freely applied fragments of satin fabrics and lace together with stem, cretan and various straight stitches, have been worked onto a background, softly coloured with fabric crayons, to suggest the view of a cherry tree seen through a window. The whole picture is framed by an appliquéd window casement and roller blind.

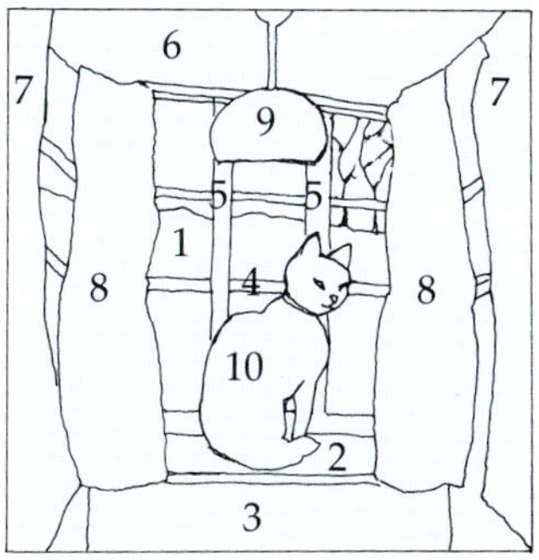

Left and above: *Snowy. This simple everyday subject, worked in felt and printed fabrics, makes an ideal beginners project. Frame the finished picture with a deep recessed surround, with or without non-reflecting glass. If without glass, then coat the picture with a silicone dust preventative spray.*

SNOWY

The image of a beautifully soft, furry cat sitting at a window–the epitome of the family pet—makes a most enchanting subject for an appliqué picture. The composition uses very few fabrics—a simple mixture including felt, spot patterns and a flowery print. The sky and windowsill are featured in spotted cottons, the whole of the window area, its recess and frame, and the cat are cut from felt, the curtains—realistically ruffled, which could be the result of a mischievous cat—are in a flower print, the view from the window and the trees beyond are also cut from felt, as are the lamp and shade. A workable size for the picture would be about 25cm (10in) square.

With a little imagination, it would not be too difficult for even a beginner to adapt any individual feature in the picture to suit a personal preference. For example, you may wish to show pink-striped curtains and a black cat, or red curtains and a striped cat—adding distinguishing marks for extra realism. Whatever your choice, the picture is easy to work and would make a very acceptable present.

For the project enlarge the drawing to the size suggested and select suitable fabrics and felt. You will also need a firm cotton backing and matching coloured threads for the appliqué.

The picture is applied in the same way as Ring o' Roses with the exception of the curtains. For these, cut the shapes slightly wider to allow for the ruffled look. You could add a little loose wadding underneath to pad out the folds, and then secure them with a few stitches hidden inside the creases before stitching the outline. Complete the appliqué and add the features. Frame the finished picture as you prefer.

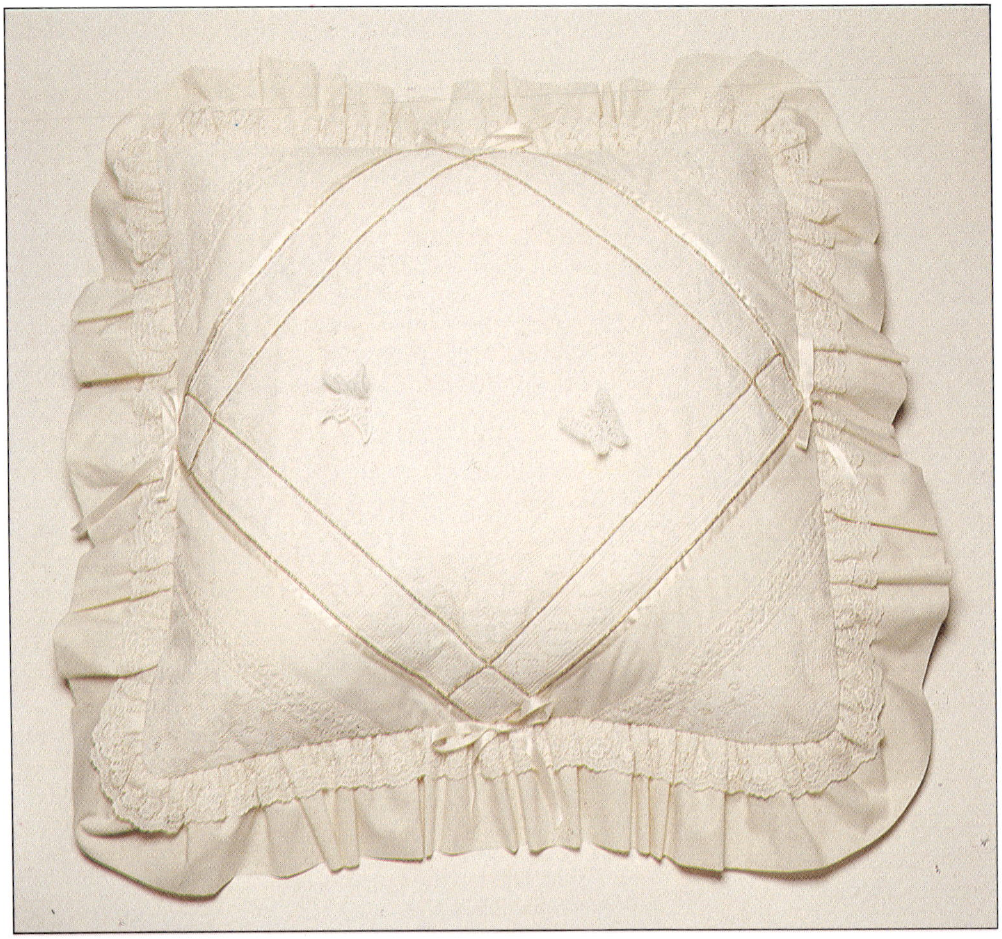

Left and below: *Garland. The design for this attractive lace pillow cover can easily be adapted to suit other shapes and sizes, as part of a set of bedroom cushions.*

• LACE APPLIQUE •

GARLAND

SOME OF THE DAINTIEST effects in appliqué can be achieved by this technique in which richly textured and highly decorative lace fabrics and trims are used, as in this prettily frilled pillow cover.

The design shows a large central diamond (with butterflies) and corner motifs cut from white cotton curtain lace and appliquéd on to a creamy cotton ground fabric. Straight-sided insertion lace is used to cover the edges of the motifs and the central border is further trimmed with gold piping and narrow satin ribbon tied in decorative bows. To complete the romantic effect, the pillow is surrounded by a deep double frill of cream cotton and scalloped lace.

Although designed to fit a large 60cm (24in) square pad, the appliqué design can easily be adapted to suit other shapes and sizes. A selection of mixed shapes combined with simple design variations would make a very attractive set of bedroom cushions.

As alternatives to lace curtaining, wedding lace, pieces of antique lace, filet net, edgings, doilies and crochet can be used for the appliqué with some stunning

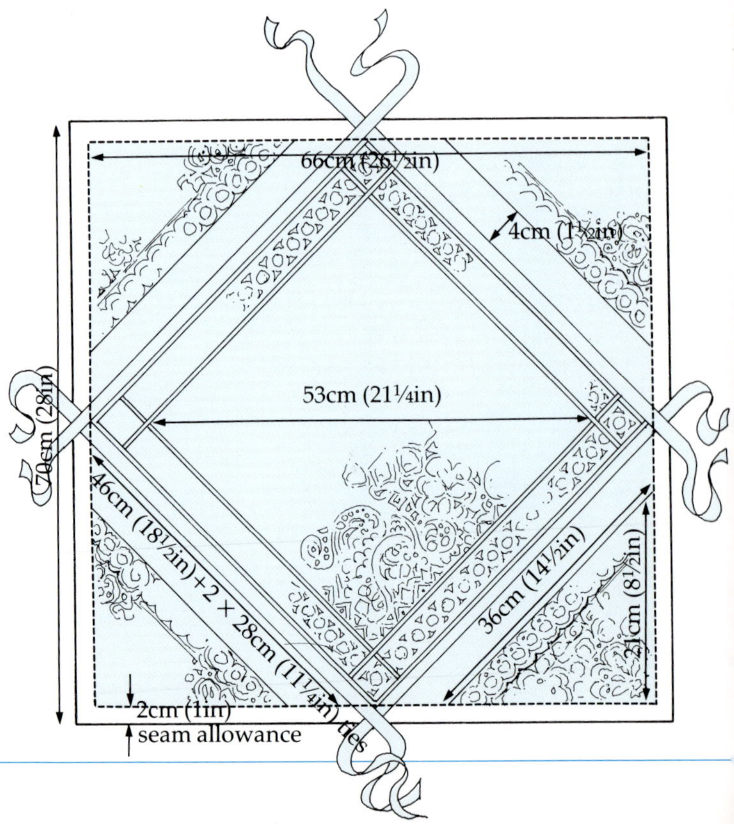

results. Other suitable ground fabrics include light- to mediumweight silk, satin, cotton and polyester.

For the project you will need sufficient main fabric for the pillow front and back plus a generous double frill about 10cm (4in) deep—for the length, allow roughly one and a half times the measurement around the pillow. Allow extra for the back, if you prefer a pocket opening, and for all seam allowances.

From lace, cut out the diamond motif and corner sections to size. Position the diamond centrally on the ground fabric, and tack to secure. Pipe the edges of 5cm (2in) wide insertion and machine stitch it over the raw edges. Pipe separate squares for each corner of the diamond and stitch on top. Stitch lengths of ribbon close to the insertion leaving the ends free for tying. When sewing, pin them away from the edge to prevent them from getting caught in the seam.

Position the corner sections with the outer edges in the seam allowance. Tack in place and cover the diagonal edges with 3cm (1¼in) wide insertion.

Large expanses of lace appliqué such as the central diamond, may need to be supported by catching it to the ground fabric with a few tiny stitches judiciously placed within the pattern.

Attach separate butterfly motifs stitching through both layers.

Finally make the frill by running a gathering thread around stitching through both layers 1cm (½in) from the raw edge. Attach a similar length of 5cm (2in) wide scalloped lace just below the stitching. Pull up the gathers to fit around the pillow, tack it to the top section and make up the cover, as preferred.

ROSE BORDER

This delightful rose-scented pillow uses the prettiest appliqué combining écru lace trim with a contrast ribbon and hand-embroidered flowers. The design is worked on a wadded ground in matching cotton and shows a centre panel filled with rows of hand quilting. This is surrounded by a lace border, edged with narrow ribbon and a daintily pleated frill.

A scalloped edging 5cm (2in) wide is used for both the lace border and the frill, where the border is simply appliquéd with mitred corners and decorated with embroidered roses and French knots. More tiny flowers and knots are embroidered on the ribbon edging to complement perfectly the rose perfume and give an extra delicate finish to the pillow. A handful of fragrant rose petals is placed inside the pad before it is made up, but this could easily be left out or substituted by any other sweet-smelling herbs or *pot pourri*.

A size of about 30cm (12in) square is ideal for the design, which is very easy to work either in the hand or an embroidery hoop.

For the project allow the perfume to escape by choosing a main fabric that has a slight open weave, such as unbleached calico. Cut out two sections to size and back the top with wadding and muslin and prepare them as for wadded quilting. Pin and tack 1.5cm (½in) wide ribbon 5cm (2in) in from the edge, mitring the corners and turning in the raw edges at one corner. Pin the lace border in position, mitring the corners and placing the straight edge just over the ribbon, and, with matching thread, slip stitch neatly in place. Then, mark parallel lines diagonally through the centre about 15cm apart and quilt using pale green coton à broder.

Following the diagram given below, work the embroidery in bullion knots and French knots, as shown, in rose pink and green coton à broder. For the frill, allow one and a half times the measurement around the edge. Pin over the edge of the ribbon in even pleats, making sure that a pleat falls on each corner. Hide the joining under a pleat and neatly hand stitch through all layers. Make up the cover and add perfume, as preferred.

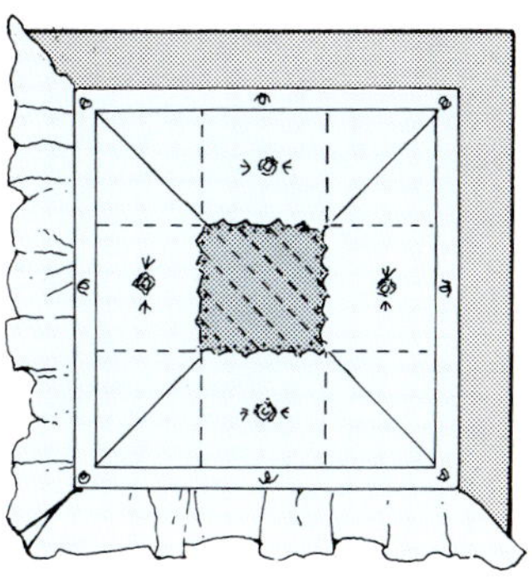

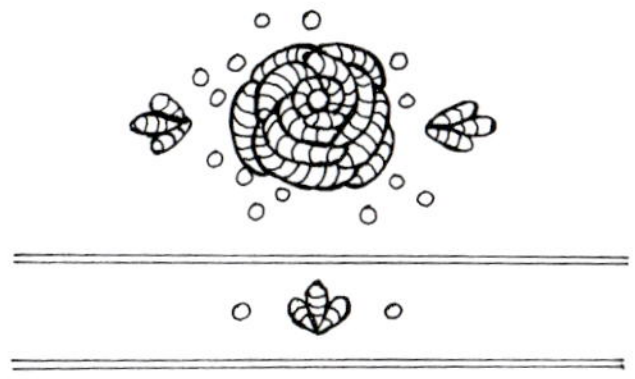

***Left and below:** Rose Border. This pretty rose-scented pillow is embroidered with tiny pink roses.*

• WHERE TO FIND EXAMPLES OF • QUILTING, PATCHWORK AND APPLIQUÉ

The Embroiderers' Guild, London
The Guild was founded in 1906 as an educational charity, and membership is open to anyone who is interested in embroidery. The Headquarters at Hampton Court Palace house a priceless collection of both historic and contemporary examples of the art of embroidery. There is also an extensive library for the use of members, as well as regular classes, workshops and seminars. There are over one hundred Affiliated Branches of the Guild throughout the United Kingdom which arrange their own programme of lectures and classes

The Victoria and Albert Museum, London
The museum was originally opened in 1857 after being built with money derived from the Great Exhibition of 1851. The museum now contains one of the world's outstanding collections of fine and applied arts. Apart from this permanent collection there is also an ever-changing programme of exhibitions, lectures and seminars. The development of English embroidery from medieval times to the present day can be studied in the many galleries and also in the specialized Textile Study Room.

Museum of Costume, Bath
An extensive collection of costume from the late sixteenth century to the present day. It includes embroidered garments of 1580–1620, and of the eighteenth century, also whitework babies' clothes of the seventeenth and nineteenth centuries.

American Museum in Britain, Claverton Manor, Bath
A large collection of American quilts, both patchwork and appliqué, also hooked rag rugs and woven coverlets. The collection includes patchwork dating from 1770 up to the mid-nineteenth century. Many of the early pieces, which were worked by early settlers, show a great similarity in design to those made by quilters and rug makers in the North of England.

Fitzwilliam Museum, Cambridge
One of Europe's major museums, the Fitzwilliam Museum houses collections devoted to the applied as well as the fine arts. The English embroideries include seventeenth century samplers, and stumpwork, and there are also examples of work from the Middle East, Greece and Turkey.

Gawthorne Hall, near Burnley
The Hall houses the collection of the Hon. Rachel B. Kay Shuttleworth—a descendant of the owner. The comprehensive collection includes fine lace and embroideries from the seventeenth century to the present day. Many specialist courses are held at the Hall.

Hardwick Hall, near Chesterfield
An extensive collection of sixteenth and seventeenth century embroideries, including work attributed to Mary Queen of Scots and Elizabeth Shrewsbury, Bess of Hardwick. Also of interest are a set of appliqué hangings depicting 'The Virtues'.

Lady Lever Art Gallery, Port Sunlight Village, Merseyside
This notable collection includes large tapestries, many elaborate examples of English seventeenth century embroideries for caskets, mirror frames, and pictures. There are also some samplers and silk panels from the late eighteenth and early nineteenth century.

Burrell Collection, Glasgow
The art collection bequeathed by Sir William Burrell to Glasgow includes some fine examples of sixteenth and seventeenth century embroidery. The collection is now displayed in a new museum building opened in 1983.

Musée des Art Décoratifs, Paris
The museum has a superb collection of particular interest to the designer and embroiderer.

Cooper-Hewitt Museum, New York
A museum of design with impressive collections of decorative art, furniture, glass, embroidery, woven and printed textiles and lace. It is designed as a reference centre for designers, researchers, scholars and students.

Smithsonian Institute, Washington, D.C.
In the American Folk Museum of the complex, there are examples of old Amerindian patchwork and appliqué and some classic American patchwork quilts.

• PICTURE CREDITS •

The illustrations are reproduced by kind permission of the following:

BEAMISH, North of England Open Air Museum, p. 18
MOIRA BROADBENT (photo by Peter Weaver), pp. 23, 73
ROSEMARY MUNTUS, pp. 26, 32, 33, 42, 60, 72
PAM DEMPSTER, pp. 57, 65, 66–67, 75, 76, 84
DOROTHEA HALL, pp. 24, 32, 39, 40, 41, 43, 44, 79, 102, 111, 120, 121
DIANA THORNTON, Goldsmiths College, p. 25
THE QUILTERY, Falconeston, Norwich, pp. 30, 38
DIEDRE AMSDEN, p. 31
DIANA HARRISON, p. 34
MARGARET RIVERS, pp. 35, 77
SUE RANGELEY, pp. 36, 112
VICTORIA BARTLETT, p. 39
SUSIE FREEMAN, Crafts Council, p. 45
JENNIFER FOX, p. 48
CHRISTINE COOPER, p. 56
ENG TOW, Crafts Advisory Council, pp. 37, 58, 85, 86, 87
ROSEMARY MUNTUS AND EIKO YOSHIDA, p. 61
AMERICAN MUSEUM IN BRITAIN, pp. 64, 68, 69, 73, 84, 100, 101
PAULINE BURBAGE, Crafts Council, p. 70
FRANCESCA KEMBLE, p. 71
MARGARET BRANDENBOURG, p. 74
JENNY BULLEN (photo by Eileen Tweedie), p. 78
WELSH FOLK MUSEUM, p. 80
VALERIE CAMPBELL-HARDING, p. 81
CHRISTINE COOPER, pp. 82, 83
HERTA PULS COLLECTION, p. 87, 91
SUE RANGELEY, Crafts Council, p. 96–97, 112
FIONA EDE, Goldsmiths College, p. 103 (below)
ARIELLA GREEN, Goldsmiths College, pp. 44, 79, 103, 104
GLENYS SIDA, Crafts Council, pp. 105, 107, 116–117, 118
PETER HOARE, Furnishing Interiors, Tunbridge Wells, Kent
SUSAN MAXWELL, Crafts Advisory Council, p. 110
DOROTHY WALKER, p. 113
VICTORIA AND ALBERT MUSEUM, p. 114
JULIE ATHILL, p. 115
DOROTHY TUCKER, p. 117

Every effort has been made to obtain copyright clearance for the patchwork, quilting and appliqué projects featured in this book. Quintet Publishing would like to thank all the copyright holders who granted clearance, and at the same time apologize if any omissions have been made.

• BIBLIOGRAPHY •

Butler, Anne: *Encyclopaedia of Embroidery Stitches*, Batsford.
Campbell-Harding, Valerie: *Strip Patchwork*, Batsford.
Coleman, Anne: *The Creative Sewing Machine*, Batsford (paperback).
Dawson, Barbara: *Metal Thread Embroidery*, Batsford (paperback).
Dean, Beryl: *Embroidery in Religion and Ceremonial*, Batsford.
Geddes, Elizabeth, and McNeill, Moyra: *Blackwork Embroidery*, Dover.
Howard, Constance: *20th Century Embroidery*, Vols. 1, 2 and 3, Batsford.
Kendrick, A. F.: *English Needlework*, A. & C. Black.
Lancaster, John: *Lettering Techniques*, Batsford (paperback).
Lemon, Jane: *Embroidered Boxes*, Batsford (paperback).
McNeill, Moyra: *Pulled Thread*, Mills and Boon.
Puls, Herta: *The Art of Cutwork and Appliqué*, Batsford.
Pyman, Kit (editor): *Any Kind of Patchwork*, Search Press.
Snook, Barbara: *Embroidery Stitches*, Batsford.
Springall, Diana: *Canvas Embroidery*, Batsford.
Thomas, Mary: *A Dictionary of Embroidery Stitches*, Hodder and Stoughton.
Thomas, Mary: *Mary Thomas's Embroidery Book*, Hodder and Stoughton.
Wardle, Patricia: *Guide to English Embroidery*, Victoria and Albert Museum (paperback).

• GLOSSARY •

Accent stitch An embroidery stitch which is chiefly used to provide a splash of colour or texture to enliven a monotone or flat area of stitching.

Acetate sheet A strong, smooth film produced in different colours. Useful for shadow work, decorating embroidery, and as a base on which to work needlepoint fillings. Available from suppliers of artist's materials.

Appliqué or **applied work** A technique in which shapes of different fabrics are placed on the ground fabric to form a design. The edges are secured by tiny stitches which are hardly seen, or by a decorative embroidery stitch.

Assisi Work A type of counted thread embroidery originating in Assisi, Northern Italy. The patterns or motifs are outlined before the background is filled in using cross stitch or long-armed cross-stitch, leaving the motifs unstitched.

Awl A sharp pointed instrument used for making holes in fabric.

Berlin woolwork A technique of working designs in coloured yarns on canvas, following a chart on which each square represents one stitch. The yarns and charts were originally produced in Germany but the work spread to the rest of Europe and to the United States and was popular during the nineteenth century.

Bias Any slanting or oblique line in relation to the warp and weft threads of a fabric. The true bias is formed when the selvedge is folded at a right angle across the fabric parallel to the weft and runs exactly at 45 degrees to the straight grain.

Binca canvas A multiple-thread embroidery canvas woven with squares formed by the warp and weft threads. It is suitable for all kinds of coarse embroidery. It is not necessary to fill the ground completely.

Blackwork An embroidery technique used on clothing and household linen during the sixteenth century and revived during the twentieth century. It consists of outline and filling stitches worked in black thread on a white fabric to create geometric designs.

Bodkin A long blunt-edged needle with a large eye, used for threading tape, cord or elastic through a channel or casing.

Bouclé A novelty yarn, spun with random clusters of uneven loops along its length, usually with a hairy or tweedy texture.

Border stitch A wide embroidery stitch which is always used in a straight line and makes a very attractive border. Multiple rows can be worked to make a more complex decorative border.

Canvas The ground material for needlepoint in which vertical and horizontal threads are woven together to produce precisely spaced holes between the threads. Canvas has a regular grid-like structure and is available in several different sizes of grid.

Closed finish The term used when an embroidery stitch is compressed in order to cover the ground fabric completely.

Common-weave fabric A fabric in which the warp and weft threads are woven too irregularly to provide a grid for working stitches by the counted thread method.

Couching A technique in which a thick thread or group of threads is attached to the ground fabric by means of a finer thread. It is particularly suitable for textured and metallic threads which cannot be stitched directly into the fabric.

Counted thread embroidery An embroidery technique in which the scale and placement of the stitches is determined by counting the warp and weft threads of the ground fabric over which each stitch is worked.

Crazy patchwork A technique in which irregularly shaped pieces of fabric are sewn at random on a ground fabric. The raw edges where the pieces join are secured by decorative stitching.

Crewel embroidery Embroidery stitched with crewel yarns on a linen background, using a variety of stitches. The designs are often naturalistic.

Crewel yarn A fine two-ply yarn for delicate needlepoint or free embroidery.

Cutwork A technique in which motifs or patterns are outlined with close buttonhole stitching and the ground fabric is cut away in various sections of the design.

Damask Reversible fabric, originally of silk, woven with an ornamental—often self-coloured design, usually a matt pattern on a satin weave background. The fibres used may also be cotton, viscose and synthetic, or a mixture of natural and synthetic.

Detached stitch An embroidery stitch which is anchored to the ground fabric at the edges only, with the main part of the stitching remaining free.

Diaper pattern Fabric woven with a small geometrical design. Sometimes applies to staggered rows which give the effect of diagonal lines, called bird's eye diaper. The same pattern is used in gold couching.

Dressing A stiffening agent of starch, gum, china clay or size found in new fabrics. Sometimes hides poor quality fabric but can also be an integral part of the fabric, as in glazed chintz.

Edging stitch An embroidery stitch used to finish a raw edge to prevent the fabric from fraying, or to decorate a plain hemmed edge.

Encroaching stitches A term used to describe the overlap of one row of stitching with the preceding row.

Even-weave fabric A fabric with warp and weft threads of identical thicknesses, which provide the same number of threads over a given area, enabling the threads to be counted to keep the stitching even.

Eyelet embroidery A type of cutwork embroidery which evolved from Ayrshire embroidery *circa* 1850, and became very popular as a decoration on children's garments and ladies' underclothes. The formalized designs consist of a series of tiny round and oval holes.

Fabric grain The line of the warp thread in a piece of fabric.

Filling stitch An embroidery stitch which is used to fill a shape on the ground fabric. Filling stitches can be light and delicate with a lacy appearance, or they can completely cover the ground fabric.

Fine crochet cotton A tightly twisted pearlized thread similar to pearl cotton but with a less lustrous finish.

Flower threads Single stranded cotton embroidery threads sold in skeins, and produced in an excellent range of colours.

Foundation grid The regular arrangement of threads laid across a shape to provide a framework for an embroidery stitch.

Foundation row A row of stitching which provides the basis for a composite stitch. This term is also used to describe the stitched outline which anchors a detached filling stitch to the ground fabric.

Frame A square or rectangular wooden frame used to keep fabric taut during stitching.

Gauge The number of threads that can be stitched in 1 inch of canvas. Also the number of threads or woven blocks that can be stitched in 1 inch of even-weave fabric.

Glass tubes Glass beads, larger than bugles, used in decorative bead work.

Grain The line of the warp in woven textiles. To cut horizontally, along the weft, is called cutting across or against the grain.

Grounding stitch A term used in needlepoint to describe a stitch that is suitable for covering large areas of background.

Ground fabric Any fabric on which embroidery is worked.

Half drop A term used in needlepoint to describe an arrangement of stitches. The top of the second and subsequent stitches aligns with the centre of the preceding stitch.

Hessian A strong, coarse fabric woven from hemp and jute in a fairly open weave. Used for ground fabrics, it is relatively inexpensive and good for experimentation and dyes well.

Hoop A round frame for stretching the ground fabric while embroidery stitches are worked.

Isolated stitch An embroidery stitch which is worked individually and can be used alone or massed together to fill a shape.

Jacobean embroidery A type of free embroidery worked on linen, popular during the seventeenth and eighteenth centuries.

Journey In embroidery, a term used to describe working a stitch along a line. Many stitches are completed on one journey but others will require two or three.

Laid filling stitch An embroidery stitch consisting of a foundation grid of spaced laid threads which are then anchored to the ground fabric in a decorative manner.

Laid-work An embroidery technique used to fill a shape. Long threads are laid across the shape and anchored to the fabric by a second thread to create a pattern.

Line stitch Any embroidery stitch which forms a line during the working.

Maquette A small, preliminary model made as a trial piece prior to making the final work.

Matte embroidery cotton A tightly twisted five-ply thread with a matte finish, always used as a single thread.

Mitre The diagonal line formed at 45 degrees to the edges of fabric joined to form a 90 degree angle, or when two hems meet at a square corner. Makes a strong, neat corner.

Mono canvas Canvas in which the weave is formed by the intersection of single vertical and horizontal threads.

Motif stitch An embroidery stitch which is worked individually, with each stitch making a distinctive shape, such as a star or triangle.

Nap Soft, downy raised surface given to some woven fabrics by a finishing process. If the raised nap looks a different shade from opposite angles, it may lie in one direction, as in a pile surface.

Needlepoint A general term for embroidery on canvas. The entire surface of the canvas is covered with stitching and a wide range of stitches is used.

Passing Metal threads, including pure gold and silver, made with a solid core. These threads are usually couched on to the surface of the fabric with decorative stitching.

Pearl cotton A twisted two-ply thread with a lustrous sheen. It cannot be divided into separate strands but it is available in three different weights.

Pearl purl (or bead purl) Hollow metal threads made from convex shaped wire that look like a string of tiny beads. Used for outlining.

Penelope canvas Canvas in which the weave is formed by the intersection of pairs of vertical and horizontal threads.

Persian yarn A loosely twisted three-ply yarn which can be divided into separate strands.

Picot A small loop of twisted thread forming a decorative edging on lace or embroidery.

Pintucks A series of very narrow tucks stitched on the right side of the fabric and used as decoration.

Plate A broad, flat metallic thread, usually gilt, with a very bright, shiny surface. Can be crimped to give texture.

Powdering A light filling for a shape made by scattering an isolated stitch over an area of ground fabric.

Pulled fabric work An embroidery technique in which stitches are pulled tightly so that the threads of the ground fabric are distorted, creating a pattern of tiny holes in the fabric.

Purl Made up of finely drawn metallic wire coiled tightly round into a spring-like spiral. It is made in lengths of about 39in (1 metre) which are then cut into lengths as needed. Purls are threaded on to a needle and stitched in place like beads.

Richelieu embroidery A form of cutwork similar to Renaissance embroidery; the main difference is the addition of picots to the buttonhole bars which join parts of the design.

Rocailles Trade name for transparent beads used in embroidery. They are divided into three groups: round rocailles, or seed beads, are round with round holes; toscas are square rocailles with square holes but are rounded outside; charlottes are faceted on the outside.

Sateen A strong, lightweight fabric with a satin weave running across it. It has a glossy sheen on one side only. It is relatively inexpensive and available in a good range of colours; it is usually made from cotton.

Seeding Small embroidery stitches worked in a random, all-over way to fill an area, or worked gradually to soften an edge.

Scrim Fine openweave canvas of a light brown colour, originally made from low-grade linen but may be cotton or a mixture of other fibres. Suitable for counted thread work backgrounds and as a backing fabric.

Shadow embroidery A type of embroidery worked on a semi-transparent fabric.

Shisha embroidery A traditional embroidery technique using tiny mirrors, which originated in India.

Silk noile Inexpensive silk fabric. The waste fibres which are too short for spun silk are carded and spun into coarser yarns, and woven into a dress-weight fabric.

Slips Traditionally, an embroidered motif showing a flower with stem and foliage and with a small piece of root attached. Ready worked slips can be cut out and applied separately to a ground fabric.

Slub An unevenly spun yarn with alternating thick and thin areas randomly placed which, when woven, gives a characteristically knubbly texture to the finished fabric.

Smocking Evenly spaced gathers in a piece of fabric which are held in place by ornamental stitching.

Soutache braid A pliable, narrow plaited braid, similar to russia braid, used for appliquéd decoration such as outlining, interlacing patterns and initials.

Stiletto A very sharp pointed tool used in embroidery for making eyelets in broderie anglaise, cutwork and eyelet embroidery. It may also be used in metal thread work for making holes in the ground fabric through which the ends of heavy threads are taken to the back.

Stranded floss A loosely twisted, slightly shiny, six-strand cotton thread. For fine embroidery, the threads can be separated and used in twos or threes.

Stranded silk A pure silk thread similar to stranded floss but with a more lustrous finish.

Tambour work Type of embroidery worked in a frame with a tambour hook. The designs are worked in continuous lines of chain stitch. It is often associated with whitework embroidery.

Tapestry needle A long thick needle with a blunt tip and a large eye.

Tapestry yarn A twisted four-ply yarn with hard-wearing properties, mainly used in needlepoint.

Tramming The preparation of double thread canvas, before the decorative stitching is begun, to make the stitched surface hard-wearing. Horizontal straight stitches are worked between the double canvas threads, using colours that match the design. Tramming fills out the stitch that is worked over it and also helps to cover the canvas ground.

Vanishing muslin Stiffened, treated muslin used as a backing or support for some hand and machine embroidery. The stitching is done through both layers and the surplus muslin vanishes when pressed with a warm iron.

Voiding Part of the design where the unworked areas define the pattern and the background fabric shows through. The technique is, in effect, similar to stencilling.

Warp The threads in a woven fabric that run lengthwise on the weaving loom.

Waxed thread A thread which has been strengthened by rubbing it against a block of beeswax.

Weft The threads running across the width of a woven fabric that are interwoven with the warp threads.

Whipping A term used in embroidery to describe the method of passing a second thread over and under a simple line stitch to give a raised effect.

Page numbers in *italic* refer to illustrations and captions

A

abrasive paper, 10
acetate, 10
Adam and Eve appliqué, 103, *103*
American patchwork, 7
Amish quilts, 68–9, *69*
applied patchwork, 48
appliqué:
designs, 90
enlarging designs, 91, *91*
fabrics, 15, 90
finishing, 97, *97*
folded patterns, 90, 96, *96*
frames, 92, *92*
hand sewing, 92, *92–3*
inlay, 90
lace, 90, 120–1, *120–1*
machine sewing, 93, *93*
motifs in relief, 96, *96*
neatening curves and corners, 92, *92*
onlay, 90, 100–8, *100–7*
origins, 6–7
padded, 90, 96, *96*, 111–13, *111*
perse, 90, 108, *108–9*, 110, *110*
picture, 116–119, *116–19*
preparing to, 91 *91*
projects, 99–121
Adam and Eve, 103, *103*
cube, 102, *102*
elm tree lane, 114, *114–15*
flower garden, 108, *108–9*
garland, 120–1, *120*
Kapa Lau, 113–14, *113*
landscape with otter, 104, *104*
Penny, 111–12, *111*
posies, 112–13, *112*
ring o' roses, 116, *116–17*
rose border, 121, *121*
salamander, 110, *110*
sea bathing, 105, *105*
Snowy, *118–19*, 119
variegated tulip, 100–1, *100*
wedding party, 106–8, *106–7*
reverse, 90, 95, *95*
shadow, 90, 114, *114–15*
styles, 90
techniques, 89–97
thread, 14
transferring designs, 90, *91*
appliqué perse, 90
flower garden, 108, *108–9*
salamander, 110, *110*

B

backgrounds, quilting, 20
bags:
appliqué, 112, *112*
quilted, 36–7, *36*
batting, 15, 19
beads, 26
binding, quilting, 26, *27*
blanket stitch, *94*
blouses, appliqué, *95*
bordered quilting, 26, *27*
borders:
patchwork, *60*
quilting, *18*, 19
broderie perse, 6
brushed cotton, 14
brushes, *10*

C

calico, 18
Canadian patchwork, 54–5, *55*
carbon paper, 10
card, 10
cathedral window patchwork, 56, *56*
Cave of the Thousand Buddhas, 6
chain stitch, *94*
chalks, 10, *10*
chamois, 15, 18
changing colours patchwork, 86–7, *86–7*
charcoal, *10*
circles and quatrefoils
quilting, 40–1, *41*
cleaning, fabrics, 15
compasses, *10*
conté crayons, *10*
corded quilting:
circles and quatrefoils, 40–1, *41*
cord for, 15
double celtic knot, 42, *42*
techniques, 25, *25*
corduroys, 14
corners:
appliqué, 92, *92*
patchwork, *61*
cotton fabrics, 14, 18, 25
cotton wadding, 115
craft knives, *10*
crazy log patchwork, 74, *75*
crazy patchwork, 53–4, *53*
Victoria, 80, *80*
crêpe-de-chine, 18
cube appliqué, 102, *102*
curves, appliqué, 92, *92*
cushions:
appliqué, 97, 108, *108–9*, 110, 120–1, *120–1*
patchwork, 78, *78*, 82, *82*, 83, *83*
quilted, *24*, 30, 32, *32*, 38, *38*, 44, *44*

D

damasks, 14
dance patchwork, 79, *79*
dancing waves quilting, 37, *37*
designs:
enlarging, 91, *91*
transferring, 90, *91*
diagonal patchwork, 64–6, *65*
dolls, quilting, 39–40, *40*
domettes, 15
double celtic knot quilting, 42, *42*
double Irish chain patchwork, 68, *68*
drawing:
enlarging, 91, *91*
equipment, 10, *10–11*
transferring, 90, *91*
dressmaker's carbon paper, 10
quilting, 21, *21*
dressmaker's shears, 14

E

early morning quilting, 44–5, *44*
elm tree lane appliqué, 114, *114–15*
embroidery frames, 14, *14*
embroidery stitches, *94–5*, 95
embroidery thread, *15*
enlarging designs, 91, *91*
equipment, 9–15
drawing, 10, *10–11*
paper, 10, *11*
sewing, *12–13*, 13
templates, *10*
erasers, *10*

F

fabrics, 14–15
appliqué, 90
cleaning, 15
patchwork, 48, 50–1
quilting, 18
feather circle quilting, 30
feeling good quilting, 45, *45*
felt, 15, 18, 26
felt-tip pens, *10*
finishing:
appliqué, 97, *97*
patchwork, 60–1, *60–1*
quilting, 26, *27*
fixatives, *10*
floating triangles patchwork, 69–71, *70*
Florida patchwork, 83, *83*
flower garden appliqué, 108, *108–9*
fly stitch, *94*
foil, 26
folded appliqué, 90
Kapa Lau, 113–14, *113*
folded star patchwork, 55, *55*
morning star, 81, *81*
frames, 14, *14*
appliqué, 92, *92*
quilting, *22*, *22*
French knots, *44*
fruit basket quilting, 38, *38*

G

garden wreath appliqué, *101*
garland appliqué, 120–1, *120*
glitter fabrics, 26
gouache, *10*
grandmother's choice patchwork, 68–9, *69*
grandmother's flower garden, 64, *64*
graph paper, 10, *10*
isometric, 10
grey shadows patchwork, 85, *85*

H

herb pillows, quilted, 41, *41*
history, 6–7
hoops, quilting, 14, 22, *22*

I

ink, *10*
inlay appliqué, 90
irons, 14
pressing patchwork, 52, *52*
isometric graph paper, 10
Italian quilting, 18, 25, *25*

K

Kapa Lau appliqué, 113–14, *113*
kimono patchwork, 77, *77*
knits, 24
knives, *10*
Kosslov, 6

L

lace appliqué, 90
garland, 120–1, *120*
rose border appliqué, 121, *121*
landscape, patchwork, 78, *78*
landscape with otter appliqué, 104, *104*
lawn, 14
leather, 15, 18
linen, 14, 25
lining, patchwork, 61
log cabin patchwork, 54–5, *54*
crazy log, 74, *75*
starry night, 74, *74*
straight furrow, 73, *73*
long diamond, 50

M

machine quilting, 23, *23*
magic markers, 10
marking, quilting, 20
mayflower patchwork, 56, *56*
stained glass, 82, *82*
moiré silk, 25
Mola blouse, *95*
morning star patchwork, 81, *81*
muslin, 14, 25

N

necklaces, quilted, 45, *45*
needles, 13
notepaper, 10
November morning patchwork, 70–1, *70*
nylon, 24, 26

O

ocean-wave with window pane quilting, 32, *32*
onlay appliqué, 90
Adam and Eve, 103, *103*
cube, 102, *102*
landscape with otter, 104, *104*
sea bathing, 105, *105*
variegated tulip, 100–1, *100*
wedding party, 106–8, *106–7*
op art patchwork, 85, *85–6*
organdie, 26
orange saddle, *23*
organza, 14
origins, 6–7

P

padded appliqué, 90, 96, *96*
Penny, 111–12, *111*
posies, 112–13, *112*
padded quilting, 18
fruit basket, 38, *38*
techniques, 24, *24–5*
Vanessa, 39–40, *40*
paint box, 35–6, *35*
paint-box quilting, 35–6, *35*
palamporé designs, 6
paper, 10, *10*
abrasive, 10

- patchwork:
  - American, 7
  - applied, 48
  - borders, *60*
  - choosing designs, 48–9
  - construction, 49
  - corners, *61*
  - crazy, 53–4, *53*, 80, *80*
  - cutting fabric, 50–1
  - estimating fabric quantity, 50
  - fabrics, 15, 48
  - finishing, 60–1, *60–1*
  - flower basket, *61*
  - folded star, 55, *55*, 81, *81*
  - hand sewing, 51–2, *51–2*
  - Jacob's ladder, *61*
  - lining, 61
  - log cabin, 54–5, *55*, 73–5
  - long diamond, 50
  - machine sewing, 50, 51, *51*, 54
  - marking fabric, 50–1
  - mayflower, 56, *56*, 82, *82*
  - origins, 6–7
  - paving stones, *61*
  - pieced, 48, 64–73
  - pleated, 48, 58, *58*, 85–7, *85–7*
  - pressing, 52, *52*
  - projects, 64–87
    - changing colours, 86–7, *86–7*
    - crazy log, 74, *75*
    - dance, 79, *79*
    - diagonal, 64–6, *65*
    - double Irish chain, 68, *68*
    - floating triangles, 69–71, *70*
    - Florida, 83, *83*
    - grandmother's choice, 68–9,
    - grandmother's flower garden, 64, *64*
    - grey shadows, 85, *85*
    - kimono, 77, *77*
    - landscape, 78, *78*
    - morning star, 81, *81*
    - November morning, 70–1, *70*
    - op art, *85–6*, 85
    - stained glass, 82, *82*
    - starry night, 74, *74*
    - straight furrow, 73, *73*
    - stripey II, 76, *76*
    - sugar bowl, 66, *66–7*
    - sunburst, 72–3, *72*
    - Victoria, 80, *80*
  - random strip, 78–9, *78–9*
  - Seminole, 48, 57, *57*, 83–5, *85*
  - shell, 52, *52–3*
  - size of block, 49
  - sewing blocks together, 51
  - strip, 76–7, *76–7*
  - techniques, 47–61
  - templates, 49–50, *51*
  - thread, 14
  - tucks, 59, *59*
  - types, 48
- pencils, 10, *10*
  - sharpeners, *10*
- Penny appliqué, 111–112, *111*
- picture appliqué:
  - ring o' roses, 116, *116–17*
  - Snowy, *118–19*, 119
- pieced patchwork, 48
  - diagonal, 64–6, *65*
  - double Irish chain, 68, *68*
  - floating triangles, 69–71, *70*
  - grandmother's choice, 68–9, *69*
  - grandmother's flower garden, 64, *64*
  - November morning, 71–2, *71*
  - sugar bowl, 66, *66–7*
  - sunburst, 72–3, *72*
- pillows, quilted, 41, *41*
- pincushions, quilted, 43, *43*
- pins, 13
- piping, quilting, 26, *27*
- plastic coated fabrics, 15
- pleated patchwork, 48, 58–9, *58–9*
  - changing shadows, 86–7, *86–7*
  - grey shadows, 85, *85*
- poplin, 14, 18
- posies appliqué, 112–13, *112*
- pressing, 14
  - patchwork, 52, *52*
- purple hearts quilting, 30, *30*
- puzzle patchwork, 53–4, *53*

Q

- quill patchwork, 55, *55*
- quilting:
  - background patterns, 19
  - backgrounds, 20
  - binding, 26, *27*
  - bordered, 26, *27*
  - borders, *18*, 19
  - by hand, 23, *23*
  - by machine, 23, *23*
  - coded, 18
  - contemporary designs, 19
  - corded, 14, 25, *25*, 40–2
  - cutting the layers, 20
  - designs, 18–19, *18–19*
  - dressmaker's carbon paper, 21, *21*
  - fabrics, 14–15, 18
  - finishing, 26, *27*
  - frames, 14, 22, *22*
  - hoops, 14, 22, *22*
  - Italian, 18, 25, *25*
  - marking, 20
  - needle marking, 21
  - needles, 13
  - origins, 6–7
  - padded, 18, 38–40
  - piping, 26, *27*
  - preparing to, 22
  - projects, 29–45
    - circles and quatrefoils, 40–1, *41*
    - dancing waves, 37, *37*
    - double celtic knot, 42, *42*
    - early morning, 44–5, *44*
    - feather circle, 30
    - feeling good, 45, *45*
    - fruit basket, 38, *38*
    - ocean-wave with window pane, 32, *32*
    - paint-box, 35–6, *35*
    - purple hearts, 30, *30*
    - rippling stream, 36–7, *36*
    - squares and diagonals, 34, *34*
    - tortoise shell and pampas grass, 33, *33*
    - trio, 43, *43*
    - Vanessa, 39–40, *40*
  - shadow, 14, 18, 26, *26*
  - shadow quilting, 14, 18, 26, *26*, 43–5
  - stencils, 13
  - stuffed, 18, 24, *24–5*
  - techniques, 17–27
  - templates, 20
  - threads, 14, *15*
  - traditional designs, 19, *19*
  - Trapunto, 18, 24, 24–5, 38–40
  - wadded, 18, 19–23, 30–7
- quilting bees, 7
- quilting cord, 15
- quilting parties, 7
- quilts:
  - appliqué, 100–1, *100–1*
  - patchwork, 64–87

R

- random strip patchwork:
  - dance, 79, *79*
  - landscape, 78, *78*
- reverse appliqué, 90, 95, *95*
- reverse stitch, 14
- ring o' roses appliqué, 116, *116–17*
- rippling stream quilting, 36–7, *36*
- rose border appliqué, 121, *121*
- rulers, 10, *10*

S

- salamander appliqué, 110, *110*
- *sashiko*, 32, *33*
- sateen, 14
- satin, 14, 18
- scissors, 14
- scrim, 24
- sea bathing appliqué, 105, *105*
- Seminole patchwork, 48, 57, *57*
  - Florida, 83, *83*
  - op art, *84–5*, 85
- sequins, 26
- set squares, 10, *10*
- sewing machines, 14
  - appliqué, 93, *93*
  - patchwork, 50, 51, *51*, 54
- quilting, 23, *23*
- shadow appliqué, 90
  - elm tree lane, 114, *114–15*
- shadow quilting, 18, 26, *26*
  - early morning, 44–5, *44*
  - feeling good, 45, *45*
- trio, 43, *43*
- shell patchwork, 52, *52–3*
- Siberia, 6
- silk fabrics, 14, 18, 26
- Snowy appliqué, *118–19*, 119
- spray diffusers, *10*
- squares and diagonals quilting, 34, *34*
- stained glass patchwork, 82, *82*
- starry night patchwork, 74, *74*
- stencils, quilting, 13
- stitches:
  - blanket, *94*
  - chain, *94*
  - embroidery, *94–5*, 95
  - fly, *94*
  - straight, *94*
- straight furrow patchwork, 73, *73*
- straight stitch, *94*
- strip patchwork:
  - kimono, 77, *77*
  - stripey II, 76, *76*
- stripey II patchwork, 76, *76*
- stuffed quilting, 18, 24, *24–5*
- suede, 15
- sugar bowl patchwork, 66, *66–7*
- suitings, 14
- summer garden appliqué, *97*
- sunburst patchwork, 72–3, *72*
  - synthetic fabrics, 14
- synthetic wadding, 15

T

- taffeta, 24, 25
- templates:
  - materials, 10
  - patchwork, 49–50, *51*
  - wadded quilting, 20
- thimbles, 13
- thread:
  - embroidery, *15*
  - quilt, *15*
- tortoise shell and pampas grass quilting, 33, *33*
- tracing paper, 10
- traditional designs, quilting, *18–19*, 19
- transferring designs, 90, *91*
- Trapunto, 18, 24, *24–5*
  - fruit basket, 38, *38*
  - quilting, 6–7
  - Vanessa, 39–40, *40*
- trio quilting, 43, *43*
- tucks, patchwork, 59, *59*
- tweeds, 14

V

- Vanessa quilting, 39–40, *40*
- variegated tulip appliqué, 100–1, *100*
- velours, 24
- velvets, 14, 24
- Victoria patchwork, 80, *80*
- voile, 14, 24, 26

W

- wadded quilting, 18
  - backgrounds, 20
  - cutting the layers, 20
  - dancing waves, 37, *37*
  - dressmaker's carbon paper, 21, *21*
  - feather circle, 30
  - marking, 20
  - needle marking, 21
  - ocean wave with windowpane, 32, *32*
  - paint box, 35–6, *35*
  - planning designs, 20
  - preparing to, 22
  - purple hearts, 30, *30*
  - rippling stream, 36–7, *36*
  - squares and diagonals, 34, *34*
  - techniques, 19–23
  - templates, 20
  - tortoise shell and pampas grass, 33, *33*
- wadding, 15
- waistcoats, quilted, *26*, 35–6, *35*
- wallhangings:
  - patchwork, 70, *70*, 79, *79*
  - quilted, 34
- watercolours, *10*
- wedding party appliqué, 106–8, *106–7*
- wool wadding, 15
- woollen fabrics, 14

Z

- zigzag stitch, 14